PEDESTRIAN PILGRIMAGE

Carn Lês Boel to Hopton on Sea

FRANK ROBERTS

Copyright ©2023 Frank Roberts

All rights reserved.

ISBN: 9798393416300

No portion of this book may be reproduced, copied, distributed or adapted in any way, with the exception of certain activities permitted by applicable copyright laws, such as brief quotations in the context of a review or academic work. For permission to publish, distribute or otherwise reproduce this work, please contact the author.

Particular thanks to Paul Broadhurst for allowing me to extensively refer to and quote from 'The Sun and the Serpent'.

Also to Gary Chapin, Elizabeth Dale, Stewart Harding and John Greening for permission to quote.

Thanks also to Richard Dealler, whose writing and directions kept me 'on track'.

And a special thank you to Graham Stephens for the artwork.

Photography by the author.

Keep an open mind. You never know what you'll find.

Preface

In 2019 I walked from the easternmost point of Great Britain (Lowestoft Ness) to its westernmost extremity on the Ardnamurchan Peninsula. As for the other two cardinal points, I already had them in my bag. Lizard Point (south) and Dunnet Head (north) are close to Land's End (northeast) and John o' Groats (southwest), respectively, so it was easy to include these on the same trails I'd previously completed.

For my next project, I intended to walk a trail between Land's End and Lowestoft, a coast-to-coast walk across the most expansive land in England and an excellent way to link the termination points of my previous two trails. With an open mind, I got out my maps and books, switched on my laptop and began searching and researching for a possible route.

Over several days, I discovered that the line between the tip of Cornwall and the easternmost point of East Anglia was far more than an arbitrary one on a map. I started to glean that apart from the physical geography, the line appeared to have profound significance as the St Michael Alignment, the most famous 'ley line' in Britain. I confess I understood very little about ley lines and was sceptical about what I knew. Nevertheless, I decided to look further into it. I soon found myself reading about ancient mysteries, myths and legends, Druids, earth energy currents, saints and sanctuaries, sacred sciences, healing, dowsing, UFOs, crop circles and 'dragon forces', to name but a few things.

I was out of my depth. I switched off my laptop and returned to the safe familiarity of studying my maps. After all, I'm used to the tried and trusted process of planning my routes, walking them, and observing and recording what I discover along the way. It's simple, but it's worked OK for me so far.

I continued forming my plans over the next two days, but for some reason, I couldn't get this ley line thing out of my head, so I thought I'd take another look. I bought a copy of the Sun and the Serpent, a book written in 1989 by Paul Broadhurst and Hamish Miller. Within hours I was hooked. From here on, my trail would be more than just a walk from Land's End to Lowestoft; It would be a pilgrimage along the St Michael Alignment.

Introduction

The St Michael Alignment is named after St Michael the Archangel. It's an astronomical line that stretches from a point just a few miles south of Land's End in Cornwall to the Norfolk coast, very close to the easternmost point of England. If a crow flew above it, the flightpath would be 350 miles long, and a remarkable country-wide linear assembly of ancient places would unfold beneath it. Once a year, the astronomical relevance becomes clear. On Mayday, the sun rises to shine its light precisely along the length of the Alignment. It's the halfway point in the calendar between the spring equinox and the summer solstice in the northern hemisphere. Mayday is the timely and relevant festival representing this when celebrations are held to welcome the new summer. In the pre-Christian Pagan tradition, May Day was the Celtic festival of Beltane, and Bel (or Belenus) was the name given to its great Sun God. Annual celebrations took place in processions and ceremonies, and fire festivals were held throughout the land. Beacons were lit on certain hilltops, which became strategic sites for defence, ritual and worship.

A theory arose that many important archaeological and historic sites were geometrically 'aligned' along this and other lines of important significance. This concept was first mentioned in the observations of Alfred Watkins (1855-1935) just a hundred years ago in his book 'The Old Straight Track'. A rational man, Watkins was nevertheless struck by how so many ancient features of historical significance appeared to line up along what he believed to be ancient pathways. Watkins was the first to use the term 'ley line', but once the idea was out, people began to explore the theory across the entirety of the British landscape and beyond.

Of course, there are sceptics of the ley line phenomenon. Since it was proposed, people have used all manner of things to disprove it. More recently and most notably, postcodes, telephone boxes and even our sadly demised Woolworth's stores have been used to suggest that anyone can draw a line on a map to link such places with equal accuracy.

But there's so much more to the St Michael line than chance geography and geometry. Below the surface are layers of history, religion, culture and tradition. St Michael the Archangel is generally regarded as the Christianised Sun God of former times. Earlier manifestations have included the Celtic Belenus and the Roman god Apollo. Michael is depicted as the Warrior-Saint, symbolically slaying a serpent or dragon, and the places of worship dedicated to him were traditionally sanctuaries in early Christian times. Many are found along the entire length of the Alignment in the form of churches, shrines and monasteries, including the spectacular hilltop sites of St Michael's Mount, Burrow Mump, Roche Rock and Glastonbury Tor. Most are now abandoned from their former function, but modern-day pilgrims can still connect with these places for their beauty, mystery and energy.

Most of these ancient sites have undergone tremendous changes, and many others are long-vanished beneath the plough or built over by modern 'developments'. Those that survive have nearly all been affected by layers of later history, conflict or restoration; fortunately, however, the locations remain, and so do some of the stones.

Somewhere in the 17th Century, as the modern era of history began to take shape following the Renaissance, people became curious about the stones beneath their feet. Pioneering antiquarians started to explore the possibility that there was more to these forms than just landmark features of unfathomable origin. First came John Aubrey (1626-1697) and then William Stukeley (1687-1765), whose interests and influence extended across many fields, including science, philosophy, natural history, and religion; and more importantly, the earliest forays into field archaeology. They studied and surveyed ancient sites, including Stonehenge and Avebury, and attributed them to the old native inhabitants of Britain rather than the Romans or the Vikings.

Avebury lies directly on the St Michael Alignment and is precisely halfway along its length. Stukeley proposed that in conjunction with other nearby sites, this extensive neolithic complex was a 'Serpent Temple' conceived and constructed by the Druids under the direction of their priests. His observations, investigations and research are recorded in great detail in his book 'Abury, a Temple of the British Druids'. Stukeley became instrumental in establishing the Druid Revival which, although marginalised, has endured in various forms for the last 300 years.

In the 1950s, the surrealist painter and mystic Ithell Colquhoun (1906-1988) wrote a book entitled 'The Living Stones: Cornwall'. In it, She wrote about earth energy currents in the landscape and described the ancient stones and monoliths as powerhouses of vital energy. This radical interpretation of the Earth as a living being soon attracted the interest and attention of others outside the conventions of the 'mainstream'.

A decade after Colquhoun wrote The Living Stones, another writer associated with Earth mysteries wrote a book called 'The View Over Atlantis'. John Michell defined and described the nature of earth energies and ley lines in more detail. He also identified that the St Michael Ley Line formed along a detectable earth energy current. Many people find they can experience such energies through dowsing.

During the late 1980s, two researchers in the vast subject of ancient mysteries and practitioners in the field of dowsing decided to explore and follow the route of the St Michael Alignment, following a course of 'earth energy' they had discovered that flows along its path. Their names were Hamish Miller (1927-2010) and Paul Broadhurst (b.1965). They called the energy current 'Michael' and planned to dowse its entire length, starting at St Michael's Mount, the famous tidal island on the Cornish coast. Over many months they followed this current to the western tip of Cornwall and then east through Devon and Somerset to Glastonbury and then on to Avebury. Their book 'The Sun and the Serpent' documents the progress they made in dowsing the current and the discoveries they made along the way. At first, they followed what they believed was the only energy current associated with the Alignment. They plotted 'Michael' as he weaved alternately north and south of the geographical line. 'Michael' changed his course to meet and pass through many different sites—ancient standing stones, stone circles, Bronze- and Iron Age settlements, medieval churches, and hilltop forts; all places with great historical significance. The dowsers discovered profoundly measurable results at such sites, sometimes unexpected or startling. Not being a dowser myself, I can't describe or interpret their experiences, but I read about how these energy channels had powerful, dynamic and interactive qualities.

When Miller and Broadhurst reached Glastonbury, their dowsing led them to and through several key sites. Here they were amazed at the complexity of the energy line's activity. At the Neolithic henge monument of Avebury, they were even more surprised when it became apparent that the current was interacting with a second energy line, so far overlooked because of its different qualities and frequency. Although equally powerful, they described these qualities as 'gentler, smoother and altogether more feminine than its counterpart'. For relevant reasons, they decided to call it 'Mary'. St Mary can be regarded the Christian manifestation of the Earth Goddess, Gaia. The discovery of this second energy had profound implications for the entire project, as a completely different energy line would now have to be dowsed along with the first.

Over many more months of adventurous dowsing, Miller and Broadhurst found that the two energy currents broadly ran in parallel to each other, but inter-weaved along the line, crossing each others paths at particular locations. In so doing, Mary and Michael would alternately travel north and south of each other with the Alignment forming the axis along which they travelled. On the ground, these two currents of 'serpent energy' were found to align with and travel through particular landmarks and landforms of geographical and historical significance. Sites of similar or even greater significance marked the points at which the two currents crossed, many known and revered in past centuries as sacred places. The two currents had their individual qualities; 'Michael' had what they described as masculine, and 'Mary' its feminine equivalence. The duality of the differing qualities appeared to be complementary: the Yin and the Yang, if you will. Where Michael represents the Sun God, Mary represents the Earth Goddess. These qualities also discern the nature of the landmarks and landforms that align with them. 'Michael' tends to travel over the higher ground and landforms, while 'Mary' channels her energy along the lower geographical features, including springs and water courses.

The dowsers termed the points where the two currents met or crossed each others' paths 'nodes'. Twenty-two were found, each marking what appeared to be the most important sites. These include St Michael's Mount, Glastonbury Tor and the Avebury complex of prehistoric sites. Others may seem less important today, but perhaps their significance has been forgotten and lost over the centuries since they were initially established. Ten nodes lie directly on the alignment, while the other twelve run either north or south of it, depending on where the two energy currents cross. The pattern of travel made by the two currents and the central axis can be likened to a pair of serpents or snakes, as depicted by the historical symbol of the Caduceus, the wand of the classical Messenger God Hermes or Mercury. This symbol is the modern-day emblem of the healing professions, with associations throughout history, not least the ancient oriental healing tradition of Kundalini.

At each of the 'nodes', the dowsers found some extraordinary results. These fusion points were powerful centres of energy, not only detectable but potently felt by those attuned to them. Here, the energy paths were found to perform in many different ways to create unique geometric patterns on the ground, often appearing to interact with each other. Furthermore, the dowsers frequently wrote of the powerful and uplifting qualities they experienced at these locations, suggesting a two-way interaction between the dowser and the dowsed. Miller and Broadhurst believed that people knew of these energies in our distant past and located their important sites in alignment with them.

Intriguingly, there are scores of churches of great antiquity dedicated to either St Michael or St Mary, directly aligned with the two energy currents. Additionally, many other churches are dedicated to St George, who can be regarded as the archangel's more human dragon-slaying revelation in post-Roman Britain. Many prehistoric megaliths and stone circles lie along both routes, as well as many more scores of other churches, ancient settlements and holy wells. Famous ancient trackways also form along these energy channels, and many of their important junctions are similarly aligned with them.

I completed my pilgrimage from west to east, but I could just as easily have done it in reverse. I walked it in two halves over the summers of 2020 and 2021. As a trail walk, the better walking was undoubtedly in the west as I traversed the magnificent modern-day counties of Cornwall, Devon, Somerset and Wiltshire. There were granite landscapes, mountain-height moors, magnificent downlands, and most of the prehistoric monuments. The walking was hard, but the rewards were spectacular. I also had the advantage of walking much of the Mary Michael Pilgrim's Way, an invaluable trail recently conceived and charted by Richard Dealler.

Further east, the second half of my pilgrimage bravely coursed its way through a far more built-up landscape, much altered by the expansion of the capital's commuter belt over the last century. The ground was lower-lying, so the walking was more accessible in some ways, but there were fewer vantage points from which to view the landscape. Towards the end, rural East Anglia had its appeal, particularly its wealth of magnificent medieval churches that the two energy currents form along. Several other remarkable places included the enigmatic Royston Cave, Eye Castle and the abbey site of Bury St Edmunds.

Before walking my pilgrimage, I had virtually no knowledge of ley lines and knew nothing about earth energies. I still don't know a lot, but I have now experienced walking to and being at many of the places and most of the node locations documented in the Sun and the Serpent. I can confirm that most of them are magical and beautiful places to discover and enjoy.

This book is a log of the daily walk reports from my pilgrimage trail, walked over two summers. I draw heavily (and necessarily) on the authors' writings in 'The Sun and the Serpent'. I highly recommend this classic publication, and I thank Mr Broadhurst for permitting me to use it extensively in my writing.

Overleaf are some guidance notes and illustrations for reference when reading.

Explanatory and Guidance Notes

I walked my pilgrimage over the two summers of 2020 and 2021. These were lucky breaks between the various coronavirus lockdowns that would otherwise have forbidden my travel. I walked my trail on a reasonably strict but necessary budget, so I relied on the limited availability of open campsites or hostelries and their reduced capacity. This was particularly the case during the first of these two summers, to the extent that I deduced that I couldn't feasibly continue my walk east of the mid-point of Avebury.

Additionally (and perhaps rightly), many of the sites I wished to visit along the way were firmly closed throughout this period. These were predominantly many of the churches along my route. As a result, I later revisited a selection of the ones I had a particular desire to, and the reviewed sites are logged and dated in the **appendix** of this book.

I'm a trail walker by familiar habit, and until this particular walk, I'd never considered myself a pilgrim. However, as my trail unfolded, I realised that by walking these ancient trackways, I was treading in the footsteps of countless unknown millions who had gone before me. 'Pilgrimage' is fortunately now a personal term for the individual, and I use the word interchangeably with 'trail'. However, I tend to view my conventional 'A to B' (boots on the ground) writing as a 'trail', while the sites and the objectives motivating me are my 'pilgrimage'. Either way, I'm just a pedestrian on a long walk.

Throughout the text of my walk reports, I have separated the 'regular' content from my extensive references to the St Michael Alignment, its associated earth energy currents and 'The Sun and the Serpent'. I have written all of these in *italic text*, but I hope the book can be read and appreciated as a whole. Please remember that all the *italicised* content is within subject areas far beyond my expertise. I have tried to ensure this content represents these subject areas correctly and that the authors are referenced accurately and not unfavourably.

Finally, **This is not a guidebook.** Please refer to the bibliography for specific publications and websites on possible walking routes, particularly the **Mary Michael Pilgrims Way**.

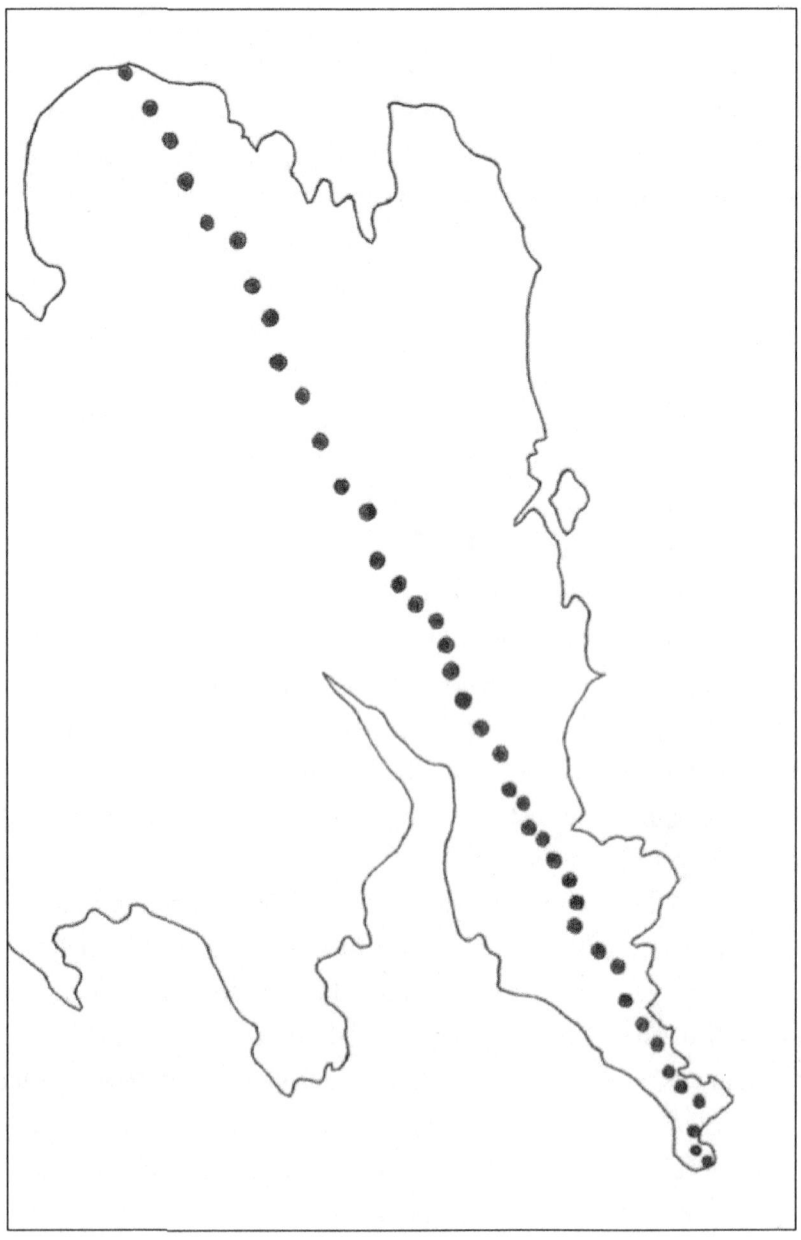

CONTENTS

DAY 1 - CARN LÊS BOEL TO ST BURYAN — 1

DAY 2 - ST BURYAN TO PENZANCE — 8

DAY 3 - PENZANCE TO GODOLPHIN CROSS — 15

DAY 4 - GODOLPHIN CROSS TO STITHIANS RESERVOIR — 23

DAY 5 - STITHIANS RESERVOIR TO OLD KEA — 26

DAY 6 - OLD KEA TO COURT FARM — 31

DAY 7 - COURT FARM TO THE EDEN PROJECT — 36

DAY 8 - THE EDEN PROJECT TO TRENANT FARM, ST NEOT — 40

DAY 9 - TRENANT FARM TO KELLY BRAY — 45

DAY 10 - KELLY BRAY TO LYDFORD — 52

DAY 11 - LYDFORD — 57

DAY 12 - LYDFORD TO OKEHAMPTON — 63

DAY 13 - OKEHAMPTON TO GIDLEIGH COMMON — 67

DAY 14 - GIDLEIGH COMMON TO CLIFFORD BRIDGE — 74

DAY 15 - CLIFFORD BRIDGE TO CREDITON — 79

DAY 16 - CREDITON TO BICKLEIGH	83
DAY 17 - BICKLEIGH TO TIVERTON PARKWAY	88
DAY 18 - TIVERTON PARKWAY TO WELLINGTON	92
DAY 19 - WELLINGTON TO ASH CROSS	95
DAY 20 - ASH CROSS TO WALTON	100
DAY 21 - WALTON TO GLASTONBURY	110
DAY 22 - GLASTONBURY TO STOKE ST MICHAEL	122
DAY 23 - STOKE ST MICHAEL TO BUCKLAND DINHAM	132
DAY 24 - BUCKLAND DINHAM TO TROWBRIDGE	135
DAY 25 - TROWBRIDGE TO DEVIZES	137
DAY 26 - DEVIZES TO ALL CANNINGS	142
DAY 27 - ALL CANNINGS TO AVEBURY	146
DAY 28 - AVEBURY - REST DAY	159
DAY 29 - BUCKLAND DINHAM TO TROWBRIDGE	167
DAY 30 - AVEBURY TO LIDDINGTON CASTLE	171
DAY 31 - LIDDINGTON CASTLE TO COURT HILL	177
DAY 32 - COURT HILL TO NORTH MORETON	182

DAY 33 - NORTH MORETON TO WATLINGTON	185
DAY 34 - WATLINGTON - REST DAY	190
DAY 35 - WATLINGTON TO PRINCES RISBOROUGH	191
DAY 36 - PRINCES RISBOROUGH TO IVINGHOE	196
DAY 37 - IVINGHOE - REST DAY	199
DAY 38 - IVINGHOE TO PEGSDON	201
DAY 39 - PEGSDON TO RADWELL	206
DAY 40 - RADWELL TO GREAT CHISHILL	210
DAY 41 - GREAT CHISHILL TO BRINKLEY	214
DAY 42 - BRINKLEY TO STONECROSS GREEN	217
DAY 43 - STONECROSS GREEN TO BURY ST EDMUNDS	221
DAY 44 - BURY ST EDMUNDS TO THORNHAM MAGNA	226
DAY 45 - THORNHAM MAGNA TO WEYBREAD	228
DAY 46 - WEYBREAD TO WARDLEY HILL	234
DAY 47 - WARDLEY HILL TO HOPTON ON SEA	238

APPENDIX
245

BIBLIOGRAPHY/REFERENCES
275

INDEX OF PLACES VISITED

Day 1

Carn Lês Boel to St Buryan

6 Miles

23.07.2020

'the granite doesn't mind.
it does not need to win.'

From 'Granite Poem', Gary Chapin

It's hard to think of a better place to start a coast-to-coast walk across England than the Penwith peninsula of Cornwall, and for an outsider like me, this is an inspiring place to visit. Geographically, it forms England's westernmost lobe of land, and historically, Penwith was, and still is, England's last Celtic outpost. Just looking at a map is enough to indicate this, for the topography is unique, with a richly Celtic language to match. Here the coastline forms starkly projecting headlands and rugged granite promontories, topped by rock piles, separated by beautiful coves and deep inlets.

I began my walk at a campsite in St Buryan, intending to return there at the end of the day. Call it cheating, but I started without all my trail gear, opting to travel light with barely more than my rainproof and a packed lunch in my empty day pack. I admit I wasn't adequately prepared to walk hundreds of miles ahead. I hadn't trained my body over the preceding weeks, and I was carrying a two-stone handicap thanks to three months of laziness, mainly due to the strictly enforced first lockdown of the 2020 coronavirus pandemic. Therefore I made this first walk even more manageable by keeping it inside single-figure miles.

To get to the start of my walk, I caught the bus from St Buryan and got off at Polgigga, a small cluster of farms and a bus stop. It's not quite the westernmost bus stop in England, but it comes close. A granite milestone with pointing hands carved onto its faces indicated Logan Rock 1¾ miles and Lands End (no apostrophe) 2½ miles. Polgigga is a surprisingly quiet settlement considering its location. It's barely a mile from the coastal tourist traps of Porth Curno and Penberth Cove, and (of course) Lands End. Arguments have raged for years on whether Lands End should have an apostrophe in its name, but thanks to a 90-minute debate in the chambers of Cornwall Council in 2018, Lands End is now officially Land's End.

A two-mile walk along farm tracks and footpaths brought me to the small headland of Carn Lês Boel and the start of my pilgrimage. I climbed up to the highest point of the small peninsula and surveyed my view out to the Atlantic. The Longships Lighthouse stood on its rocky perch a mile off-shore. Nanjizal Bay lay immediately to my north and beyond it (partially obscured by another headland), Land's End. I could make out the assembly of clifftop buildings that serve the 400,000 visitors who visit the place every year. To my south, Carn Barra ended its seaward stretch above Zawn Kellys, its chaotic jumble of fractured rocks spilling into the waves. Seduced by the beauty of this still summer's day, it was hard to imagine what it must be like to stand here in a winter storm, but I surmised that it would be alarming.

Carn Lês Boel is two miles south of Land's End and lies on the South West Coast Path. It was once the site of an Iron Age fort. Traces of a ditch and bank remain on its northern side, and a single standing stone that once formed part of the entrance. There's also a large boulder perched on a rock platform near the cliff edge.

__Carn lês Boel__ is where the Michael and Mary energy currents enter England and join to form the __first__ of the __22 node points__ that lie along the course of the St Michael Alignment. These are the precise locations where the two currents converge and cross as they weave east. Between here and the next node point of St Michael's Mount (see Day 3), Mary travels north of Michael, and for this day's walk, I was approximately following the Michael energy current inland and into the Penberth Valley. I then met the Mary current further east at the site of Alsia Holy Well. My final destination for the day – St Buryan – lies between the two currents but directly on the Alignment itself.

Hamish Miller and Paul Broadhurst first discovered this location as a node point while dowsing the Michael energy current west from their starting point at St Michael's Mount in the late 1980s. It was a profound discovery, described as a moving experience beyond their comprehension. In The Sun and the Serpent, the two authors describe their experiences:

'What we found at this spot was inexplicable. The broad band of energy converged to a point at a great slab of horizontal granite and apparently disappeared into the ground. Then, slightly further on, it re-appeared in precisely the same manner, heading off into the reddening glow of a late winter sunset. On further investigation, and with a strange sense of unreality, we found that a five-pointed star was clearly dowseable in the earth's field at the point where the line converged and disappeared.'

I Sat on the highest clump of rocks and listened to the waves. The sky was overcast, but the air was warm, with hardly a breath of wind. I allowed myself ten magnificent minutes of stillness, quietening my mind to appreciate the timeless, natural quality of the place and to give the commencement of my trail a degree of formality.

It would have been a bonus to think I'd continue this walk all the way to the Norfolk coast, but this would be a trail of two summers. I'd only planned this one as far as the halfway point of Avebury, primarily due to the scarcity of camping opportunities available in the wake of the year's coronavirus pandemic. My route to Avebury was over 300 walking miles, mainly following the beautifully conceived Mary Michael Pilgrims Way (see Introduction). I still had to plan the stages beyond Avebury to the east coast, but that would have to wait.

I added another five peaceful minutes to my ten, unwilling to break the spell of this magnificent time and place. I had a joyful feeling of anticipation for the adventure that lay ahead.B

From the promontory, I descended to join the coast path and walked onto the secluded sandy beach of Nanjizal Bay, exposed by the receding tide. Still feeling ceremonial, I walked to the shoreline and paddled my boots in the Atlantic. I reminded myself I'd have to take time to repeat this coast-to-coast ritual in the North Sea at the end of my pilgrimage.

I walked over to a small cave and back up to the path before joining another, taking me inland for my six-mile, half-day walk back to St Buryan. This route took me through a tranquil farming landscape back to Polgigga. I followed a series of country lanes east, down into the attractive Penberth Valley, and on to Bosfranken Farm. My MMPW trail guide suggested that the half-mile of 'public' footpath leading from the farm to Alsia Well may be of dubious interpretation by the landowner, so I opted for the three-quarter-mile road route. This brought me to Alsia Mill, where I picked up an almost indecipherable route leading to the next feature of my walk, Alsia Well. Without prior research, I'd never have found it.

Following an invisible path over a stile and along the edge of a field, I located a barely visible gap in a hedge and a rusting iron gate. Beyond that, I found the well lying at the bottom of a dark, leafy dell. A few almost-buried stone slabs paved the ground in front of the trickling spring, which formed a small pool, almost completely hidden behind an abundant growth of ferns. The only apparent indicators were a few tattered ribbons hanging from an adjacent hawthorn.

Alsia Well is one of many holy wells found along the course of the Mary line, but none are located on its masculine counterpart. This would affirm the nature of the two forces at work. The Michael force can be seen as powerful masculine energy associated with the Sun God, tending to travel over the higher, protruding landforms. The more subtle, lunar-associated energy of its feminine counterpart takes the formless force of Mary. This force is associated with the Earth Goddess. It tends to channel itself through the depths of the land where the Earth's waters flow. These two forces can be seen as complementary opposites.

The well was a traditional location for divining. Young girls would congregate to drop pebbles or pins into the water and count the number of resultant bubbles that would rise to determine how many years they would wait before providence might grant their romantic wishes. Such practices are undoubtedly the surviving legacy of the ancient rites and customs associated with such springs. A cross once stood alongside the well; its water was reputed to cure rickets.

As I stood by the well, I listened to the trickling water, the strong earthy smell of damp vegetation filling my nostrils. With plenty of time and no other pressing objective, I made my pause a long one. Wherever the opportunity allows, I like to connect with the places I visit and here was a glorious chance to do so. Like my seat on the rock just two hours earlier, another half-hour of timeless joy.

From the well, I picked up a very overgrown and neglected path towards St Buryan. I presumed this was the old path that links the well site with the church in the village, but it was an arduous walk. My map navigation was useless, and I frequently wasted many minutes negotiating ditches, hedges and vicious brambles as I tried to make my way along field edges towards the church tower in search of a proper path. The spring of 2020 may have been nature's opportunity to claim back a lot of its territory as seldom-walked country tracks became even more rarely walked during the recent 3-month lockdown (or maybe I wasn't on the right path). After a while, I progressed better and walked my last mile across open meadows towards St Buryan. I returned to my tent at the campsite and with plenty of time to spare, I walked into the village. The afternoon sun was shining brightly, and I was pleasantly surprised to find that the church was open for visitors.

The church is named after the 6th Century female Irish Saint Buriana, who, according to tradition, was buried here after perishing while being kidnapped. It's believed there was a shrine to her dating from this early period of Celtic Christianity. The first church on the site was founded in the 10th Century by King Æthelstan after he stopped at the shrine. Remnants of an earlier church survive in the fabric of the present building, which was built in the 16th Century. The white-painted interior is clean and bright, and among other things, my attention was drawn to the ornately carved Victorian wooden screen running the entire width of the church between the choir and the nave. I also noticed a large upright grave slab with a brass plaque mounted alongside:

THE INSCRIPTION ON THIS TOMBSTONE READS...

Clarice la femme Cheffrei de Bolleit git ici:

Dev de la me eit merce:

ke pvr pvnt di lor de pardyn avervnd

Clairi the wife of Geoffrey de Bolliot lived here:

God on her soul have mercy:

who pray for her soul shall have ten days pardon

There is no date on this stone, but the cross and inscription in Norman French are of 13th-century style.

In the late 17th Century, the sexton of this parish, while sinking a grave four feet deep in the churchyard,

met with this large flat stone which he

lifted out of the ground

I sat on a pew and enjoyed my third memorable pause of the day. Sitting in the silence of a beautiful old church is always a peaceful and contemplative experience for me, and I don't know why. It's been many years since I've done it for religious reasons, but while I'm no longer a churchgoer, I'm an avid visitor to old country churches. St Buryan's was the first of at least 200 I passed or stopped to visit on this coast-to-coast pilgrimage. Parish churches must be the most abundant and prolific physical testament to our country's history. There's something special about being within the walls of a space unchanged and deemed sacred by countless others for centuries. Besides, these days there aren't many other buildings you can still visit just for shelter, or rest and for free without being expected to buy something. I sat down and enjoyed another half-hour of peace, quiet and stillness, then walked back outside.

A 10th Century Celtic cross stands on a stepped platform in the churchyard. Another can be found in the centre of the village, taking the form of a standing stone, similarly shaped into a Celtic cross. Twelve still exist around the parish, and the stones may be Neolithic.

Two miles to the south of the village stand the Merry Maidens stone circle (easily accessed and well worth a visit). It's just one of many other prehistoric sites on the West Penwith peninsula of Cornwall; there are no less than 700 ancient sites in this tiny but unique corner of England. Many of these form alignments with each other. Some extend to the Scillies, the rest of Cornwall and further afield. Our Neolithic and Bronze Age ancestors may have had the skills to exploit the Earth's natural forces, and the various sites might have been located and constructed for this reason.

With my short day's walk over, I headed back to camp. My pilgrimage had begun, and lots of proper walking lay ahead. The next day wouldn't be a long one but perhaps more of a challenge. I'd be taking my camp with me.

Day 2

St Buryan to Penzance

9 Miles

24.07.2020

The sun was shining intermittently between the clouds as I left the campsite at St Buryan. On my back, I now carried everything I needed for the next month; fit or not, I was taking this seriously. Even if my body wasn't adequately prepared, I ensured my kit was. It's nice to think you can throw everything into your bag and shoulder it, but long-distance trails require significant discipline, planning, and attention to detail; otherwise, on unpredictable occasions, you can end up in tricky situations like getting lost, tidal cut-off, hypothermia and even squashed sandwiches.

As with most of the days on my trail, this one followed part of the Mary Michael Pilgrims Way route, and as with all of them, I headed east. My main objectives for this one were two magnificent sites of great age; the Boscawen-un Stone Circle and a large, solitary standing stone known as the Blind Fiddler. After visiting them, I continued east to reach the coast at Newlyn and then walked on to Penzance, where I finished my day's walk.

As usual, I planned my route using a 1:50,000 scale paper map from the collection of them I had for my trail. I also had both volumes of the MMPW guidebook, which soon proved invaluable in keeping me oriented and informed all the way to Avebury, over 300 walking miles away. I'm not a fan of GPS devices, and I feel lost without a paper map in my hand.

This day's walk closely followed the course of the Mary energy current.

Here she travels north of Michael. The two sweep west to leave the land at the western end of Mount's Bay; Mary does so at Penzance and Michael further south beyond the site of a disused quarry. The two currents then travel towards each other before merging at St Michael's Mount to form the second node on the St Michael Alignment (see Day 3). Using my MMPW guidebook, I followed the course of the Mary current, taking in the aligned sites of Boscawen-un Stone Circle and the Blind Fiddler standing stone before ending with the parish church of St Mary in Penzance. I visited all three locations, but the church was unfortunately closed.

Setting off from St Buryan, I picked up a path heading north through a series of fields, following some necessarily complicated directions in my guidebook. Without them, I think I'd easily stray off-course, but within a mile, I reached the woodland track that brought me successfully out at the stone circle, the first highlight of my walk. Clouds were starting to fill the sky, but the morning sunshine lingered for a few minutes, allowing me to see this magnificent assembly in all its glory.

The monument stands in a grassy clearing, surrounded by bracken and gorse bushes. A tall, central menhir stands prominently, surrounded by nineteen smaller stones. All of them are granite, apart from one composed of quartz. The main stone leans obliquely and uniquely at a 45-degree angle towards the northeast, and small carvings, clearly weathered and ancient, can be made out at its base. These have been interpreted as possible representations of axe heads or human feet.

Much has been researched and written about this remarkable monument, and its documented history is fascinating. The Circle was erected in the Bronze Age and is mentioned in medieval manuscripts known as the Welsh Triads. These early texts contain much earlier fragments of folklore and mythology, indicating that the circle was a meeting place for one of the three great Gorsedds of Britain. These were Bardic groups of Celtic origin, the relevant being the Gorsedd of Beisgawen of Dumnonia. Dumnonia was a kingdom in post-Roman Britain which likely included Cornwall, Devon and parts of Somerset. In 1928 a new Cornish Bard Association was inaugurated at the site by Henry Jenner, the chief originator of the Cornish language revival. It was known as the Gorsedd of the Bards of Cornwall (Gorseth Kernow). In the 18th Century, the pioneer antiquarian William Stukeley (see Introduction & Day 27) somewhat ambitiously asserted that the monument was the work of Hercules, who he believed was the leader of the Phoenician Druids and had landed in Western Britain in ancient times.

Since the 16th Century, documents have consistently described the stone circle in its present form. Stukeley suggested that the leaning angle of the central stone may have resulted from disturbance by treasure hunters. However, subsequent Victorian excavations and later scientific reports determined that the stone has always had this striking inclination. Until the 1860s, a Cornish hedge ran through the circle. The landowner thoughtfully removed this and planted a new one that still surrounds the site today.

As with so many ancient sites, Boscawen-un has attracted a lot of speculation about its original purpose. The angle of the central stone, the singular oddity of the one quartz stone, and aspects of the precise geography of the site have attracted many theories about its possible astronomical and ceremonial significance. A burial site was discovered near the stones in the 19th Century containing several urns.

In The Sun and the Serpent, Miller and Broadhurst eloquently describe how dowsing the site produced some remarkable discoveries. Here, they found that the Mary current enters the monument but channels its force by interacting with the stones in particular ways. They also found that apart from the Michael and Mary energy currents, other subtle forces were at work at this and other major prehistoric centres:

'It had long been apparent that whichever line was being followed,

'Michael' or 'Mary', they were only arteries of a vast interconnected system. Main arteries, perhaps, and with enormous significance. But like a river, tiny tributaries and large streams join the main flow in a way that is totally synonymous with the organic metaphor of the planet's waterways. Major sites marked by prehistoric remnants always seem to be places where these streams of energy merge and interact, often in a way unique to that particular spot'.

Fascinating information, but leaving it aside, I spent twenty minutes walking among the stones, enjoying the peace and beauty. I walked over to the central slanting stone and sat at its base. I stretched my legs on the grass and rested my back on it, perfectly angled for five exquisite minutes of 45-degree reclining. Before long, I was joined by a family of other visitors, and after a few minutes of pleasant conversation, I went on my way while the children ran and chased each other between the stones. I wondered if their Bronze Age ancestors had done the same.

Feeling energised, I left the Circle and rejoined the track on which I had arrived. My next pilgrimage objective was another ancient monument, this time a solitary standing stone known as the Blind Fiddler. Reaching it involved a roundabout route of two miles along footpaths and quiet country lanes to avoid taking my life in my hands on the main A30 road. In due course, I reached the monument, attractively standing with dignity in the far corner of a green meadow strewn with white daisies.

At eleven feet, the Blind Fiddler is the largest of several standing stones found within a few miles of the locality. The story goes that a musician was turned to stone for playing music on the Sabbath, a parable familiar with many other ancient standing stones. Eternal petrification seems like a rather harsh punishment for such a minor contravention.

Miller and Broadhurst found that the Blind Fiddler directly aligns with the Mary current. They describe it as a 'magnificent menhir', 'exceedingly powerful, and the energy field surrounding it is so potent that it can be detected a very great distance away.'

Leaving the site, I headed southeast, following more paths and farm tracks. I crossed a shallow valley and then a series of fields to reach the small settlement of Kerris, where I found a quiet grassy spot to sit down for half an hour's rest and some lunch. On continuing my walk, I passed through a cluster of very old farm buildings and noticed the covered head of a well with granite posts on either side, each with grooved slots that would once have held the winding mechanism. It must have been in use for decades, if not centuries. Nearby stood an ancient granite cross.

Another mile of paths and quiet lanes brought me to the tiny hamlet of Tredavoe, which hosts an attractive, whitewashed chapel in beautiful surroundings. From here, the sea came into view, and another short walk brought me above the coastal town of Newlyn. From the clifftop, I could see Mounts Bay stretching away to Penzance, Marazion and the dramatic outline of St Michael's Mount, crowned by its castle.

I walked down into Newlyn, passing the School of Art and joining the coast road at the town's bold, bronze statue of a fisherman casting his line towards the sea. The Fisherman Statue was built to honour upwards of 20 local men who died while fishing from Newlyn since 1980. The work is by Tom Leaper and was erected in 2007. Nearby, I noticed a plaque on the harbour wall:

> **To honour Capt RICHARD NICHOLLS and**
> **the Epic voyage of the Lugger MYSTERY**
> **which sailed from this harbour on the 18th**
> **November 1854 and arrived at Melbourne,**
> **Australia 116 days later on 14TH March 1855**

The Mystery was a lugger built for inshore fishing but modified for its 'Epic voyage'. Despite severe damage along the way, her passage to Cape Town was so fast that she was commissioned to take the mail from there on to Australia. In 2008, a vessel replica was sailed to recreate the journey.

The Spirit of Mystery sailed from Newlyn on 20th October 2008. She reached Cape Town on 25th December and arrived in Melbourne on 9th March 2009. Although this voyage took place over a century and a half later than the original one, it took 24 days longer to complete.

The authors of The Sun and the Serpent dowsed the nearby point at which the Michael current leaves the eastern coastline of the Penwith peninsula. It's now a large disused quarry where once there was a small hilltop or headland. The current continues seaward across Mounts Bay and heads directly to St Michael's Mount. Meanwhile, Mary continues overland to Penzance, aligning herself with the Parish Church of St Mary.

I remembered this section of coastline from when I walked the South West Coast Path three years earlier, and that a mile away (in the wrong direction) is the Penlee Lifeboat Memorial Garden, which commemorates one of the nation's worst sea tragedies in living memory. I recall standing silently reading the inscription on its polished marble tablet.

On the night of 19th December 1981, the eight-man crew of the Penlee Lifeboat made a valiant attempt to rescue the eight passengers and crew of the cargo ship Union Star, which was floundering in a hurricane-force storm in Mount's Bay. Tragically, all sixteen souls were lost to the sea. The heroic actions of the lifeboatmen are simply beyond words. At the time, the Penlee lifeboat station was located near Penlee Point, but it now operates from the harbour in Newlyn.

I continued along the coast to Penzance from Newlyn and headed for St Mary's Church. Her tall tower dominates any view of the town. Well worth a visit, the present building dates from the 1830s, but a much earlier chapel once occupied the site. An arson attack destroyed the interior in 1985 but it was wholly restored afterwards. Although closed on my visit, I'd previously seen inside the church in 2017.

Heavy rain was now falling, which soon turned into a torrential downpour. I marched through it to reach a campsite at the far end of the town and sheltered under an awning for an hour until the rain eased enough for me to pitch my tent without soaking everything. I then decided to walk back into town and eat a meal under a solid roof. I was wet, but at least the weather had stayed dry for most of my day's walk.

On returning to my tent, I planned my next day's walk. I knew I had a long stage to reach my next night's camp at Godolphin Cross, and I had hoped to pay a visit to St Michael's Mount. Unfortunately, access to the Mount was severely restricted at this time due to coronavirus restrictions. Furthermore, it's only accessible along a causeway at low tide, and the tide times for the following day were unfavourable. Regrettably, I knew I'd have to give this magnificent place a miss; I wouldn't have found the time even without these limitations.

Day 3

Penzance to Godolphin Cross

14 Miles

25.07.2020

'God calls us, and the day prepares
With nimble, gay and gracious airs:
And from Penzance to Maidenhead
The roads last night he watered.'

From 'An English Breeze', Robert Louis Stevenson

Most of this section of the Mary Michael Pilgrims Way route shares its way with the South West Coast Path, which I had already walked three years earlier. To re-walk it and reach my intended camping location would be straightforward enough, but I recall this stage was one of the most disappointing of all the 46 days I took to walk this spectacular 630-mile monster. That day was meteorologically very similar to this: a constant drizzle that didn't seem to want to cease as long as I walked in it. On both occasions, my views were tempered by a thin mist, concealing much of the beauty this coastline offers on any brighter, clearer day. In some respects, this day's walk was doubly disappointing. The coast was shrouded in a dull mist, but my schedule and timing forbade me from visiting St Michael's Mount (see **Appendix Day 3***), one of the essential destinations on my pilgrimage.

My damp day began with a wet, 2½-mile trudge along the coast to the small town of Marazion. This short walk section is historically significant in that it shares the course of St Michael's Way, a pilgrimage route that developed over centuries. Travellers from Ireland and Wales would seek safe passage overland from the north Cornish coast, thus avoiding the dangerous sea route around Land's End. Their immediate destination would be St Michael's Mount before joining other ways to reach Santiago de Compostela in Northern Spain eventually. The course is waymarked to this day, identified by the logo of a scallop shell, the emblem used by those particular pilgrims. However, I can't say I felt the historical significance as I trudged beside the railway line using the cycleway this section now forms.

As I approached Marazion, the grey outline of St Michael's Mount grew in stature but not so much in detail as the drizzly rain continued to fall. The causeway it serves at low tide was now submerged, so I couldn't even approach to see the legendary sanctuary at close quarters. I walked past the large parking areas to reach the nearest point I could get to the causeway. Dozens of people were standing at various vantage points, taking photos of the Mount, of each other and themselves, while the endless stream of vehicles passed along the town's coast road. I pondered that maybe St Michael's Mount is now a victim of its commercial success. Admittedly on this day, I'd failed to 'connect' with it in both senses of the word. However, I knew it would be worth another visit when the opportunity arose. St Michael's Mount is perhaps the most renowned of all the St Michael sanctuaries on the Alignment. Its history and significance are not easy to summarise in a few short paragraphs, but here goes:

Evidence suggests the Mount was a hill in the landscape rather than a tidal island in a far distant time. The subaquatic remains of ancient tree stumps can be found in the bay. Little is known about the early history of the Mount, but many legends are attached to it. Perhaps most notable are the claims that in the 5th Century, the Archangel Michael appeared before local fishermen on the Mount. Another is the famous tale of a sleeping giant that inhabited the island until it was slain by a bold young local named Jack. The Mount has long been considered a place of extraordinary power. Medieval scribes have written accounts of miraculous healing taking place, and the skeletal remains of a giant-sized man were said to have been uncovered and reburied during the 14th Century. The Mount has many striking parallels and links with the St Michael sanctuary on the smaller tidal island of Le Mont-Saint-Michel in Northern France, not least from its bequeathment to the Benedictine order by Edward the Confessor in the 11th Century. Legends of the apparition of St Michael are associated with both places.

Soon after the construction of a church and monastery on its summit in the 12th Century, the Mount became a flourishing monastic community and a strategically important asset. It was taken from Richard I by Sir Henry de la Pomeroy in 1193. After much late medieval political turbulence (and geological turbulence in the form of an earthquake in 1275), Henry V severed all links between St Michael's Mount and Mont Saint Michel in 1414. The monastery on the Mount was finally dissolved in 1535 by Henry VIII and from then on, it became little more than a coastal fortress.

Through the subsequent centuries, St Michael's Mount gradually moved from a Cornish fortress to a comfortable manorial residence under the ownership of the influential St Aubyn family, who remain its custodians. The much altered 15th Century chapel survives as a museum. There is also a private cemetery and a collection of later buildings. Chapel Rock at the foot of the Mount marks the site of a shrine dedicated to the Virgin Mary. The Mount also has extensive terraced gardens (see **Appendix, Day 3***). St Michael's Mount is imbued with all the romanticism of the 19th (and the commercialism of the 20th) Century. Pandemics permitting, It has never been more accessible to the general public than it is today.

*Travelling from west to east, **St Michael's Mount** is the first point where the Mary and Michael energy currents merge and cross after Carn Lês Boel and, therefore, the **second node** on the Alignment. The Michael current heads northeast to re-enter the mainland just beyond Marazion, while Mary gains the land at Perranuthnoe before continuing east. Following the coast, my walking route passed these two entry points before* *heading inland and further east to meet the Mary current at Germoe, taking in the landmark sites of Germoe church, Tregonning Hill and Godolphin Cross.*

When Paul Broadhurst and Hamish Miller began their quest to dowse the entire length of the St Michael Alignment, they started at St Michael's Mount. They knew it was a vital energy centre, and the St Michael alignment was a well-established proposition. However, they had yet to learn of the nature of the energy currents they would come to find. It was the beginning of a trail of discovery.

When dowsing on the Mount, the authors located a powerful energy centre at a large rock some distance below the summit buildings on the island's west side. They later discovered that this somewhat secret point had the added significance of marking the flow of the 'English' St Michael currents that run from west to east and their 'European' counterpart alignment, an earth energy ley line with a more north-south orientation. This has become known as the 'Apollo-Athena' line. It stretches across Europe, taking in the historical sites of Skellig Michael in Ireland, Mont-Saint-Michel in France and other St Michael sanctuaries.

In the busy town of Marazion, I found little of interest, but my attention was drawn to a wooden sign affixed to the wall of a house bearing the following engraving:

PRINCE CHARLES – LATER CHARLES II
IS REPUTED TO HAVE SPENT
THE NIGHT OF 2ND MARCH 1646
IN THIS HOUSE BEFORE
ESCAPING TO THE SCILLIES
AFTER THE ROYALIST
DEFEAT AT NASEBY

I walked through the town and located the path I needed to take me down to the rocky beach in Trenow Cove. Hands up, I wasn't particularly looking forward to the walk ahead. At this early stage of my trail, I knew I lacked the fitness to enjoy the ascent and descent required for Cornish coastal walking. The weight of my pack didn't help, nor did the seeping dampness of the drizzling rain. I now had two options; continue to moan about the weather and my payload and get on with it, or just get on with it. Thankfully I chose the latter.

I took the path and walked down to the cove. I walked along the stony shoreline, and at its end, I ascended a metal stairway up to a low cliff. I then followed the coast path around a headland to reach a car park below the attractive village of Perranuthnoe. I decided to make a short detour into the village to look at its beautiful medieval church dedicated to St Piran and St Michael. Sadly, the building was locked, but the churchyard is attractive even in the drizzly rain.

Perranuthnoe is the first landmark the Mary current reaches after returning overland from St Michael's Mount.

I returned to the car park and walked along the low cliffs above Perran sands. A further half-mile cliff walk above the rocky shoreline brought me around the dramatic headland of Cudden Point (the drama somewhat muted by the misty drizzle). My final two miles of coast walking above Prussia Cove and then Kenneggy Sands were impressive enough, but they would have been spectacular in fairer weather. Prussia Cove is no less than four individual coves designated as an Area of Outstanding Natural Beauty. Historically the Cove is associated with the notorious 18th Century shipwrecker and smuggler John Carter, also known as the 'King of Prussia'; hence the name.

After rounding the final coastal headland of Hoe Point, I descended to Praa Sands, and before heading inland, I noticed the Sunderland Flying Boat Memorial. This Granite stone bears a lengthy inscription commemorating the crew of a stricken Sunderland flying boat that crash-landed near this spot in June 1943. The plane had taken part in an 'epic' air battle with German fighter planes over the Bay of Biscay. Severely damaged and with one crewman killed and most of the others wounded, the plane headed for home but had to ditch on the beach.

A short walk through the nearby dunes brought me onto the road, which I followed out of the village. After a mile, I crossed the main A30 road to reach the quiet settlement of Germoe. I located the church, pleasantly situated by the village green.

This beautiful church is dedicated to its namesake, St Germoe, and like Perranuthoe, a few miles to the west, it's aligned directly with the Mary energy current. Miller and Broadhurst dowsed the current through the length of the church and out into the churchyard, where it reached a curious and ancient stone feature known as St Germoe's Chair.

Although the church was locked, I had the consolation of enjoying this delightful churchyard and its equally delightful curiosity. St Germoe's Chair is a tiny medieval building with a double-arched 'entrance'. Inside, a raised stone ledge forms inside three arched recesses. It has a gabled roof with a small carved head at its apex, and the whole structure adjoins the churchyard wall. It's smaller than a bus shelter but, thankfully, just big enough to squeeze into and shelter from drizzling rainfall. I used it for a few peaceful minutes, enjoying my view of the church.

As for the Saint, Germoe (or Germochus) was one of several 6th Century Irish missionaries located to a Celtic settlement on nearby Tregonning Hill. From there, they established an early Christian mission for the local area. Germoe preached from here throughout the rest of his life.

The existing church is mainly of 14th Century construction. Over the centuries, the weathered grey granite has accumulated thick coatings of lichen, giving a natural enhancement to the many sculptural forms found in the masonry. Across the road from the church is an old sacred well restored by the parish residents in 1977 to commemorate Queen Elizabeth II's Silver Jubilee.

I headed northeast along a quiet lane from the church before joining a footpath through woodland up to the top of Tregonning Hill. As I approached the summit, the woods gave way to gorse, bracken and heather, and my views began to open out nicely. It was now late afternoon, still cloudy, but fortunately, the rain had finally stopped. A gentle wind was blowing, and the air was clear. At 194 feet, the height is modest, but the hill stands aloft from the rest of the surrounding land, affording some excellent views out to sea and across the surrounding countryside. A large stone platform surmounted by a Celtic granite cross stands on the summit. It commemorates the men of Germoe killed in action during the two world wars. I sat down to enjoy the panoramic view and ate the sandwiches I had prepared before the walk. Tregonning Hill was once the site of Castle Pencaire, an Iron Age hill fort.

With barely a mile left of my walk, I descended the hill with a spring in my step. As I did so, I noticed a rock amongst the bracken by the side of my path. On it was a plaque bearing the following inscription:

WILLIAM COOKWORTHY 1705-80

This stone commemorates the 300th anniversary of the birth of William Cookworthy, a Plymouth Quaker Chemist, who discovered China Clay at Tregonning Hill in 1746.

China Clay enabled the production of English porcelain and is an international business exporting to over 100 countries. Today its use is widespread in the manufacture of paper, paints, rubbers and plastics as well as ceramics

A short distance further on, I reached the remains of a quarry, part of which became a preaching pit. Here, Methodist services were conducted every Whitsunday, and John Wesley was said to have preached here. The pit is still used for multi-denominational services.

After descending the hill, I soon arrived at the village of Godolphin Cross and, beyond it, the campsite that marked the end of my day's walk. I booked myself in, pitched my tent and took advantage of a hot shower.

Godolphin Cross lies on the course of the Mary current. Its Victorian church is now redundant, and the churchyard contains an ancient stone cross.

Day 4

Godolphin Cross to Stithians Reservoir

13 Miles

26.07.2020

This day was one of careful navigation to get across thirteen miles of agricultural Cornwall.

As with the previous day, my route primarily followed that of the Mary current while Michael makes his way east a few miles north of where I walked. I directly encountered just one of Mary's significant landmarks, the church at Crowan, which was unfortunately closed to visitors.

I began my walk in high spirits, loaded up and fuelled. From the campsite, I retraced my previous day's final steps back to the quiet road leading east out of Godolphin Cross. I then followed it for two miles to reach the village of Nancegollan. I picked up a footpath by a disused railway line beyond the village. Hopping over a stile, I found the magnificent ivy-clad remains of a tall engine house perfectly set in an otherwise empty meadow. It commanded my attention and that of my camera for ten minutes. This impressive stone-built ruin consists of the main engine house and a separate stone and brick chimney stack. The building once served an underground tin mine during the 19th Century. I often find such ruins remarkably dignified places, testimony to a once-thriving landscape, but now silently at rest from their long-abandoned operations. Cornwall is full of these ghosts from its industrial past, in some ways as mysterious as its ancient one.

Carefully following my guidebook instructions, I continued through field, meadow and wood to reach Polcrebo Downs, an attractive area of heathland hosting a solitary chimney stack that served another tin mine. I continued north through more fields, carefully following my guidebook's directions to reach the village of Crowan. There I located the church, which was unfortunately locked.

Crowan Church (**see Appendix Day 4***) is dedicated to Saint Crewenna, her image depicted in a stained glass window. Little is known about her, apart from her arrival in Cornwall from Ireland in the early 6th Century. This attractive granite building is of 15th Century construction and occupies a beautiful setting. I allowed myself half an hour's rest in the beautiful churchyard and ate my lunch. Nearby, I noticed an epitaph for a young woman who died in 1779:

> **Afflictions forelong Time I bore,**
>
> **Physicians were but vain;**
>
> **Till God did please that death should seize**
>
> **And ease me of my pain.**

From Crowan, my route followed a series of paths running south of an outcrop called Black Rock and the higher elevation of Crowan Beacon, upon which is a triangulation column *(Both hills directly align with the Mary current)*. Many hills are named Beacons, where traditionally (and practically) there would have been fire beacons on their summits. Further along the crest can be found the Nine Maidens stone circle and the massive Bronze Age burial site of Hangman's Barrow, later the site of a double murder and the perpetrator's subsequent grisly gibbeting.

I now had a tortuous two miles of stiles, gates, hedges, ditches and fields to contend with as I navigated my way, completely lost on my map and utterly reliant on the details in my MMPW guidebook. The red-dotted paths on an Ordnance Survey 1:50,000 map always look straightforward, but the reality on the ground is never short of uncharted and unwanted surprises. On occasions like this, those lovely, posh expensive 1:25,000 maps are often a safer bet. Safer still, I imagine, are the latest GPS devices that strap to your wrist, tell you where you are in Farmer Giles's field, simultaneously monitor your blood pressure and tell you what the weather's like in Toronto. But I'm still an old paper map man.

Finally clear of menacing farmland, I reached the higher ground of Wheal Rock. I passed another disused chimney and the crumbling remains of another engine house, almost entirely encroached by a vigorous growth of brambles. I then descended towards the small village of Penmarth and joined a quiet road leading to Stithians Reservoir. This large, tranquil stretch of water was created in the 1960s by engineered flooding, which lost 274 acres of farmland. In times of drought, the remains of the once-thriving farmsteads are exposed above the waterline, and some fascinating contemporary archaeology can occur. It's now a popular location for water sports; fortunately for me, the water sports centre has a campsite. I pitched up, took advantage of a shower and treated myself to a meal in the next-door pub. My day had been uneventful, but it had also been rain-free, giving me a chance to dry out properly after the previous day's deluge. I was feeling fitter. I had nothing to complain about and every reason to feel grateful. I ate like a king. Afterwards, I walked along the shore of the lake. The moon was visible as a crescent. The water was almost as still as the sky, and the stars shone above me from zenith to horizon. I slept like a log.

Day 5

Stithians Reservoir to Old Kea

13 Miles

27.07.2020

'Ruined churches, cottages and farms. There is something endlessly interesting, something that sparks my imagination, about broken down, forgotten buildings. How they came to be there. How they once looked. Who touched their walls, walked their halls. How they fell into disrepair. Old Kea Church Tower is one such place'.

Elizabeth Dale

The fifth day of my pilgrimage took in the churches in Stithians, Perranarworthal, and finally, the ruined church at Old Kea. My day would finish near the west bank of the Truro River, which forms part of the extensive tidal inlet of the River Fal.

All three churches are located directly on the Mary current and the one at Devoran, but this was a mile off my walking route. Meanwhile, Michael continues to run further north, directly passing through the City of Truro and its Cathedral (see **Appendix Day 5***), among other significant landmarks.

I began my day early, walking into the village of Stithians for breakfast 'on the hoof'. A mile-long road via the hamlet of Hendra limbered me up and brought me to the church of St Stythians (the village and the reservoir have an 'i', and the church and the saint have a 'y').

Unsurprisingly, the church was locked. It's substantially 15th Century, but there's been a church on the site for 1600 years. Saint Stythian was a female Celtic hermit, but very little is known about her. I noticed an ancient stone bearing a carved Christ figure encrusted with lichen in the churchyard. This was located to its present position in 1910. the village war memorial stands by the entrance to the churchyard.

Miller and Broadburst dowsed the Mary current to the church. Continuing west, they describe how it became 'ever more sinuous' until it abruptly reconnected at 'an exquisite Celtic Cross' in a nearby field. A short road detour of barely a mile would have enabled me to visit this cross, but I didn't realise it was so close to my trail route at the time of walking (see **Appendix Day 5****).

From Stithians village, I walked east to Kennall Vale. This small but picturesque nature reserve bears the name of the river that cascades through it. The water of the River Kennall powered a series of mills producing gunpowder in the Victorian Era. The mills and their associated buildings went into an abrupt and spectacular decline in 1887 when five blew up, one after the other. Parts of the buildings were found over a mile away, but only one person was killed. A second explosion a few years later resulted in the gruesome dismemberment of a man whose head was found over a quarter of a mile from the incident. A small granite quarry operated in the Vale in the early 20th Century, which also fell into decline. The substantial remains of these industries can still be found, now beautifully overgrown and given up to nature.

At the end of the Vale, I reached the village of Ponsanooth and followed the directions in my guide to Cosawes, where once stood a chantry chapel before it was dissolved in the Tudor Era. Further directions took me onto a lane leading to a curious wooden turnstile at the head of a path leading down to an exquisite holy well.

Approached by a flight of stone steps, St Piran's Well rests in an attractive leafy recess. On the wall beside the issuing spring is a small plaque:

ST PIRANS WELL c15TH CENTURY

RICH IN IRON SALTS

SAID TO HAVE MEDICINAL PROPERTIES

ESPECIALLY FOR CURING SICK CHILDREN
WATERS NOW USED FOR ALL BAPTISMS
AT ST PIRANS CHURCH

I watched and listened to the water trickling down over the moss-lined walls of the wellhead while birdsong filled the air. A light rain shower cooled my head. I recalled my pause at Alsia Well on my first day walking the trail, an equally perfect opportunity to connect with the present moment. At Alsia, I had considered imbibing in the spring's water, but I decided it was best not to because it flowed sparingly over the ground. Here I had no such qualms. I cupped my hands under the flow and drank.

After a few more perfect minutes, I made my way back up the lane and walked to Perranarworthal church. It lies in a quiet setting in a most attractive churchyard, out of view from the few buildings nearby. The church was locked, but its porch afforded me some sheltered sit-down rest.

Perranarworthal church is dedicated to Saint Piran, who arrived from Ireland in the First Century, like Saint Germoe (see Day 3). Among many legends associated with the saint, perhaps the most significant claim is that he rediscovered the art of tin smelting. His black hearthstone was a slab of tin-bearing ore from which tin smelt rose in the form of a white cross. This became the origin of the Cornish flag's white cross on a black background. Piran is the patron saint of tin miners.

Traditionally, the patron of Cornwall was Saint Michael the Archangel, the spiritual warrior, champion of justice and guardian of the church (and a lot more besides). In comparatively recent history, however, he was supplanted as patron by the itinerant figure of Saint Piran. In the Sun and the Serpent, the authors assert that this reflects humanity's shift from the spiritual to more material values. It's an example of a theme that frequently appears in their writing; somehow, we have lost our knowledge of and connections with the Earth that our ancestors had.

Perranarworthal church was substantially rebuilt in the 19th Century, but its medieval tower remains. I wandered among the graves in the churchyard and noticed one of a ten-year-old boy named Samuel Rowe, who died in 1846. The headstone is inscribed with a simple but profoundly moving question:

Why didst thou fade with youth
and joyance on thy radiant brow?

Perhaps I'm sentimental, but I stood still over the grave in complete silence for more than a minute.

Walking on, I followed a track north from the church and soon arrived at the village of Perranwell, where I bought myself some lunch and a few provisions for the following day(s). The village is named after a different well from the one I visited earlier, but this was sadly destroyed in Victorian times. From here, I made my way by road to Carnon Downs, a village very much expanded in recent decades. I then walked east to a tiny hamlet with the delightful name of Come-to-Good. Here stands a beautiful, thatched quaker house built over 300 years ago. I sat on a bench in its garden and enjoyed some pleasant sunshine. There had been little of this since St Buryan.

A mile of bridleway brought me to the shore of a tidal inlet of the River Fal called Cowlands Creek. The tide was out, exposing a vast stretch of mud exploited by a sizeable population of wading birds. By the shoreline, a sign occupied a small grassy area no larger than a few square yards declaring 'Cowlands Creek Village Green'. I made my way along a combination of footpaths and a quiet road to Old Kea, my destination for the night and the end of my day's walk.

Old Kea church is a ruin of which only the tower remains after its demolition in 1802. It shares the site with a small mission church built in the 19th Century, still used for occasional services. Nearby stands a tall, round-shafted stone discovered during the demolition. A monastery was founded here by Saint Kea in around 500 AD, and the ancient stone is believed to date from this time.

Saint Kea was a 5th Century British saint active in Wales, the West Country and Brittany. Several legends are associated with him, including that of King Arthur. He settled at Old Kea for much of his later life as a hermit but died at Cleder in Brittany.

It's easy to imagine that this quiet corner of Cornwall has hardly changed in centuries. Bounded by tidal creeks on three sides, Old Kea effectively occupies a natural peninsula no bigger than a couple of square miles. There are only a handful of buildings within a mile's radius of this tiny settlement. A small campsite is run by the farm next to the ruined church. It wasn't officially open, and its associated facilities were closed. However, I'd phoned a week previously and begged for a night's camp, promising to be self-sufficient with all my natural needs. I'm used to wild camping and carry a small, folding trowel for burying my deeds.

With the Sun shining out from a clear, blue afternoon sky, I pitched my tent and relaxed for an hour before cooking myself a meal. Later, I took a nice aimless walk and took pictures of the tall, crumbling, ivy-clad church tower shining magnificently in the evening sunlight.

Miller and Broadhurst write eloquently on the delights of Old Kea. They dowsed the Mary energy current to the tower and described the place as quite special, having 'the effect of imbuing strength and spirit'.

I must concur. Old Kea is indeed a special place.

Day 6

Old Kea to Court Farm

19 Miles

28.07.2020

This day's walk from Old Kea involved considerably more miles between the start and finish than would be flown by a crow due to the necessity of diverting south to cross the River Fal. It began with a walk south along the west side of the tidal inlet to the King Harry ferry crossing and then a walk northeast through the Rosedale Peninsula towards St Austell, finishing at a campsite a few miles west of the town.

This long walking day mainly followed the Mary current. The significant locations were the Roundwood Iron Age fort and the churches of Ruan Lanihorne and Creed. Further on, the **third Node** *point at which the two currents cross was* **Resugga Castle**, *another ancient hill fort. My final destination was the village of Coombe and the campsite at Court Farm. These two locations align directly with the Michael Current.*

My day began under a sky of nicely broken clouds and plenty of early morning sunshine. The old church tower's east face shone brightly, and in the wind-free stillness, a constantly changing soundtrack of birdsong filled the landscape in every direction. I had a wet-wipe wash, dressed, and made a simple breakfast. Another half-hour for breaking camp, and I was on my way, following the route of my MMPW guidebook around the headland formed by the various inlets (creeks) of the River Fal.

My route took in roads and paths, inland and creek-side, all extremely quiet but for the sounds of nature. The river banks were heavily wooded in places, but my guidebook kept me on track. The route eventually led me back to Cowlands Creek, the point I'd reached the previous afternoon. Continuing around the shoreline, I arrived at the next low-lying headland of Roundwood and the woodland site of an ancient fort, the earthworks of which now lie clothed under the roots of the trees. The site is owned and managed by the National Trust and includes a level stretch of land with a fire pit. My guidebook indicated it was suitable for informal (wild) camping, but the ground looked very stony. I saw two large cargo ships anchored along the river through the trees.

Hamish Miller dowsed the Mary current to and through the fort's location. It lies south and west of Old Kea, so these first few miles had taken me in reversed direction as far as the Alignment goes.

Rounding the next inlet of the river, I continued along the wooded bank and soon reached the quayside crossing point of the King Harry Ferry. I now have several country-length coast-to-coast walks under my boots, and invariably there's a short river crossing somewhere, where a boat is the only viable means required to get to the other side. Such junctures break the continuity of the walking line, if only by distances measured in yards. The first time I had to board a boat on the trail, I felt like a cheat, but now I take it in (or instead of) my stride.

The King Harry Ferry is a chain ferry, one of only five in England. It's propelled by attachment to a continuous iron chain, driven between the two riverbanks. Vehicles have to pay for their passage, but walkers and cyclists go free with the expectation of a charity donation. The origin of the name is believed to go back to the reign of Henry IV, who had a nearby chapel built in his honour in the early 15th Century. In time, the crossing became known as the King Harry Passage. It only took ten minutes to cross the river, and I was back on my way.

The river crossing brought me south of the Mary current, which continues west after crossing the Fal further north, before continuing east to reach the church at St Michael Penkevil. It's worth mentioning that Old Kea lies west of the river (see Day 5), and a crow's flight of barely two miles separates the two places. The pedestrian requires a walk of twelve and a ferry ride, however. This made it impracticable for me to visit the place while on my pilgrimage, but its remote location attracted my interest (see **Appendix, Day 6***).

I still had a lot of distance to cover from the ferry crossing, so I aimed to do most of the rest of my day's walk by road. The directions in my guidebook seemed similarly road-based, so I decided it would be safe enough to rely on my map.

I passed through Philleigh (named after Saint Fili, another local saint). The main body of the church is of the 15th Century, with an attractive 13th Century tower. I continued walking to Ruan Lanihorne, a tiny hamlet at the furthest reach of another tidal inlet of the Fal, the Ruan River. A quiet and sleepy place, Ruan has a late medieval church (unfortunately locked as I passed).

Ruan church aligns with the Mary current, as does the next church in the village of Tregony.

I reached Tregony by the road along the River Fal's east side. The village was once a thriving and significant port, trading in shipments of wool until its decline several centuries ago. Early mining activities further up the valley eventually caused the harbour and quay to silt up with mining waste. Tregony Bridge, which spans the Fal, was once a scene of vengeance for the prayerbook Rebellion of 1549. The disenfranchised catholic population resisted the form of worship imposed in the English Reformation's Book of Common Prayer. It was brutally suppressed with harsh consequences. Over five thousand Catholics were killed nationwide, including Cuthbert Main, a priest killed for his mission practices in the locality. He was hung, drawn and quartered, and his dismembered remains were displayed, suspended from Tregony Bridge as a warning to others. Main was canonised, but that took another 400 years.

Tregony's church is dedicated to St Cuny, another 5th Century saint with local connections. I'd say 'yet another', but there are no less than 170 saints associated with Cornwall, so it's probably too soon. The church was locked, so I could not view the interior, but I read that it houses an inscribed stone from the 5th Century and some medieval carvings of animals. Near the church is a much overgrown holy well.

From Tregony, I took a riverside footpath which led me to the tiny settlement of Creed and its beautiful church *(aligned with the Mary current)*. It was open, so I entered the building and noticed a display of early photographs from the late 19th Century. They recorded the building before and during its restoration in 1903. There was also some information on the Rev. William Gregor (1761-1817). He was a rector of Creed and an eminent scientist credited with discovering titanium. On the wall was a board recording a letter of thanks from Charles I written from Sudeley Castle to his royalist supporters in 1643.

Outside, I sat in the churchyard, took off my backpack, and had lunch in the sunshine. I then lay down on the grass, and with the sounds and smells of summer filling my senses, I stretched my body into a comfortable position for an untimed, peaceful pause.

After what I assumed to be half an hour or so, I resumed my walk. I continued north along the quiet road on the east side of the valley of the Fal, passing through the village of Grampound. I crossed the A390 road and continued north for another two miles, passing along the east side of the ancient hilltop fort of Resugga Castle.

Resugga Castle marks the point at which the two energy currents cross and the third node along the alignment after Carn Lês Boel and St Michael's Mount. Broadhurst and Miller describe Resugga as 'one of Cornwall's hidden beauties' and 'a secret place'. They suggest that the crossing of the two currents indicates a greater significance to the site than merely a fort:

'It was clearly an important ritual centre where ancient ceremonies had once invoked the Earth Spirit at crucial times of the annual cycle. One can feel a presence at the place as if it is somehow protected.'

It would have been nice to climb the hill, but the site is on private land, and I couldn't see any easy way to do so from where I walked.

With the sun still shining, I completed my last stretch of road walking to reach the next village of Coombe and beyond it, the campsite at Court Farm, my destination for the night. On arrival, I booked in, ensuring I followed the prescribed hygiene and social distancing rules. As with all the other accommodations I would use on my trail, I'd booked my place well in advance. These sites had only recently been re-opened, with a strict limit on the number of places available.

Day 7

Court Farm to The Eden Project

9 Miles

29.07.2020

'The first impression of the Eden Project seemed enhanced by the effort of having walked to get here. It is a relevant destination for pilgrimage encouraging as it does a visionary sense of the sacredness of life, the potential of humanity and our responsibilities towards the earth, each other
and future generations.'

Richard Dealler

On this day, I had an undeniable highlight in my sights. The Eden Project was a place I'd always wanted to visit since it opened in 2001. Given its proximity to my route, not putting it on my trail would be unforgivable, not just for its co-incidental location. Regarding the theme of Earth Energies, Eden ticks all the boxes and brings the subject nicely into the 21st Century.

As for my route, it was a short one. I walked east to the outskirts of St Austell, where I continued north to visit the Menacuddle Holy Well. I then made my way across a vast area of china clay pits that once scarred this part of the Cornish landscape but were now reclaimed by nature with some help from the conservationist wing of humankind. Most of my afternoon was spent enjoying the Eden Project before I completed my walk at a campsite a couple of miles north of the complex.

My walk mainly followed the Michael current, taking in a Quaker burial site and Menacuddle Holy Well. Meanwhile, the Mary line continues several miles to the north throughout, passing through St Stephen and the hilltop ruin of Roche Rock (see **Appendix Day 7***).

The first part of my walk was road-bound and of limited interest. The only feature that attracted my attention almost went unnoticed was a small clearing beyond the verge of the busy A390, which hosted a couple of benches and a memorial. This was once the site of a historic Quaker burial ground dating from 1706. I sat on one of the benches. As the traffic thundered past, I tried to imagine what the place would have looked like 300 years earlier, but it wasn't easy, with engines roaring in my ears and diesel fumes filling my nostrils.

Approaching St Austell, I turned north at the town's historic west bridge. I called into a shop for food and provisions and continued my road walk. I eventually escaped the tarmac at the attractive landscaped gardens of Menacuddle Holy Well. Menaccudle was one of the most important medieval religious sites in Cornwall, but it's only recently that the site has been cleared of the bushes and weeds that overgrew the Well and its surroundings. The Well locates beside a stream inside a small, 15th Century gable-roofed well-house that Admiral Sir Charles John Graves-Sawle restored in honour of his son, who was killed in action during the First World War. I stooped inside the stone well-house and found its spring water pool formed within the moss-covered walls. On the other side of the stream is a solitary granite boulder sculpted into the form of a seat known as The Druid's Chair. I would have stopped to use it, but it was presently occupied. Menacuddle is a popular place, and in addition to me, several other walkers, families and groups were enjoying the site.

Menacuddle is located directly on the Michael earth energy line. Miller and Broadhurst write of it:

'It is one of those special, inspirational places where mysterious ideas which seem to have been created in another dimension creep into the mind...Whether this special atmosphere is due to the ghosts of those who once inhabited the place or to the presence of the Earth Spirit is difficult

to know; perhaps it is a combination of both.'

Leaving the gardens, I picked up a woodland path/cycle track. The surrounding land is strewn with disused china clay works, and many are now returning to a more natural state with various nature trail routes crossing the area. I followed one, heading east for three or four miles to reach the access road for the Eden Project. With over a million visitors every year, Eden might not need an introduction, so I'll be sparing with mine:

The Project occupies the site of an abandoned china clay pit that was nothing more than a sterile bowl of land at the end of the last Century. It was the brainchild of Tim Smit and was designed by Nicholas Grimshaw. Numerous teams of engineers, consultants and environmental specialists worked on the Project for over 2½ years before it finally opened to the public in March 2001. The substantial structures are two enormous 'biomes' housing thousands of plant species in the world's most giant conservatories. The largest of these recreates a rainforest environment, featuring a tall, cascading waterfall. A second biome simulates a Mediterranean setting. The diversity and interdependence of plants and people are strongly themed throughout. There are over a thousand plant species, and the beautifully landscaped site covers over thirty acres.

A geothermal electricity generating plant is currently under construction, which will be served by a well sunk beneath the granite crust below the complex. The water required for everything collects from the rainwater that would otherwise pool at the bottom of the quarry. Such schemes place the Eden Project at the forefront of renewable energy technologies.

After being allowed to leave my backpack inside the ticket office, I spent nearly three hours exploring the site. First of all, I was amazed by the sheer scale of the place. The cathedral-sized biomes are filled with too much to notice in one go. It was an almost overwhelming experience; the beauty of the natural, living forms, the colours and the smells, even the changes in temperature and humidity. Beautiful artworks and creative installations throughout the site serve to astound, fascinate, and educate.

Before I was halfway around, I had to take myself out to a quiet corner of the site and rest for ten minutes before continuing.

The Eden Project wasn't in existence when the two energy currents were first dowsed. It may be a powerful earth energy centre in future centuries. Perhaps it is already. I'd like to know.

At the end of my tour, I left the site, and after half an hour's road walking, I reached the campsite I'd booked for the night. As at Old Kea, the facilities were strictly out of bounds, but when I'm on the trail, I'm not averse to going without soap and water for the odd night or two. I conjured up a simple tent-side meal and settled down for the night, a contented pilgrim with intent, content within tent.

Day 8

The Eden Project to Trenant Farm, St Neot

15 Miles

30.07.2020

This walk was longer than the previous one, taking in an impressive section of the Luxulyan Valley and the villages of Luxulyan and Livery before reaching the historic town of Lostwithiel. I continued east over Goonzion Down and through St Neot village before finishing my walk at a beautiful campsite in the tiny hamlet of Trenant. The weather remained warm and bright throughout the day, with plenty of sunshine.

When Miller and Broadhurst dowsed the two energy currents, they discovered that not only do they interweave, but in some places, they don't just travel on either side of the Alignment. With both currents to its south, here was one such section. For the first half of the day, my walk mainly followed the course of the Mary current as far as **Lostwithiel***. The town marks the point of the* **fourth node** *where the currents meet, located within the parish church and, more precisely, at its lavishly carved stone font. Beyond Lostwithiel, my walk stayed close to the Michael current, joining it at St Neot and finishing a mile east of the village.*

From the camp location, I walked east to cross the spectacular Teffrey Railway Viaduct, which once served the copper mining industry. It stands impressively, spanning the Luxulyan Valley with superb views on either side of its 650-foot length. This steep, wooded valley was given World Heritage status in 2006. Evidence of its industrial past can be found in the remains of abandoned copper mines, tramways and a waterwheel. The viaduct also served as an aqueduct.

At the head of the valley, I reached the village of Luxulyan. The parish church is dedicated to the migratory Welsh saints Cyricus and Julitta (son and mother). The church was locked, but I noticed a tall Celtic cross in the churchyard. Nearby is the site of a long-abandoned well.

Here, the two energy currents come within a quarter of a mile of each other, but Mary runs through the church and the cross. It carries on in an easterly direction, taking in the next village of Lanlivery before reaching its next crossing point with Michael at Lostwithiel.

I walked on to Lanlivery. The church (dedicated to St Brevita) was locked, but the exterior, with its 14th Century tower, was a magnificent sight. It's also a significant landmark. Seen from the sea, fishermen have used the 197-foot tower for navigation for centuries. Luxulyan and Lanlivery lie on a southern spur of the ancient Saints' Way, a longitudinal, 30-mile coast-to-coast trail associated with the St Michael's Way (see Day 3). Close by is the Crown Inn, a pub as old as the church and much associated with it. Pilgrims would find board and lodging there, and so too, drovers taking their stock to boats sailing from the port at Fowey. A holy well is located near the church, and four ancient stone crosses stand within the parish.

Another two miles of walking brought me to Lostwithiel, the medieval capital of Cornwall. The River Fowey runs through the town, spanned by one of the oldest bridges in the county. The parish church (dedicated to St Bartholemew) stands prominently at its centre. Its 13th Century tower is the oldest part of the church, crowned with a 14th Century spire. A medieval lantern cross occupies the churchyard and the head of an ancient stone cross, moved to its present position in the Victorian Era. The high altar was removed during the reformation and buried upside down beneath the entrance to the church. People still step over it as a mark of respect when entering the building. I was pleasantly surprised to find the church open when I visited, so I decided to look inside.

The interior is a pleasant, airy space, but I was utterly drawn to the stone font. Mounted on a columned base, it has eight highly decorated faces. I've seen some fantastic examples of similar ones with intricate, masterly carvings stretching around them, some telling biblical stories or representing particular religious themes and events.

But this one is unique. Its bold and somewhat crudely executed carvings stand out in stark relief. They include a huntsman with a hawk, a crucifixion scene, a 'Green Man', two charging lions and a wolf goring a rabbit. However, the most remarkable is a grotesque, gargoyle-like protruding face with a massive stone forehead (or 'third eye'?) with serpents writhing around it, projecting disproportionately from the rest of the work. The forehead has a spiral carved into it and is discoloured by centuries of hands rubbing it out of intrigue or superstitious gesture. Without even thinking, I found myself doing the same.

Miller and Broadhurst dowsed the Michael energy current to the font and later discovered it was precisely where Mary and Michael crossed to form the fourth node point along the Alignment. They describe the head as 'like no other ecclesiastical gargoyle in the country...it seems to leer out from another time, a time so strange that it beckons to some atavistic urge within, with its swirling vortex of energy carved exactly where the third eye is located. The existence of such a curious object in a Christian church is remarkable. But its effect upon the energy flow was even more so.'[1]

My guidebook mentions that the church was desecrated during the civil war. Parliamentary horses were stabled in the church, and one was 'baptised' at the font in an act of deliberate indignity.

Elsewhere in Lostwithiel, I noticed a local history museum (closed to visitors at the time) located in a Georgian building. This same building has served as the town's Corn Exchange, a school, a butcher's and a magistrate's court. A room in the rear of the building was also once the Town Gaol. Among the many old buildings and alleys, I found a house on one of the streets bearing a cornerstone with a boldly carved inscription on its two faces:

WALTER·KENDALOF·LOSTWITHIELL·
WAS·FOVNDER·OF·THIS·HOVSE·N·1652
HATH·A·LEASE·FOR·THREE·THOVSAND
YEARES·WHICH·
HAD·BEGINING·THE·29th·OF·SEPTEMBER·ANNO·1652

Without considering Britain's adoption of the Gregorian Calendar in 1752, I calculated that the lease should be good for another 2,630 years and sixty days.

From Lostwithiel, I headed north, hoping to pay a visit to Restormel Castle or view it at close quarters. Unfortunately, it was closed, and a barrier forbade my approach. I had also considered locating the cross on Druid's Hill *(which aligns with the Michael energy current),* but I knew this to be on private land. After a few more miles, compensation was eventually gained when I reached Goonzion Downs, an attractive area of moorland with open access and some great views, particularly on a nice sunny day like this one. I made it the location for my late lunch and rested for nearly an hour, as my final destination was only a couple of miles away, beyond the village of St Neot.

The Michael energy current aligns with an ancient tumulus located on Goonzion Down.

A steep descent brought me into the village. Here I followed a path to St Neot's Holy Well. It stands beneath a rocky outcrop in a meadow by the St Neot River in a tiny building restored in 1852. Behind the rickety old wooden door, water flows into a small pool, its floor strewn with coins.

The healing properties of the well are associated with the first three mornings of May when sickly children were bathed in its waters. I read a notice beside the well:

SAINT NEOT HOLY WELL

Legend has it that an angel told Saint Neot there will always be three fish for him in this well, provided he only took one a day to eat.

But when he was ill in bed his servant Barius took and cooked two. When Saint Neot found out,

he prayed for forgiveness.

Barius returned the fish to the well, whereupon they miraculously came back to life.

The window facing the entrance to

our church portrays this legend.

On walking to the church, I couldn't get in to see the interior or the saint's window, but in the churchyard, I noticed two ancient crosses and a third stone carved with a Celtic interlace pattern.

From St Neot, I took the road heading east out of the village and soon reached the small campsite I'd previously booked for this date. I was one of only three parties using the site, which had reduced its numbers to meet post-lockdown coronavirus requirements. It was a quiet and peaceful place to camp, on a par with Old Kea, but this time with facilities and a much-needed power point to charge up my electrical equipment. I pitched my tent by a stream that runs gently through the picturesque site, knowing that the peaceful sound of the trickling water would guarantee me a good night's sleep. After my tent-side routines, I enjoyed a pack-free evening walk back to St Neot for a pub meal. So far, my plans had worked out nicely, and I slept like a baby.

DAY 9

Trenant Farm to Kelly Bray

18 Miles

31.07.2020

> 'See to the north, the south.
> At the moor's crown
> Thin field, hard-won, turns on
> The puzzle of stones.
> Lying in dreamtime here
> Knees dragged to chin,
> With dagger, food and drink -
> Who was that one?'
> *None shall know, says*
> *bully blackbird.*
> *None.*
>
> From 'Trethevy Quoit', Charles Causley

In 2020 Camping and accommodation were at a premium, and sometimes I had to divert from my route. Here was one such occasion. The first half of this day's walk took in many fascinating places to visit and things to see. The second half, not so much; it was an unavoidable detour off-route to enable me to camp. My guidebook proposed that I head onto Bodmin Moor and visit a series of nearby sites. This I could do, but to continue north over the moor to the village of North Hill was far too much north for me. From my research, there were no suitable opportunities for accommodation within my budget, and no campsites were open in the area.

I could have wild camped on the moor, but that would have committed too much rescheduling further on. With no other choice, I booked into a site further west, several miles from the path I'd prefer to tread.

I awoke to another bright, still morning, and before long, I was making my way along the empty lane that heads east from Trenant. After a mile, I reached the car park and entrance to Golitha Falls, an attractive woodland reserve through which the River Fowey flows in places cascading in a series of small waterfalls. To reach the falls would have used up about forty minutes, so I decided not to detour and walked on, joining a path that led me through more woodland and onto another road, where I found a small walled enclosure within which stands King Doniert's Stone. It's actually two large wayside stones, probably once part of the same Celtic cross. They're richly carved, and one contains an incised inscription commemorating Dungarth, King of Dumnonia. The script is insular and commemorates the king's untimely death by drowning in 875 AD. The cross appears to be contemporary with the time.

A short walk from the stone brought me to the village of St Cleer and its 15th Century church (dedicated to St Clarus). It was closed, but I located its holy well on the roadside nearby. The well is inside a small granite well house and baptistery with a gabled roof, not unlike Menacuddle. It was vandalised during the Civil War but restored in its present form in 1864. An ancient cross stands alongside.

Miller and Broadhurst dowsed the Mary energy current through the church, the well and the cross.

From the well, I continued east to join a sunken bridleway leading to the next significant landmark on my trail, Trethevy Quoit. This huge dolmen (the largest in Cornwall) stands in a clearing close to several domestic buildings. Coming upon it suddenly is quite a surprise. This magnificent assembly of huge boulders has been motionlessly holding its ground for over 5½ thousand years. Its original purpose was known by those who made and used it, but now it's in the realm of historians' 'thought to have been's. Here are the current ones:

This 'Portal Dolmen' is thought to have been a focus of ritual and ceremony and also served to contain human remains. Six huge standing stones create an interior supported by a colossal slanting capstone. One of the standing stones has fallen back. The capstone has a curious round hole, which suggests it may have been used for astronomical observations. When built, the entire structure would have been covered in earth. It's never been archaeologically excavated and is considered one of the best-preserved chambered tombs in Cornwall.

I walked around the dolmen and shuffled myself between two of the stones to stand underneath the capstone. I looked up through the hole in the stone at the sky above. It was strange to imagine that I was aligning my footsteps precisely with those of people who had gone before me hundreds of generations earlier.

Miller and Broadhurst dowsed the Mary energy current directly through the Quoit:
'The realisation that the Mary line flows through this remarkable structure, though, appears to indicate that its original use was far less prosaic than that of mere burial'.

The Quoit was known locally as 'The Giant's House'. A legend states that a giant threw the stones into their position. Quoits is a traditional game where rings (or horseshoes) are thrown onto spikes set in the ground.

From the monument, I made my way north through the village of Darite, passing the historically famous Crow's Nest inn. I ascended onto the southern end of Bodmin Moor below Caradon Hill, in sight of several chimneys and buildings from its abandoned copper mining and quarrying past.

Cutting across the magnificent Craddock Moor, I located Longstone

Cross or 'Long Tom'. This superb, nine-foot example of an ancient wayside cross stands in its original position near the ancient trackway that still crosses the moor, now a tarmacked minor road. The granite cross may once have been a tall pre-Christian standing stone later carved with a cross-head in its present form. Curiously, it appears to align with the three stone circles of The Hurlers, just half a mile to the north. I sat beneath Long Tom for ten minutes' rest, enjoying the peaceful surroundings and the company of grazing sheep before joining the ancient trackway leading to the small settlement of Minions.

Minions is now a tourist centre with a pub, a shop and a parking area. From here, I intended to explore the local landmarks and features in my trail guide, but before doing so, I donned my face mask, entered the shop, and purchased some food items. I then asked the proprietor if he would take custody of my backpack in the hope that I could explore the area for an hour or two, unencumbered by the weight on my back. I received an emphatic "No".

Fully laden, I walked back to the car park and out onto the open moor. After a short distance, I reached the first of the three magnificent stone circles known as The Hurlers. They stand in a beautiful moorland setting, supported by a liberal scattering of grazing ponies.

The three circles of granite stones date from the late Neolithic or early Bronze age and are strikingly arranged in a row running from north to south. They may have formed part of a processional route for ceremonial gatherings. Their north-south alignment appears to extend to two other ancient sites; the hilltop settlement of Stowes Pound to the north and Caradon Hill barrow cemetery to the south. Initially, the monument comprised 65 granite stones, all smoothed by hand. With 29 stones, the central circle is the largest of the three and was restored in the 1930s. The northern ring has only eleven stones standing, and the southern circle has just nine.

Miller and Broadhurst discovered that the Michael and Mary energy *currents cross over precisely inside the central circle of **The Hurlers**, thus forming the **fifth node** on the alignment. Here, they describe the flow of the Michael energy current:*

'As on the cliffs at Land's End, it tapered to a point and disappeared into the ground where an oddly-shaped five-pointed star was dowseable, and re-emerged to head towards the third circle'.

Rather than enter the northernmost circle, the authors found that the current abruptly bypassed it, heading away to the west. They describe how inside the north circle, 'a seemingly infinite succession of shapes are dowseable, from geometric designs to inexplicable organic patterns.'

In the Sun and the Serpent, the authors mention the seemingly erratic behaviour these two energy currents presented when dowsed at particular locations. Perhaps most remarkably, they explain how they appear to dance, even fuse, and symbolically mate, as at Glastonbury (see Day 22). At the time of these discoveries, they described them as beyond the dowsers' understanding, so you can be sure they're way beyond mine.

I wandered among the stones, the sun periodically shining and the sound of larks singing directly overhead. My surroundings were a panorama of unspoilt moorland in every direction, the horizon broken here and there by the solitary ruins of abandoned mine buildings. To my north, the land rose to terminate at the sharply defined outcrops of granite on the southern edge of Stowes hill, one of which is known as The Cheesewring. I readily identified its bold and striking shape and made my acquaintance.

The Cheesewring is a granite formation that looks almost like a gigantic cairn of piled-up boulders, each precariously balanced on top of the one beneath. It certainly looks top-heavy. It stands strikingly on the edge of the plateau of Stowe's Hill, which once contained an extensive Neolithic settlement. Immediately below this magnificent rock pile, the hillside has been quarried for centuries, leaving it dangerously close to the edge of what's left. It's easy to imagine how people assumed this outstanding piece of natural sculpture to be the megalithic work of giants in pre-history.

I made my way up the hill but briefly paused to explore the remnants of an interesting artificial feature; a stone-built dwelling known as 'Daniel Gumb's House'. Gumb was an 18th Century amateur astronomer, mathematician, and stone-cutter by trade. He lived a very eccentric life out on the moor in a small stone-built hut; the scarce remains mark his home among the rocks. Its roof consisted of a large block of granite under which he excavated the quarters where he lived with his wife and family. Part of the granite roof remains at the site, and some of the geometric patterns he carved on it. Highly intelligent but unsocial, Daniel Gumb lived a very isolated existence. He showed no interest in the conventional ways of life and spent all his days studying the night sky and working on theorems concerning his discoveries. His family life was dogged by tragedy, with his wife and many of his children dying young.

The ruins of Daniel Gumb's 'house' are no longer in the precise location of the original site, removed to their present position during previous quarrying activities. A small cavern has been re-assembled, surmounted by a section of the actual granite rooftop. I could make out some of the geometric shapes Gumb had carved on it, but I failed to locate a nearby stone that's said to remain, bearing his name and the dated 1735.

I walked up to the Cheesewring and walked around it. If anything, it looks even more impressive and gravity-defying at close quarters. My views looking south were magnificent. From my high point, I stood still beneath the rocks, a gentle wind blowing in my face and the morning sun shining across the expanse of the moor. It was a memorable experience.

Miller and Broadhurst discovered that after bypassing the northernmost circle of the Hurlers, the Michael energy current directly flows through the original site of Daniel Gumb's House, the Cheesewring and Stowe's Pound. The authors speculate that the prominence and location of the Cheesewring could suggest it was revered by Pre-Christian Druids. It aligns with the Michael energy current but is also located precisely on the straight alignment of the St Michael Ley Line. This fact (more than co-incidentally) connects the Cheesewring with Glastonbury Tor, St Michael's Mount, and Avebury.

From the hilltop, the MMPW route continues north past Sharp Tor and towards the village of North Hill. However, my plans involved retracing my steps back to Minions and then a walk east to reach a campsite decidedly off-route but necessary for my accommodation and the continuation of my pilgrimage. The walk back to Minions was pleasurable, and the larks were still singing and fluttering high above the Hurlers. I ate my lunch, resting my back against one of the central circle's tall stones.

From Minions, I walked a footpath around the north side of Caradon Hill before joining a road heading east. The clouds were building, and drops of rain began to form. Before long, a steady drizzle started to fall, which continued for the rest of the afternoon. I made my way along a seven-mile stretch of road-walking, eventually trudging into the village of Kelly Bray.

I took a road going around the south slope of the conical-shaped Kit Hill to reach the campsite I had booked for my night's accommodation. It was a caravan and motorhome-biased site, but I was glad of the pitch, the facilities and a restaurant in which to eat and dry off.

Day 10

Kelly Bray to Lydford

18 Miles

01.08.2020

*'a church, full bleak, and weather beaten, all alone,
as if it were forsaken'*

St Michael de Rupe, Tristram Risdon, 1625

Being somewhat off-route, I spent much of my walking day heading northeast to reconnect with the Mary Michael Pilgrims Way. It meant I would miss the opportunity to walk from Cornwall into Devon via the villages of North Hill, Coad's Green, Lezant and the historic Greystone Bridge over the River Tamar. I'd also fail to visit Milton Abbot, but I would reconnect with the route at Brent Tor.

All of the above places lie along the Mary earth energy current, while the route for my walk would be closer to or directly on the Michael current. It was a shame to miss these places, but adequate compensation would be forthcoming in the form of **Brent Tor** *and its historic hilltop church dedicated to St Michael. This is the* **sixth node** *on the St Michael Alignment, and what a gem it is!*

Overnight, the weather had improved, and the morning began clear and bright. From the campsite, I walked along the road before picking up a footpath that took me into Kit Hill Country Park and up the southern slope of Kit Hill. I reached the top in less than half an hour, marked by an ornate mine chimney, now somewhat despoiled by a plethora of transmitters and aerials. However, the view from the 1095-foot summit was superb. My panorama took in far-stretching rural views in every direction, with Bodmin Moor and Dartmoor in the distance. Kit Hill is the most dominant feature in East Cornwall, and I could see why.

Leaving the summit, I descended the hill's northern slope and joined a road that brought me down into the valley of the River Tamar at the tiny village of Luckett. I entered a section of the Tamar Valley Discovery Trail as it flanked the edge of the flood plain and headed upstream. I reached and crossed the historic, 15th Century packhorse bridge into the aptly named village of Horsebridge, and in so doing, I also crossed from Cornwall into Devon.

Miller and Broadhurst Dowsed the Michael energy current to a point nearby, and my first mile of Devon followed it closely to reach the church at Sydenham Damerel. The church is dedicated to St Mary.

The church was closed, so I continued on my way, meandering along quiet country lanes in a north-easterly direction. With no significant landmarks or features to distract me, I settled into a steady march that became even steadier when I reached the small settlement of Longcross. From here, I had a 2½ mile, dead-straight road ahead of me, and in the distance, the mound of Brent Tor and its hilltop church were clearly in my sight. Forty minutes later, I reached the car park below the tor. I was now on the edge of Dartmoor.

St Michael de la Rupe (of the Rock) is well-named as it stands 1,100 feet above sea level on a steep, extinct volcano. It was founded in 1130, and although restored in Victorian times, the building substantially dates from the 14th-16th Centuries. During its restoration, forty skeletons were found beneath the church floor.

At the foot of the hill on which the church stands are the unfinished earthworks of an Iron Age fortification. There are other later earthworks on the hill, believed to be from the Michaelmas fairs held annually between 1231 and 1550.

Broadhurst and Miller dowsed the Michael and Mary energy currents to Brent Tor, but they found the precise node location where the two crossed to be at a point in the earthworks at the base of the hill. As with the node points at Carn Lês Boel and The Hurlers, they dowsed what they describe as a curious pentagram-shaped pattern on the ground. From here, they found the Michael energy current ascended the tor and passed through the rock on which the church stands.

I made the short but steep climb up to the church. Services are still held, and attendees must make this unavoidably steep ascent to join the congregation in one of the smallest churches in England. The view from the top is as breathtaking as the climb is literally. A few gravestones surround the church, two solitary hawthorns, a wooden cross and a bench facing out towards the beautiful Devon landscape. The whitewashed walls and stone floor give the place a nice, unspoiled feel. There is an old stone font, some simple wooden pews and a plain altar. A beautifully executed and coloured stained glass window depicts a winged St Michael, complete with sword and scales of justice. James Paterson designed it in 1971. A plaque on the wall bears the simple inscription:

**O GO YOUR WAY INTO HIS GATES
WITH THANKSGIVING,
AND INTO HIS COURTS WITH PRAISE.**

Unsurprisingly, St Michael's Church attracts quite a lot of visitors. Although I didn't have the place to myself, I allowed for a few minutes of mental, if not physical, solitude by sitting quietly and still, contemplating this beautiful place.

With some reluctance, I made my short but steep descent from the church and continued, taking the quiet road into North Brentor. A Victorian church *(also aligned with the Michael energy current)* stands down in the village, closely associated with the church on the rock but unavoidably far more mundane than its high-level, medieval counterpart. It was built as a chapel of ease to provide the parishioners with an alternative to scaling the hill for worship in lousy weather.

The rest of my day's travel was a four-mile walk to the village of Lydford, my destination for the night. I took a footpath below the west slope of Black Down, which runs parallel to the dismantled railway line that once linked Lydford with Tavistock. Black Down's summit is called Gibbet Hill. For centuries, this was the site of executions by hanging or the public display of hanged corpses left to rot in cages suspended from the gibbet that stood on the hill. It was the ultimate destination for many victims of the notorious Lydford Law, administered from the castle in the village just four miles away (see Day 11). At the end of the footpath, I joined the road alongside Lydford Gorge, a two-mile stretch of the valley owned by the National Trust (and a Site of Special Scientific Interest). As I approached the village, I crossed over the Gorge at the historically famous Lydford Bridge.

Lydford Bridge spans the river Lyd at the northern end of the Gorge above a deep chasm through which the river dramatically squeezes into an impressive white torrent known as The Devil's Cauldron. The bridge has attracted the attention of artists, writers, and poets for centuries. It's also been the scene of many legends and fables, including romantically documented tragedies.

Broadhurst and Miller dowsed the Michael energy current to the Gorge, the bridge and the river (see Day 11).

On crossing the bridge, I could look down at the Cauldron far below, partially obscured by the valley's abundant summer foliage. I could make out part of the walkway that passes above the torrent, and I determined that a visit would be an excellent idea for the following day. Besides, I was staying locally overnight, and I had booked my pitch at the local campsite for two consecutive nights to allow myself the first rest day on my trail. I planned to use this to explore the delights of Lydford Gorge and the surrounding area before continuing further west.

I arrived in the village, noticing the castle and the church. I made a mental note of them, and knowing I could visit at leisure the next day; I continued to the campsite. Within half an hour, my tent was pitched. The site was expensive (by my standards), but the facilities were spotless and adequate for my needs, including a well-stocked shop. I booked in, following all the mandatory requirements operating concerning the coronavirus pandemic.

Day 11

Lydford

Rest Day

02.08.2020

'Let Lydfor' men mind Lynfor' roogs, and by Lynfor' law if they will, hang first and try after.'

'Westward Ho!', Charles Kingsley

Lydford Gorge is a nature reserve owned by the National Trust. It forms a deep, two-mile-long section of the valley through which the River Lyd flows in its upper reach, with access for paying visitors at either end. The Devil's Cauldron is at its northern end (see Day 10), while further downstream, the young river plunges in a 90-foot drop called White Lady Falls. I looked up the relevant information about visiting and found that the place was open during the day, but visitor numbers were reduced to comply with coronavirus requirements. Furthermore, access was only available at the southern end of the reserve, and the Devil's Cauldron was closed to visitors. Visiting was by pre-booked tickets only. Disappointed but not completely dissuaded, I decided to chance my luck by playing the trail walker card, indicating my non-vehicular status, having travelled a long way on foot, and see if this could get me into the Gorge.

I set out from the campsite, pleased to be enlightened from 10 days of being laden like a packhorse. Retracing my steps from the previous day, I walked back through the village and crossed the bridge, getting another tantalising glimpse of the white water of the Cauldron flowing far below. I passed the closed northern entrance to the Gorge and continued along the road for another mile to reach the southern entrance. I walked down to the car park and made my negotiations with a young attendant. She happily allowed me to visit with a welcoming response, trusting that I pay the entrance fee as an online donation and follow the one-way system in place with appropriate social distancing. I thanked her and entered the reserve in compliance with all the conditions.

A network of well-maintained footpaths (some steep in places) provide access around the Gorge, and I spent an hour walking them. With the Devil's Cauldron out of bounds, the accessible highlight was the White Lady waterfall. Legend states that anyone who falls in the river here will be saved from drowning by the ghost of a woman dressed in white.

In The Sun and the Serpent, Miller and Broadhurst describe how this white lady figure has been interpreted:

'Such visions seem to be a classic manifestation of the Earth Spirit all over the world, where the woman-in-white is often interpreted as the Virgin Mary who replaced an earlier image of the shining Earth goddess. It came as no surprise to find that the current of energy passed within a few feet of this waterfall, and included half the bridge that spanned the river.'

Standing at the foot of the waterfall, it was easy to see how it came to bear its name, if only by appearance. The force of the water is a dazzling white against the shaded backdrop of dark rock. It's a beautiful sight and certainly a popular one, judging by the concentration of visitors, most of them careful to avoid sharing their two metres of personal space.

As I returned to the entrance to the Gorge, I noticed a sign providing information about the path on which I stood. It shared its course with that of a now-dismantled branch of the Great Western Railway line, which at one time ran along the length of the Gorge. It closed in the 1960s, and now nature has its way. Lydford was formerly served by a railway station which is now a Site of Special Scientific Interest known as Lydford Railway Ponds. The Gorge also contains some interesting industrial archaeology, including a deep, fenced-off shaft from which copper was mined in the 18th and 19th Centuries.

From the Gorge, I walked back into Lydford. I passed a roadside stone surmounted with a modern, circular monumental feature incorporating an axe. Beneath it, a plaque in Gothic-style writing spelt the place name:

Llydanforde
SITE OF DANISH SAXON CONFLICT. 997AD

At the end of the 10th Century, Lydford was a powerful and prosperous town under the rule of Æthelred II ('The Unready'). It was also a royal mint site and a sure target for Viking raiders. Sure enough, the mint was indeed raided in a skirmish in 997, during which the Saxon stronghold was destroyed, along with the church. Tavistock Abbey was also destroyed in the same raid. Another stone on the opposite side of the road near the church marks the event. It takes the form of a granite stone bearing runic script. Both monuments were created in 1997 to commemorate the millennial anniversary of the event.

I paid a visit to the castle ruins (free to enter). These date from the 12th Century, but the earthworks of an earlier fortification can be found nearby. The castle stands on a grassy knoll and is famously known for its dark history. Notoriously it was used as a prison and courtroom. In the 14th Century, it acquired an infamous reputation for its administration of the 'Lydford Law', a very extreme and notorious form of justice that appears to have prevailed for centuries. Those deemed to have transgressed this law would attend a court meeting held every 40 days. The court would then make presentments to a second court that met every four months. If this court found the presentments true, the offender would be deemed guilty. Sentences should only have been pronounced at a third court, but this only met every three years. With little doubt that the sentence would be hanging, many offenders would be summarily executed in anticipation and usually well before the formal judgment.

Miller and Broadhurst give a vivid account of what dowsing the castle was like:

'In the castle an intense black atmosphere pervaded the gloomy building,

and an almost physical nausea affected us both. It was emanating from a dungeon on the side next to the road, a stark stone pit that one can peer into from above.'

The authors explain techniques that those sensitive to such dark energetic forces have used to help counteract them and bring them back into a more harmonious state. They also describe how such techniques can transmute the frequency into clear, balanced, healing energy.

As I looked around the castle ruins, I was aware of the dark history associated with the place, and as I looked down into the dungeon cell, it did feel a bit eerie but not particularly upsetting. Fortunately (in this instance), I didn't have the same level of sensitivity.

A short distance from the castle, Lydford Church is dedicated to St Petroc, a 6th Century Welsh saint and British prince. I was pleasantly surprised to find it open, so I took a tour. The oldest parts of the building are Norman, with substantial later additions and alterations. Inside, I noticed the beautifully carved 19th Century chancel screen and bench ends from the same period. The font is pre-Norman. One feature that particularly attracted my attention was a large tombstone fixed to the wall. Initially located in the churchyard, this early 19th Century stone marked the grave of George Routleigh, a local watchmaker who died in 1802. The stone was relocated inside to display and preserve the lengthy epitaph, which reads:

Here lies in horizontal position

The outside Case of

George Routleigh Watchmaker

Whose abilities in that line were an honour

To his profession

Integrity was the main spring

And prudence the regulater

Of all the actions of his Life

Human generous and liberaL
his hand never stopped
Till he had relieved distress
So nicely regulated were his motions
That he never went wrong
Except when set agoing
By People
Who did not know
his key
Even then he was easily
Set right again
he had the heart of disposing his time
So well
That his hours glided away
In one continual round
Of pleasure and delight
Till an unlucky minute put a period to
His existence
He departed this Life
Nov 14 1802
Aged 57
Wound up
In hopes of being taken in hand
By his Maker
And of being thoroughly cleaned repaired
And set going
In the world to come

Sadly, the epitaph is not unique. It appeared in an American almanac a few years earlier, and only recently it was discovered to have been published in the Derby Mercury in 1786. Remarkably, at least one still-working clock exists, made by George Routleigh.

Elsewhere nearby can be found a recently restored spring and the 16th Century Castle Inn, which appears to have a lot of ghosts. There was once a mill in the village; its granite millstone lies in the churchyard.

Day 12

Lydford to Okehampton

10 Miles

03.08.2020

'Wild Dartmoor! Thou that 'midst thy mountains rude Hast robed thyself with haughty solitude,
As a dark cloud on summer's clear blue sky,-
A mourner circled with festivity!
For all beyond is life! -- the rolling sea,
The rush, the swell, whose echoes reach not thee.'

From 'Dartmoor', Felicia Hemans

For this day's walk, I closely followed the high-level route indicated in my MMPW guidebook, which took me deep into the National Nature Reserve and the highest point of Dartmoor. It was a welcome romp into southern England's last remaining wilderness.

My route closely followed the course of the Michael earth energy current. In the Sun and the Serpent, Miller and Broadhurst dowsed the current as it flowed east from Lydford and across the high tors of North Dartmoor. However, much of the line taken by the Mary current across the moor remained undiscovered. From the west, it was dowsed only to a point two miles northeast of the church at Mary Tavy, while in the east, the line heading west into the moor stopped short at a point west of Throwleigh. The authors decided to leave this missing link to allow others the opportunity to participate in the quest to dowse Mary across the moor: 'It occurred to us at this point that it might be interesting to leave a section of the route untracked, in order to give others the opportunity of entering into the spirit of the quest'.

In due course, others did dowse the current and published their reports elsewhere (see Bibliography).

Leaving Lydford, I walked along a lane heading east to cross the A 386 road. I continued east onto the moor, ascending steadily for one mile to reach the summit of Bray Tor, where the tall granite monument known as Widgery Cross stands. The visibility from here was clear, and my views were excellent. I could see for many miles from my vantage point of 1,332 feet. Looking west, I could see Brent Tor and the Church of St Michael on its summit and, far beyond in the distance, the plateau of Bodmin Moor. The skyline to my west rose before me, promising even higher viewpoints yet to reach. While I admired the scene, a man joined me on the hill, and we began to talk. He was a keen mountain walker, and now in his 70s, he'd bagged all 282 Scottish Munros and much more. His achievements were exceptional, and our ten-minute talk left me feeling inspired and decidedly pedestrian by comparison. There were only about twenty Munros in my bag when I last counted.

On this calm August morning, Dartmoor was showing its peaceful, friendly face for my first venture onto these particular hills. They may be only half the height of Scotland's highest, but they are without question a severe and potentially dangerous challenge in adverse conditions. The author of my guidebook made this one of the considerations in giving the reader both high and low-level route alternatives. There are plenty of websites and publications on walking the hills in safety; the British Mountaineering Council's New Hillwalker's Booklet can be ordered or downloaded free of charge. The advice is always the same, but there's one additional potential danger for Dartmoor that needs to be considered. The Ministry of Defence operates live firing exercises occasionally during the year, so it's best to check to ensure these are not happening when you plan to walk.

From Widgery Cross, I continued east over the moor along a track identifiable as a recessed channel in the otherwise featureless ground. It was formerly a track for packhorses used by tin miners of old. I passed a boundary stone and headed north along a small valley to the crumbling ruin of a building called Bleak House. Dartmoor litters with the marks of past human activity, but in such a vast upland mass, they always appear isolated in the otherwise near-featureless terrain. Whether they are the ruins and wastes of abandoned industries or what remains of much earlier ancient settlements and activities, the evidence is everywhere.

As the morning progressed, I continued to make my way, reaching greater heights. At Kitty Tor, a notice at the base of a flagstaff warned me that I was approaching a military firing range, out of bounds if a red flag was flying from the pole. I continued north, past some storage huts and descended into a steep valley before climbing up the other side. I climbed and reached the summit of High Willhays, the highest point of all Dartmoor.

At 2,037 feet above sea level, High Willhays is not only the highest of Dartmoor but also the highest land in Britain south of the Brecon Beacons or England south of the Dark Peak. I sought a sheltered spot and sat down to rest and eat my lunch. Nearby, two ponies grazed; otherwise, I had the place to myself. For miles in every direction, I could see my views enhanced by the sunshine and the shadows of clouds rolling across the landforms below. I took some photos, using the summit rocks as a foreground feature for the panoramic landscape before me. I then sat quietly for ten minutes, feeling great gratitude for the freedom to be here and now (or there and then).

From the top of southern England, I walked half a mile north to reach the summit of Yes Tor. It's just six feet lower than its neighbour, but it boasts a triangulation pillar which I assume levels it up by another four feet. It also forms a more clearly defined peak. The view from it was just as good and even better looking north. I allowed myself another ten-minute pause to appreciate the view. Yes Tor is believed to derive its name from Saxon roots, which would translate the word to Eagle Tor, But no eagles were sharing my rocky perch. Unfortunately, they are no longer found on Dartmoor.

Perhaps unsurprisingly, Miller and Broadhurst discovered that the Michael energy current channelled directly over Yes Tor's summit. By now, I was beginning to recognise the subtle differences in the nature of the two energies, if only by the different geographical features on which they tend to align.

The rest of my walk was reasonably straightforward; a gradual descent north to Okehampton. I had my night booked at the town's youth hostel, where I intended to use its camping facilities. I also hoped to acquire more provisions, as apart from the small range of food items at the campsite in Lydford; I hadn't been near a proper shop in over three days. I also needed to acquire a new bottle of gas for my stove.

Well-defined tracks marked my four-mile descent, most of them vehicle grade and tarmac-surfaced further down the hill. These lanes serve the military transport activities on the moor, and an extensive training camp locates nearby. I passed the base before finding the site of a 16th Century holy well known as the Fitz Well, entirely obscured by vegetation. The well lies a few feet from the roadside beside an older stone cross. It's named after Sir John Fitz, a wealthy landowner who became (somewhat less holily) a notable murderer.

In Okehampton, I booked myself into the youth hostel. The hostel is located on the site of the town's railway station in an old converted goods shed. The railway ceased its regular passenger services in the 1970s but re-opened in 1997 with a sunday heritage passenger service during the summer months. This ended in 2019, but the station has since re-opened, and regular services resumed in November 2021.

Day 13

Okehampton to Gidleigh Common

15 Miles

04.08.2020

Having sampled the heights of Dartmoor the previous day, I got another chance to do so. This day's walk continued east along the northern edge of the moor, taking in the villages of Belstone, South Zeal, Throwleigh and Gidleigh. I finished it with a wild camp back on the moor at the end of the day.

Wild camping is technically illegal in England, but Dartmoor is a unique exception where it's allowed in specific areas. Over the years, I've extensively camped wild as a solitary pedestrian, particularly in Scotland, where it's legal and generally tolerated. You have to use your common sense, though. I always ensure I camp with minimal environmental impact and leave no trace, and I never camp on enclosed land. If you're interested in wild camping, responsible social media groups offer plenty of helpful advice and guidance.

I connected with the Michael earth energy current on the moor above Belstone and again at South Zeal on this walk. Meanwhile, further south, Mary returns from her 'uncharted' journey across the moor (see Day 12) to align with the churches at Throwleigh and Gidleigh. I visited both places before heading up onto the moor to finish the walk.

My first pressing task was to acquire a can of gas for my camping stove. I'd looked around Okehampton the previous afternoon for some but failed to find an outlet selling the stuff. Later, one of the wardens at the hostel advised me that I could probably get a canister at a local equestrian and outdoor centre a couple of miles east of the town. I studied my map and guidebook and saw I could walk a footpath from the hostel alongside the railway that would take me onto the A 30 near the store. I could then walk to my first objective; the Dartmoor village of Belstone. I phoned the store to confirm they had the gas I wanted and set off on my walk. Having acquired my fuel, I walked south along a quiet road to reach this remarkably well-preserved Devon village.

Belstone is situated nearly a thousand feet above sea level and only accessible by minor roads. It sits in tranquil surroundings at the foot of the tor that shares its name. A 13th Century church dedicated to St Mary and a cluster of traditional stone cottages surround the village green, complete with stocks and a tall standing stone. A holy well can also be found in the village. I remember watching 'The Belstone Fox' as a child, a film based on a novel by David Rook about a fox the hunt couldn't catch. Most recently, the local pub in the village (The Tors Inn) achieved national fame by altering the name of its Ploughman's Lunch to Ploughperson's Lunch in a brilliant piece of marketing publicity.

In Belstone, I approached the church to find it unsurprisingly closed (see **Appendix, Day 13***), so I decided to detour from the village to visit the Nine Stones Stone Circle. I took a lane heading southwest, and within a mile, I found the monument a short distance from my path. The ring is relatively small, as are the stones, but I counted significantly more than nine. The ground is very uneven within and around the stones, and it's believed that they mark the remains of a round burial cairn dating from the Bronze Age. Standing by the monument, it exuded a quiet, small presence within the vast moorland landscape. I sat on one of the stones and quietly contemplated my surroundings. Nearby, a pony trotted past and stopped to graze the grass, its unkempt mane gently blowing in the wind. As with the Blind Fiddler (see Day 2), the legend of these stones decrees that they were once people turned to stone for breaking the Sabbath, a common theme for monoliths in the West Country.

The Nine Stones circle aligns directly with the Michael earth energy current. Curiously there are more than nine of them, but when dowsed, the authors of the Sun and the Serpent found that only nine had energy lines connecting them to the centre within.

I walked back down to Belstone and took a path into the wooded valley of Belstone Cleave, through which the River Taw flows, before reaching the village of Sticklepath. This beautiful glade has several paths and forms a small section of the Tarka Trail. Half-way along the valley, I gained a footbridge over the river, its wooden rails attractively engraved on either side with quotes from Henry Williamson's 'Tarka the Otter':

'Amid rocks and scree that in falling had smashed the trunks and torn out the roots of willow, thorns and hollies.'
'It wandered away from the moor a proper river, with bridges, brooks, islands and mills.'

At Sticklepath, I passed the Museum of Water Power (closed), which occupies a historic mill site. I then walked along a road to the next village, South Zeal. Here can be found the Oxenham Arms, a public house with a very long history. Two ancient standing stones are located within the building, or perhaps more accurately, over which the building has been built. The place was originally a 12th Century monastery, the fabric of which remains a substantial part of the inn. Standing prominently in the village is St Mary's Chapel, an ancient guild chapel. Its small churchyard (now an attractive garden) contains the original 14th Century market cross.

From South Zeal, I took a lane heading south before taking the second of my day's detours up onto the open moor to the east of Cosdon Hill. I climbed up to about 1,450 feet and located the Cosdon Beacon Stone Rows, a remarkable example of the many Bronze Age rows of standing stones found throughout Dartmoor. Most of these take the form of double rows running parallel with each other, but here there are three, each comprised of stones between two and three feet high. The three rows descend (or ascend) the hill in a slight curve for over 150 yards. A cairn marks the top of the rows. Much impressed, I retraced my steps down from the moor and connected with a road along which I continued south to the village of Throwleigh.

Throwleigh Church marks the first significant point on the Mary energy current east of the moorland mass through which it flowed uncharted by Miller and Broadhurst (see Day 11). Many of the numerous stone rows and circles, cairns and other ancient sites across Dartmoor have been found to align with each other, and those who dowse have found that energy currents connect them.

On reaching the village, I entered the churchyard through an attractive, thatched lych gate. To my surprise, the church (aptly dedicated to St Mary) was open. Inside, the clean, white walls give the space a light and harmonious feel. The timbers of the barrel-vaulted roof of the chancel contain ornately carved bosses, some depicting pagan symbols, including a Green Man and the Three Hares. On the wall, a plaque provides details of the church bells, and above it, a wooden panel bearing a notice in hand-painted lettering, old and faded:

THE RINGERS ARTICLES

I

Whoever in this place shall swear

Six pence he shall pay therefore

II

He that rings here in his hat

Three pence he shall pay for that

III

> Who overturns a bell be sure
> Three pence he shall pay therefore
> IIII
> Who leaves his rope under feet
> Three pence he shall pay for it
> V
> A good ringer and a true heart
> Will not refuse to spend a quart
> VI
> Who to not those rules agree
> Shall not belong to this bellfree
>
> *JOHN HOLE, WARDEN.*

I sat on a pew and hoped that John Hole's Bell-ringing was better than his poetry. I was relieved to be unburdened by the weight I carried over the moor. The silence was exquisite. Outside, I noticed a bronze sundial on the wall above the porch entrance, bearing a Latin motto and, below it, the date 1663 and VIVAT CAROLUS SECUNDUS.

Some fingertip post-trail research enlightened and disappointed me in equal measure, for according to the British Sundial Society, the one at Throwleigh is not what it seems. The date and the 'VIVAT CAROLUS SECUNDUS' are to be ignored, as a more accurate inscription should likely read 'VIVAT VICTORIA'. According to the society's sleuths, the sundial was bought from a junk shop in 1910, and a similar sundial at Shaldon gives the game away by bearing a 'VIVAT CAROLUS PRIMUS' and the date 1635. In England, Carolus Primus was just Carolus until the Restoration of the Monarchy in 1660. The designs of both sundials copy that of a genuinely old sundial made in 1663.

From Throwleigh, I walked on to the tiny village of Gidleigh. This church was also open *(located on the Mary energy current)*. Smaller than

St Mary's, the Church of the Holy Trinity stands in a delightful setting with a stream trickling through its churchyard. The interior is plain but attractive and retains a 16th Century chancel screen. A short distance from the church stands a once-fortified manor house.

I planned to walk up onto the moor again from the village as the last stage of my day's walk, but I was in no hurry. I would be camping on the moor, and several hours of daylight remained. My guidebook indicated that the ruins of a 13th Century chapel were located a short distance to the north of the village, involving a detour of only thirty minutes.

I found the remains of this chapel tucked away in the corner of a meadow. The roofless ruin still has the lower courses of its stone walls. A notice explained that these were the remains of the 13th Century chapel of La Wallen, dedicated to the Blessed Virgin Mary. It also mentions that the chapel fell into disuse in the 14th Century, later to be used as a cattle house.

Additional information in my guidebook suggests that a church clerk called Robert de Middlecoat raped a local girl at the site, and consequently, the chapel fell into disuse. Other sources say the girl was also murdered. The building has been a ruin for many centuries. More recently, six oak trees were planted inside it, but they no longer stand.

I walked back to Gidleigh church and took the lane leading up to the moor. Soon I was back on the open moorland, and a gradual ascent of no more than half a mile brought me to the Scorehill stone circle. This assembly of stones is considerably more extensive than the Nine Stones circle I visited earlier in the day. It's located at a similar altitude, and with the sun out and the stones illuminated, somehow, it had greater prominence in the landscape. I decided to stay awhile. I noticed that the springy turf surrounding the stones was level and dry, ideal for camping, but I had no intention of doing so. That would be wrong and spoil the setting for others wishing to enjoy it.

After twenty minutes, I walked on and soon found an ideal spot, hidden away from view alongside the young River Teign. I pitched my tent and organised my kit before cooking a simple tent-side meal. Later, I walked back to the stone circle, hoping to catch the sunset, but a broad layer of cloud obscured it from view. Still, the night stayed dry, and the stream's sound ensured me another fantastic night's sleep.

Day 14

Gidleigh Common to Clifford Bridge

13 Miles

05.08.2020

I woke to the sound of the river and a gentle breeze rippling on the wall of my tent. Outside, I said my good mornings to two nearby ponies and went for a short walk to properly wake myself up. This day's hike would take me east beyond the moor, mainly following the valley of the River Teign, but I would remain within the Dartmoor National Park throughout the day.

From Gidleigh, the Mary energy current runs north to an ancient burial chamber called Spinster's Rock (see **Appendix Day 14***) *before heading east along the valley of the River Teign, while Michael sweeps further north and east. I was walking some distance south of both lines and remained doing so for most of my day until I rejoined the Mary current at Fingle Bridge, further along the Teign Valley.*

Once my morning camp routines were out of the way, I studied my map and guidebook to work out my route for the morning. My guidebook mentioned that close by was a riverside feature known as the Tolmen Stone, a rock 'holed out' by the force of the water over what must have been a very long time. The hole in the rock is big enough to squeeze through, the act of which is reputed to have healing powers. The book indicated the location of the stone to be within 50 yards downstream of the Clapper Bridges, historic granite slabs spanning the river to afford its crossing. I found the bridges but couldn't find the stone despite searching the riverbank for a hundred yards. Perhaps it hid behind the abundant growth of bushes lining the river's edge.

Not disheartened, I crossed the granite bridges and took myself further south onto the moor. I climbed onto Shovel Down, where I found more ancient stone rows. Maybe not as impressive as the Cosdon row, but they still make a striking image as they channel through the landscape. I then walked to the top of Kes Tor, where granite outcrops take on some unusual wind-worn features. Some of the boulders have deep bowls sunk into their surfaces, caused by the action of wind and ice over millions of years.

I walked back down to the young River Teign and joined a road beside which I found the extensive stone remains of what would have once been a large Iron Age building called Round Pound. Its circular form can be discerned among the stones that sprawl across an acre of ground. Archaeological excavations have proved it would have had a timber structure and a thatched roof.

I continued walking east, following a two-mile section of winding lanes that share their course with the Two Moors Way. As can be imagined, this trail route runs from coast to coast, taking in Exmoor and Dartmoor. My path rejoined the south bank of the Teign further downstream, but you'd need a ridiculously massive granite block to span it here. Another mile brought me into the town of Chagford.

Historically, Chagford was a stannary town, subject to the local stannary laws, where tin coinage was the currency used to pay for the tin mined and smelted across Devon and Cornwall. In addition to Chagford, there were nine other stannary towns, including Penzance (see Day 3) and Lostwithiel (Day 8).

According to the New Scientist (1987), Chagford has the most radioactive toilet in the world.

I bought some provisions and explored the town. On the high street, I noticed the Three Crowns Inn. The Cornish Royalist MP Sidney Godolphin was killed here in a skirmish during the Civil War. He died in the inn's porch, which remains unaltered. The nearby church is dedicated to St Michael the Archangel. A statue of the saint adorns the tower, and inside there are several tombs and a 16th Century monument to Sir John

Whiddon, a judge of the King's Bench. On the floor is the grave slab of Mary Whiddon, who was tragically killed on her wedding day in 1641 by a jealous suitor. Her memorial reads:

> **Reader wouldst know who here is laid**
> **Behold a Matron yet a Maid**
> **A Modest looke A pious heart**
> **A Mary for the better part**
> **But dry thine eies Why wilt thou weepe**
> **Such Damsells doe not die but sleepe**

Elsewhere in the church, I noticed another beautiful chancel screen and one of the roof bosses carved with the Tinners' Rabbits. It takes the form of three rabbits in a circle, each with two ears but only three in the design. Its origin may be the much older 'Three Hares' symbol from pagan times. As at Throwleigh (see Day 13), there are numerous examples of this feature in churches across Devon.

The rest of my day was a seven-mile riverside walk along the banks of the River Teign. This wooded valley makes an enchanting walk at any point along its length. The National Trust owns parts of the valley, including Castle Drogo, which stands on a hill north of the river. This 20th Century castle is described as the last to be built in England. Another very different 'castle' is a few miles to its east. Prestonbury Castle is an Iron Age fort sited on a large hill that rises above a bend in the river. There are, in fact, two more 'castles' from the Iron Age elsewhere nearby; Cranbrook Castle and Wooston Castle. Down in the valley is Fingle Bridge, a very popular beauty spot and the site of a picturesque stone packhorse Bridge dating from the early 17th Century.

Prestonbury Castle aligns with the Mary energy current. When Miller and Broadhurst write of such places, they question the assumption that their primary functions were defensive. The authors believe such sites were more ceremonial in ancient times when people had a greater insight into, and connection with the Earth and the forces of nature.

At Fingle Bridge, I stopped for a rest. I treated myself to a pub meal before continuing my riverside walk to the next crossing point of the River Teign. Clifford Bridge spans the river at a junction of quiet country roads in another beautiful woodland setting.

The bridge precisely aligns with the Mary earth energy current.

I located a nearby campsite where I'd pre-booked my pitch for three consecutive nights. Logistically, my trail was about to get a bit complicated. I had hoped to continue my walk, camping from stage to stage over the coming days, but I couldn't find any conveniently placed campsites to enable me to do so. The only way to cover the ground over the next five walking days was to camp for three nights at Clifford Bridge and then another three at a site near Ash Cross, near Taunton in Somerset, transporting myself by bus to and from the various planned start and finish points. The planned itinerary reads as follows:

Day 15: Walk from Clifford Bridge to Crediton. Bus to Exeter, bus to Dunsford. Walk from Dunsford to Clifford Bridge.

Day 16: Walk from Clifford Bridge to Dunsford. Bus to Exeter, bus to Crediton.

Walk from Crediton to Bickleigh. Bus to Exeter, bus to Dunsford. Walk from Dunsford to Clifford Bridge.

Day 17: Walk from Clifford Bridge to Dunsford, bus to Exeter, bus to Bickleigh. **Walk from Bickleigh to Tiverton Parkway.** Train to Taunton, bus to Ash Cross.

Day 18: Bus from Ash Cross to Taunton, train to Tiverton Parkway. **Walk from Tiverton Parkway to Wellington.** Train to Taunton, bus to Ash Cross.

Day 19: Walk from Ash Cross to Taunton. Bus to Wellington. **Walk from Wellington to Ash Cross.**

Believe it or not, this was the easiest way to ensure an unbroken walking line between Clifford Bridge and Stoke St Mary. My walking included

Dunsford and Taunton, so I also put them on my trail. Further on, I had more shenanigans to encounter involving the use of buses when I had to base my camp for two nights at Stoke St Michael (Days 22 & 23) and Devizes (Days 24 & 25).

Once my camp routines were out of the way, I decided to take an evening walk into Dunsford, two miles away. The roadside church (dedicated to St Mary) was locked, but I looked around the churchyard and noticed a section of a medieval cross. I also made a point of seeking out the grave of one Jonathan May, who was murdered in 1835. May was mugged as he returned home from the fair at Moretonhampstead and tragically died from the injuries he received. Two men were later arrested and convicted of the crime. One, known as 'Buckingham Joe', was hanged at Exeter gaol, and the other, Edmund Galley or 'Turpin', was transported to Australia. Forty years later, a new investigation proved that the convicted men were innocent of the crime and at the age of 80, Galley received a Royal Pardon. The case is well-documented and proved to be a significant landmark in the history of British law. May's plain gravestone bears the following inscription:

ERECTED
TO THE MEMORY OF
JONATHAN MAY
OF SOWTON BARTON IN THIS PARISH
WHO WAS MURDERED
AS HE WAS RETURNING FROM
MORETON FAIR ABOUT
TEN O'CLOCK ON THE EVENING
ON THE 16TH OF JULY AD 1835
AGED 48 YEARS

St Mary's Church directly aligns with the Mary earth energy current (see Day 15).

Day 15

Clifford Bridge to Crediton

11 Miles

06.08.2020

This relatively straightforward walk took me out of the Dartmoor National Park and on to Tedburn St Mary, Posbury Clump and Crediton.

I took a road northeast out of the Teign Valley from my camp. After a mile or two, I reached the road between Cheriton Bishop and Dunsworth, which marks the eastern border of the Dartmoor National Park. I crossed over and continued northeast for a few more miles to reach the village of Tedburn St Mary. This settlement is much more recent than Town Barton, its predecessor a mile to the west. St Mary's Church and a small handful of cottages remain in the original village.

Miller and Broadhurst found that the Mary energy current travelled north from Dunsford before curving west, avoiding the modern village to pass (perhaps unsurprisingly) through Town Barton and St Mary's Church.

The church was closed, so I continued on my way, heading for Crediton, the first town on my trail since Lostwithiel. Quiet, winding lanes brought me through the tiny settlements of Venny Tedburn and Posbury, where I detoured to look at the remotely isolated St Luke's Proprietary Chapel. I sat on a bench in the attractive garden, taking half an hour's rest. Nearby, the wooded hilltop of Posbury Clump rose for several hundred feet above the surrounding landscape. The hill is a 250 million-year-old extinct volcano. The Iron Age hill fort of Posbury Castle once occupied its summit.

Posbury Castle also aligns with the Mary current, which continues north and east to reach Crediton, where it meets the Michael current arriving from the west. The two energy lines then cross at the church of St Creda in the centre of the town to form the seventh node along the Alignment.

To reach Crediton, I walked south of the Clump and down into the village of Uton. Here, my guidebook indicated the presence of a holy well dedicated to St Mary that once served a long-vanished 12th Century chantry chapel. Through a gap in the roadside, I located the secluded well. Its water now issued copiously from a pipe, and someone had thoughtfully left a cup for any thirsty pilgrims. Traditionally, the waters of the Lady Well are reputed to have healing properties for the eyes. I filled my bottle and enjoyed a refreshing drink before soaking my open-eyed face under the flow. I lingered for ten minutes, enjoying the peaceful sounds of the water.

My last two miles into Crediton involved crossing the River Yeo and climbing a hillside to reach a network of roads that took me into the town centre. As I did so, I noticed that the ground beneath my boots was rust-coloured, quite different from the grey soil to which I'd become accustomed. Red sandstone is the rock hereabouts and features in the local building stone, including that of Crediton parish church.

The Church of the Holy Cross (or, to give its former full title, 'The Collegiate Church of the Holy Cross and the Mother of Him who Hung Thereon') is a large, impressive building containing many monuments and a Norman font. The building dates to the 15th Century, retaining some 12th Century work. Its history and significance go back to the 10th Century when it was the location of the Cathedral for Devon and Cornwall. The church and the town are primarily associated with St Boniface, an 8th Century missionary born locally but later became a leading figure in the church's foundation in Continental Europe. Boniface was murdered in Holland when on his final mission in 754. Born in Crediton under the name of Winfrith, he is the patron saint of Devon.

Miller and Broadhurst dowsed the Michael energy current through the centre of the north tower of the church and later found the Mary current joined it at this same precise node point. Mary then flows west from the church to pass through the site of a holy well dedicated to St Boniface on nearby parkland. Meanwhile, Michael continues east towards the ancient hilltop settlement of Cadbury Castle (see Day 16).

The church was closed, but I walked around the large churchyard, a little distracted by the noise of the traffic carried along the busy roads that run through the town. I still enjoyed the otherwise pleasant, sunny surroundings. Two more Holy Wells are located nearby. One is Libbet's Well (dedicated to St Elizabeth), just a short distance from the church. It was the site of an ancient priest's hostel, possibly a leper hospital. The other is St Boniface's Well. I found it in the town park, beneath an unattractive stone housing surrounded by a temporary metal fence. The lintel bears a difficult-to-read inscription:

TRADITIONAL WELL OF WINFRITH
ST BONIFACE
BORN AT CREDITON
A.D. 680

Nearby is a white stone statue of St Boniface.

Having completed my comparatively short day's walk, I located the bus stop I needed to get to Exeter. I didn't have the opportunity to look around the city, but I managed to glimpse the cathedral from the bus as I passed. My final bus ride of the day brought me back to Dunsford. I found St Mary's church (see Day 14) was open this time, so I looked inside.

In The Sun and the Serpent, the authors photograph an old chair made of black oak. This was located in the church at the time of their visit. They describe the ornately carved piece:

'A pagan 'Green Man' spills greenery from its mouth. Dragons and serpents writhe all over it. And a Celtic 'Bishop' or early Saint thrusts his cross down the throat of a large dragon in a style that indicates great antiquity,'

This *'striking dragon chair'* is just one of many examples that Broadhurst and Miller provide in themes and references found in churches or on other Christian sites that hark back to a time before the arrival of Christianity on our shores. So many ancient sacred traditions and folklore are doubtless re-adopted into later Christian narratives.

I looked for the 'dragon chair' inside the church, but sadly it wasn't there. I can only assume (or hope) it has been safely removed or stored in the intervening years. Elsewhere in the church, I noticed some rather austere-looking tombs and memorials to the Fulford family from the 17th-19th Centuries. There's also a modern sculpted bronze head of Christ adorned with a crown of barbed wire.

I finished my day with a walk back to Clifford Bridge, where the campsite owner kindly allowed me to charge up my electrical equipment and use his Wi-Fi. I planned my next day's walk, showered, and cooked a meal before taking a short sunset walk along a magnificent stretch of Teign Valley. I figured that my walk from Carn Lês Boel to Avebury was now half-completed.

Day 16

Crediton to Bickleigh

13 Miles

07.08.2020

This day's walk began at Crediton, but I had to get there first. I walked to Dunsford once again and took a bus to Exeter before getting another back to Crediton, the point where I finished my previous day's walk. Under the circumstances, it was the best (and only) way to go about it, and as with the day earlier, once I reached the endpoint at Bickleigh, I'd have to get buses back to Exeter and Dunsford and walk back to camp. Still, there's no point in complaining, and at least I found it was all feasible. Besides, for the second day in a row, I travelled light, with barely more than sandwiches and a coat in my rucksack. The bus rides out were uneventful.

From Crediton, I had a relatively short day's walk to Bickleigh via Shobrooke, Thorverton and the highlight of my day, Cadbury Castle.

Crediton, Cadbury Castle, and Bickleigh all align with the Michael earth energy current, while Mary remains several miles north of where I walked.

At Crediton, I started my walk at the church and made my way east. Just outside the town, I took a footpath across an area of land called Lord's Meadow on my map. I then crossed the River Creedy to reach a permissive path through Shobrooke Park, a restored Victorian garden that once hosted a 19th Century mansion. The walk was pleasant, and the morning air was sunny and still. At the end of the park, I reached the small village of Shobrooke.

Shobrooke is an interesting place. The well-kept village has an exceptionally well-kept wooden roadside bus shelter. It incorporates a wooden bench and chair, complete with cushions and magazines. All it needed was a tea and coffee-making station to neutralise the disappointment of the Devonshire bus services. Noticeboards provide information on the local area and a bus timetable. There's even a functioning clock mounted on the wall.

Of greater interest is the unique nature of the buildings in the village. Many of these are made from cob, a mixture of clay, water and straw. The churchyard wall has been made of the same material and topped with a tiled roof. It bears a plaque:

> "**Your people will rebuild**
>
> **the ancient ruins and**
>
> **will raise up the age-old**
>
> **foundations.**
>
> **You will be called**
>
> **Repairer of Broken Walls,**
>
> **Restorer of Streets and Dwellings."**
>
> **(Isaiah 58, v12)**

Shobrooke's church (locked at the time of visiting) is dedicated to St Swithin. A short distance away stands a roadside holy well. A stone arch frames the spring, which issues from behind an attractive wrought iron gate. The church hosts harvest celebrations during which well blessing services take place.

From Shobrooke, I walked east, passing below the Raddon Hills to reach the village of Thorverton. Here I stopped for a short break. This sleepy Devon village saw much action during the Civil War because of its strategic position as an essential crossing point on the River Exe. It was taken over by Parliamentary forces in 1644 when they besieged Exeter but fell to the Royalists the following year, only to be retaken by the

Roundheads as Exeter fell following a second siege in 1646. Thorverton later played another vital wartime role in the build-up to D-Day when American artillery troops were billeted in the village.

After a short rest, I headed north. The most picturesque route to take to Bickleigh would have been to follow the Exe Valley Way above the valley's west side, but my main objective involved diverting to connect with the spectacular Iron age hill fort of Cadbury Castle. Approaching it from the south, I picked up the path that gradually led me to its 830-foot summit. It's a magnificent walk with stunning views in every direction. The grassy area on which the fort once stood covers the level top of the hill surrounded by earthworks, which now grow mature, leafy trees.

I sat on one of the grassy banks beneath the shade of an oak tree and rested against its wrinkled trunk. A few yards away, a gathering of sheep quietly grazed, complementing my view across the Devon landscape. It was a quintessential English summer scene, and I was in no hurry to leave, so I made a picnic of my time and ate my packed lunch.

The early occupants of the site were pre-Roman settlers. Illustrated notices explain what it would have looked like for the people from the Dumnonian tribe living here two and a half thousand years ago. Interestingly, the information refers to the Cadbury Dragon, a legend of an enormous winged beast said to fly over the Exe Valley, lighting the night sky with its flaming breath. The Dragon is supposed to guard a hoard of treasure buried on the hill.

The hill is also one of several places believed to be the site of King Arthur's Camelot. Here the legend may partly have its roots in Victorian archaeological excavations. They indicated that the site was reoccupied and fortified in the 6th Century when Arthur was believed to be active in the region. In the classic Arthurian legend, Cadbury is one of several hills under which Arthur and his men are said to sleep, awaiting the time when they shall rise once more and fight for the nation.

Broadhurst and Miller mention something of these legends and go on to describe their experience of being at this unique location, which aligns with the Michel energy current:

'After spending some time within the enclosure, the mood was indisputably mystical. It seemed as though we were being given glimpses into another way of existence, a world where a mutual co-operation with nature had laid the foundation for civilisations whose quality of life was almost unimaginable.'

After an enthralling half-hour, I reluctantly descended the hill to reach the church at its foot; St Michael's, Cadbury. Regrettably, the building was closed, so I walked around the churchyard. Having now spent many days on my pilgrimage visiting churches almost invariably built from grey granite, I quickly noticed the striking change. There was a red sandstone tower. Day by day on the trail, not everything changes all at once, but often subtly. The building materials and styles, the accents, the unique landscape features and the tourist leaflets; everything is subject to change. So too, the seasonal. Buds turn into leaves, lambs turn into sheep, pounds turn into pence, and my beard grows.

From Cadbury, I made my way to Bickleigh, the final destination of my walk for the day. I can't remember the precise route, but I recall walking along an exceedingly long concrete drive alongside acre after acre of orchards. Before reaching the village, I passed near Bickleigh Castle. The 15th Century fortification is now a private venue centre.

Bickleigh village is built along the east side of the River Exe, south of the bridge that bears its name. I terminated my walk here and had a break at the inn that overlooks the historic, five-arched edifice. The Exe flows in a picturesque cataract, as impressively wide as the bridge is long. Until recently, Bickleigh Bridge was widely believed to be the inspiration for Simon and Garfunkel's 'Bridge over Troubled Water', but an interview with Art later confirmed that the song had no connection with Bickleigh. By consolation for our nation, he did confirm that the railway station in 'Homeward Bound' was Widnes Station.

The bridge is inspirational, nonetheless. Its five historic arches beautifully span the silvery Exe in a steep section of its valley. It carries the traffic of a busy main road, squeezed into a single lane with no room for pavement, yet with far more character and dignity than the map would have you assume. The bridge dates from the 16th Century, and the present structure was rebuilt in 1809.

I walked over the bridge, timing my crossing to avoid a squeeze between the traffic and its wall. On the other side, I found the bus-stopping lay-by from where I caught my bus to Exeter (and beyond). On my third day's visit to and through the city, I was beginning to feel like a commuter. My bus rides back to Dunsford were as uneventful as the outward ones, and my walk back to Clifford Bridge was starting to feel very familiar.

Day 17

Bickleigh to Tiverton Parkway

13 Miles

08.08.2020

I was up nice and early for this, the 16th walking day of my trail. The logistics to get to the start would require a walk to Dunsford and buses to Bickleigh via Exeter. Then at the other end, a train to Taunton and a bus out to a campsite at Henlade, four miles southeast of the county town of Somerset. Annoyingly, I would have to take all my kit. I don't mind walking with it; that's part of the deal, but carting a 40lb rucksack on a chain of public transport journeys is inconvenient. Also, this day was easily the hottest I'd experienced so far. Weather records for the UK suggest that the previous day was hotter, but not where I was walking. Yesterday was hot, but this afternoon was going to be stifling.

I left the camp by my now familiar two-mile walk to Dunsford, and my bus journeys in and out of Exeter brought me back to Bickleigh at around 9.00 am. My walking route was relatively straightforward. I followed the Exe Valley Way north to Tiverton and headed east, primarily by the footpath alongside the Grand Western Canal. I finished my walk at Tiverton Parkway railway station.

Leaving Bickleigh, I joined the valley path, passing the Devon Railway Centre, a popular family attraction of restored railway buildings and narrow-gauge rail service. I also passed Bickleigh Mill, once a Georgian watermill now converted into a large shopping attraction. From here, I walked along the valley of the Exe, my path warping up and down through attractive woodland in places or passing through fields alongside the river. After an hour and a half, I reached the outskirts of Tiverton and walked into the town.

Miller and Broadhurst found that the Michael energy current travels along this stretch of the valley between Bickleigh and Tiverton. In the town, it aligns directly with St Peter's church and the adjacent castle.

I continued along the east side of the river into the town centre, which seemed surprisingly quiet for a Saturday. I passed the town's museum (closed), but by the side of the road, I noticed a very ancient-looking timber beam, above which was a plaque:

Timbers from the EXE BRIDGE, TIVERTON
Found in the river-bed during the
building of the new bridge 1970.
Probably dating from the early 15th Century
when ST MARY'S CHAPEL
stood on the bridge.

I located St Peter's church in the town centre, which was closed to visitors. However, looking around the exterior was quite intriguing. In the 16th Century, a chapel was added to the existing building, which mainly dates from the 15th Century. John Greenway, a wealthy Elizabethan wool merchant, provided this. The work is highly ornate and, fortunately, extends to the exterior of the south wall and the central porch. I stood in front of the wall and surveyed the sculptural carvings on the white stone, dazzling in the bright sunshine. All manner of mercantile symbols and imagery are recreated in the form of ships, anchors and emblems of the cloth trade, along with religious and secular subjects. It made an impressive, ostentatious display featuring (of course) relief sculptures of the donor and his family.

I sat down on the grass and had my lunch. Amidst the gravestones and the well-clipped yew trees, I noticed the medieval font that initially stood in the church before an extravagantly carved Victorian replacement consigned it to its present position. It seems they've thrown the bath out, if not the baby and the water.

A short distance to the north of the church stands Tiverton Castle. It was built by Henry I in 1106 and much altered over the intervening centuries. The parliamentarians besieged it under Sir Thomas Fairfax during the Civil War, the only time it saw battle in its long history. The castle is privately owned but opens for summer visitors (pandemics permitting) and private functions. It was closed at the time of my visit.

The Michael energy current continues north for two miles from the church and castle before making a tight loop to the east and turning back on itself. It returns to Tiverton, this time on the east side of the town and then heads east. Mary does something similar in a broader loop further north. Both currents then continue east, Mary above Michael. The rest of my walk intercepted the Michael current at the churches of Halberton and Stampford Peverell.

The day's heat made me sweat as I walked east of Tiverton. I walked a disused railway line (now a cycleway) and joined the towpath of the Grand Western Canal south of the village of Halberton. Walking alongside a canal has a certain predictability, but it's always a pleasant experience. However, this stretch tends to meander in wide loops, so I edited a mile of footage by short-cutting into the village of Halberton to look at the church. The building was closed, but I took a welcome break in the churchyard beneath the shade of a Horse Chestnut tree. The beautiful red sandstone church is dedicated to St Andrew and dates from the 14th Century.

The 18th Century Grand Western Canal was built to form a link for canal boat traffic between the Bristol Channel and the English Channel. The plan was to link the Bridgewater and Taunton Canal with the Exeter Ship Canal, but with the development of the railways, not all the projects were completed. The Grand Western Canal was successfully built from Tiverton to Taunton, straddling the counties of Somerset and Devon, but now only an eleven-mile section remains, entirely within Devon. This section was suitable for broad-beam barges carrying up to 40 tons between Tiverton and Lowdswell. In contrast, the Somerset section could only serve smaller tub boats due to the incline and the engineering of seven boat lifts between Lowdswell and Taunton. The Devonshire section remains navigable to this day.

After my short rest, I rejoined the canal and continued east to the village of Stampford Peverell, where I took another break, this time for refreshment and shade in a pub garden. Social distancing requirements meant waiting, but I had plenty of time. I only had a mile left to walk to the end of my day's walk, although I also had to get to my camp location by public transport afterwards.

Before heading on, I visited the Church of St John the Baptist. Although closed, I was interested to see that efforts have been made to landscape the churchyard with nature conservation in mind. A notice gave information about how this was achieved, and the rare species of butterflies frequenting the churchyard. Tucked away by the wall, I also noticed a small memorial of crosses and poppies made by the local children of the parish. It was marked with a small brass plaque containing lines from Laurence Binyon's 'For the Fallen'.

My last walking mile brought me to the modern commuter railway station of Tiverton Parkway, a slightly confusing name given that it's over six miles east of the town. I then had a hot and sweaty journey by train and bus to the campsite at Ash Cross, a few miles south of Taunton.

Tiverton Parkway station appears to align directly on the Michael energy line, but it was just a railway junction when the current was first dowsed.

Day 18

Tiverton Parkway to Wellington

10 Miles

09.08.2020

This day was a Sunday, and I had some wheel-based travelling to do before the start of my walk. I also had to do some more afterwards to get back to camp. I relied on the Sunday public transport timetables, so I only had a few hours of walking time. Although I now camped in Somerset, my walk was still back in Devon, and there were two full days of walking still to cover the ground in between. Before hiking, I had to take a bus into Taunton and take the train to my starting point at Tiverton Parkway station.

As for the walk, I extended my trail east to Wellington via another section of the Grand Western Canal before crossing from Devon to Somerset at Lowdswells Lock. I also visited the villages of Holcombe Rogus, Greenham, Thorne St Margaret and Holywell Lake.

Tiverton Parkway aligns with the course of the Michael energy line. From there, I walked north along the path of the Grand Western Canal to join the Mary line at Holcombe Rogus. Before finishing my walk at Wellington, I continued to Greenham (also aligned with Mary). The town lies between the two energy currents, but to its south, the unmistakable Wellington Monument occupies the summit of Wellington Hill, directly aligned with the Michael energy current.

A short road walk from the railway station brought me back onto the

Grand Western Canal at the hamlet of Ayshford. Before joining the towpath on the south bank, I crossed a bridge to visit the 15th Century Ayshford Chapel. As expected, the building was closed, but it was still an interesting place to see and read about. This stone chapel stands in a meadow by the canal. Long disused, the building is now under the care of the Friends of Friendless Churches, a marvellous charity that acquires leases for the protected ownership of redundant parish churches. Major conservation work has taken place to restore the interior.

My canal-side walk was uneventful but quietly peaceful. Before long, I reached Fenacre Bridge, where I left the waterway and followed my guidebook directions across farmland to reach the village of Holcombe Rogus. The two buildings of interest are the parish church dedicated to All Saints and Holcombe Court, a Tudor manor house established by the Bluett family, to whom several monuments are dedicated inside the church. The manor house is privately owned, and the church was closed during my visit.

Beyond the church, I rejoined the Grand Western Canal for a short distance. Here it's less popular with boaters, so the weeds and the algae give it a beautifully neglected feel by comparison with the smart and commercially functional channel I'd walked the previous day. I noticed the large stone arches of some 19th Century lime kilns on the far bank. These were used to fire the limestone extracted from nearby mines and brought to the kilns by pack horses. Apart from general agricultural and industrial use, these kilns provided the materials needed to make the puddle clay that lined the canal. The kilns' stonework has recently been structurally restored.

A short way beyond the kilns, I reached Lowdswells Lock, marking the waterway's highest point and the meeting point of John Rennie's broad canal with James Green's tub boat canal. The section east of this point is now dry land, but Green's channel was once navigable to Taunton, where it joined the Bridgewater and Taunton Canal. The lock gates have gone, but the basin is delightfully grown over and returned to nature.

Although Green's canal has vanished, a public footpath follows much of its former route, so I used it to approach Taunton. It made a fascinating walk; in places, I could walk what remained of the towpath or tread the ground that now forms the infill of the vanished waterway. I passed the site of the Greenham Lift, one of seven boat lifts that enabled the barges to be raised by a total of 265 feet between Taunton and Lowdswells (see also Day 17). The best-preserved site of these sites is the Nynehead Lift, located a few miles east.

A short distance beyond the lift site, I crossed from Devon into Somerset and diverted into the village of Greenham to look at its Victorian church *(aligned with the Mary energy current)*, dedicated to Saint Peter. It was built in the Gothic Revival style, and its octagonal tower is topped with a spire.

I continued along the course of the vanished canal for another mile, but with time beginning to run short, I decided to take a road walk into Wellington. As I approached the town, I could see the colossal hilltop monolith of the Wellington Monument perched above the valley (see Day 19). At first glance, the massive obelisk looked a bit fuzzy from several miles distance until my brain engaged with my eyes to deduce that it was clad entirely in scaffolding.

On my road walk into Wellington, I passed through the small villages of Thorne St Margaret and Holywell Lake. They share the parish church dedicated to St Margaret. The church was closed, but inside, a roll of honour lists the names of all the parish men who fought in the First World War. Holywell Lake is one of England"'s only 56 'Thankful Villages' to which all its servicemen successfully returned after the conflict . Across from the village pub (the Holywell Inn) stands a holy well. The villagers maintain that its water ensured that all the men returned safely.

Upon arrival at Wellington, I bought some provisions. A 20-minute bus ride brought me to Taunton and another back to my campsite at Ash Cross.

Day 19

Wellington to Ash Cross

14 Miles

10.08.2020

'The grass that has oftentimes been trampled underfoot,
Give it time it will rise up again,
Give it time it will rise up again.'

Somerset folksong

Another day involving public transport, but only to get me to the start point of my walk in Wellington town centre. Once there, I headed south onto the Blackdown Hills to reach the highlight of the walk; the Wellington Monument. I then made my way east to my camp located south of Taunton.

My walk joined the Michael energy current at the monument, and I remained close to it throughout the day, visiting the churches at Corfe, Orchard Portman and Stoke St Mary. All three align directly with the current. Further north, Mary travels in a line north of Wellington and then across the south side of Taunton, aligning with the churches at Nynehead, Bradford-on-Tone, Trull (see **Appendix, Day 19***) *and Ruishton. The two currents eventually meet to form the eighth node along the alignment at Creech St Michael (see Day 20).*

I started my day early with a brisk walk into Taunton, putting the County Town on my trail. Over three days, I'd got no more than a glimpse of the place from the top deck of an omnibus, but it contains a mine of interest stretching back for over a millennium. Much of its well-documented history revolves around the castle. Initially, it was the site of a significant monastic foundation, but it became an essential fortification in Norman times. It saw action during the Barons' Wars of the 13th Century and later conflicts that had left it in ruins by the turn of the 17th Century. The Royalists besieged it during the Civil War. However, it's primarily famous for Judge Jeffrey's Bloody Assizes, held in the Great Hall following the well-documented Monmouth Rebellion of 1685 (see Day 20). One hundred and forty-four supporters of James Monmouth were tried and hanged, their remains displayed across the county to ensure no such event would be repeated.

The castle has been much-altered over the centuries, particularly during the Georgian era. The Great Hall and the inner ward remain, now as a museum, which I sadly didn't have time to visit on this, and either of the other two days I passed through the town. Fortunately, After completing my trail, I was able to return to Taunton and immerse myself in there for a good two hours and learn all about the town, the county and its history (see **Appendix, Day 19****)

My bus ride to Wellington was uneventful, and by nine o'clock, my boots were back on the ground. The weather was warm and, once again, dry. I'd hardly seen any rain in over a week and nothing substantial since Day 3. I bought some food and set out towards the south end of the town. Picking my way through the urban landscape, I crossed the A38 and followed a footpath through fields and a tunnel under the M5 Motorway. Now firmly in the Somerset countryside, I followed a woodland path gradually steepening towards the summit of Wellington Hill. I appreciated having no load to carry as the last few hundred yards were alarmingly steep. The hillside and the Wellington monument are the property of the National Trust.

Approaching the summit, I could see the obelisk entirely enclosed by a massive cage of scaffolding. My first thoughts strangely reminded me of the televised images from my childhood of a Saturn V Moon rocket flanked by its umbilical tower. Scaffolding doesn't usually suit classic buildings, but here was one striking exception. Eight miles of it were needed as part of a £3 million, three-year restoration project to bring the monument back to full-functioning glory. Once completed, and for the first time in twenty years, visitors can ascend 235 steps up to the top of the 175-foot tower, the tallest three-sided obelisk in the world. Sadly, for me, it was closed and still under repair, and once up close, the place looked more like a building site than a sacred one.

The monument was built as a memorial to the Duke of Wellington. It was begun in 1817, but funds ran out, and the work remained unfinished. With the Duke's death in 1852, renewed interest and a revised design provided the necessary means to continue the project, but it wasn't until 1892 that the work was finally completed.

Miller and Broadhurst dowsed the Michael energy current to the hilltop site, and they write about their discovery and its apparent significance in the landscape:

'It was Egyptian. The juxtaposition of a great Egyptian obelisk in the middle of the English countryside seemed tantalizing. Why such monuments should occur in considerable numbers across the land, built on hills as echoes of an ancient culture so far removed from pastoral Albion has often teased the minds of romantics and students of the landscape. They appear to harbour a secret significance.'

On the summit, I stood by a panoramic direction and distance indicator and tried to identify the various locations within my view. I could make out the Quantock Hills to the north (11 miles), but the sky was too hazy to see the more distant landmarks listed. These included Glastonbury Tor (26 miles) and even the Black Mountains of South Wales (no chance). I imagine the views from the top of the tower on a clear day would be breathtaking.

From the monument, I walked east along the top of the thickly wooded northern edge of the Blackdown Hills, joining a road that reached the highest point at 915 feet. At Forches Corner, I took a road descending gradually to the hamlet of Lowton, and then a combination of quiet country lanes brought me through Sellick's Green, Pitminster and Corfe.

At Pitminster, I stopped to look at the church dedicated to St Andrew and St Mary. Interestingly this beautiful building shares the same features as the Victorian church I visited at Greenham (an octagonal tower surmounted by a spire). The fabric of this church dates back to the 13th Century, however. Set in the delightful surroundings of a sun-baked churchyard, I contentedly prepared myself for a half-hour's rest and a bite to eat, but I was surprised to find the building was open.

Inside, I found the 15th Century font, richly decorated with stone carvings. I also noticed some impressive-looking tombs commemorating and depicting members of the Colle family, the lords of the manor during the 17th and 18th Centuries. One, in particular, caught my attention. The decoratively dressed husband and wife lie alongside each other, their hands cupped in prayer. Sculpted effigies of their children kneel beneath them. Two slate panels bearing poetry in honour of the couple conclude with the following lines:

THOVGHE MEN IMAGINE THEY ARE DEADE & GONE:
THEY SHALL OVT LIVE THIS MONVMENT OF STONE.

Outside I sat down on the close-cropped grass and allowed myself half an hour of quiet time to recharge my body using solar power.

Corfe was the next village on my walk. Here I was pleasantly surprised to find that, as with Pitminster, the church (dedicated to St Nicholas) was open. The building is of Victorian construction in a Norman architectural style, rebuilt on the site of its medieval predecessor. There's a simple but harmonious quality about it. Well-proportioned throughout, a Rose Window fills the centre of the west wall, while the chancel features a trio of Lancet Windows. Norman arches frame the other windows and doors, and the square stone tower is topped with a pyramidal slate roof.

Inside, the stone font is the only remaining artefact from the earlier church, but it doesn't look out of place. Everywhere, the attention to Norman architecture can be found in the detail. The finely carved chancel arch is modelled on that of the original church. I also noticed a Georgian Royal Coat of arms painted on a panel on the wall with an interesting display beneath, explaining its historical significance.

Miller and Broadhurst dowsed the Michael current through the church and write, 'Inside, a powerful, almost electrically charged atmosphere envelops the visitor.'

I couldn't have put it better myself. I sat down and enjoyed approximately ten minutes of immeasurable timelessness. There was something special about this place.

Taking a path leading east from the church, I joined a road heading north to the Taunton racecourse at Orchard Portman. A manor house once stood in the village, but now there's little more than a scattering of homes and the church dedicated to St Michael. The building dates mainly from the 15th Century. It was closed, but the walled churchyard made for another pleasant break in the afternoon sunshine. Among the graves, I located the family grave of Dr Thomas Bond (1841-1901), the famous physician regarded as the world's first offender profiler for his work investigating the notorious Jack the Ripper murders in 1888.

A couple more miles of walking along quiet country lanes brought me to the next small village of Stoke St Mary. The 13th Century church stands in beautiful surroundings below the wooded slopes of Stoke Hill. The building was locked, but the grassy churchyard was a charming place to take yet another short break and enjoy the views.

As with the church at Corfe, those at Orchard Portman and Stoke St Mary directly align with the Michael earth energy current.

Another quiet mile of road walking brought me back to Ash Cross for my third and final night at the campsite.

Day 20

Ash Cross to Walton

20 Miles

11.08.2020

This particular day was quite a long one. Firstly, I walked north to Creech St Michael, a large village in the valley of the River Tone east of Taunton. I then followed the bank of the river east to the smaller settlement of Ham and then along the roads that link a series of villages that line the ridge of low-lying ground that runs northeast above the vast expanse of the Somerset Levels.

The highlight of my day was Burrowbridge Mump, a solitary hill that rises above the otherwise flat land like an island, strikingly topped by a ruined church. Most of my walk was almost exclusively at near sea level across the heart of the Somerset Levels, finishing at a campsite near the village of Walton, west of the town of Street. In the afternoon's heat, my last few miles were a little uncomfortable, exacerbated by the busyness of the passing traffic.

Regarding the St Michael Alignment, two of the node points were visited. I joined the Michael energy current at the village of Thornfalcon and headed north to the church at **Creech St Michael**, *where it enters and crosses with the Mary current to form the* **eighth node** *of the Alignment (it was unfortunately closed). From here, I picked up the course of Mary and passed the churches on which it aligns at North Curry and Stoke St Gregory. I then climbed* **Burrow Mump**, *where the two currents join for a second time, forming the* **ninth node point**. *On its summit stands a ruined 17th Century church dedicated to the saint. East of the Mump, I* *walked between the two currents, visiting two more aligned churches; Othery (Michael) and Middlezoy (Mary).*

I woke up early with the sun heating the interior of my tent to the point of discomfort. Still mornings like this are lovely, but my four-season tent can have disadvantages with no wind. The overnight condensation can be considerable, and the best thing to do is get up and out, open the doors and let it all burn off in the sunshine. I enjoyed my three nights here. The site was spacious, and the facilities were excellent for the price paid. If this was Cornwall or any of the National Parks, you could easily have to pay double or even treble the fees.

With all my kit packed and re-acquainted with my back and shoulders after two days of travelling light, I went on my way. I crossed the busy A358 and walked a quiet road to Thornfalcon. Here the Church of the Holy Cross *(aligned on the Michael current)* stands quietly in pleasant surroundings, but it was closed as I passed by. Although heavily restored in Victorian times, the building dates from the 14th Century.

Continuing north, in little more than a mile, I reached St Michael's church at Creech St Michael; this building was also closed to visitors. The church stands in a fairly built-up village close to the River Tone, and this one dates to the 13th Century. It's a sizeable building, much enlarged over time.

It was disappointing to find this particular church closed, as Miller and Broadhurst had dowsed the Michael and Mary energy currents to this precise location, noting:

'Mary came in through the west and ran right across the altar, crossing the Michael current at a 90 degree angle – a 'Celtic cross'. This was the first time we had found a node in a humble parish church.'

A tour of the churchyard confirmed another interesting observation they made; a set of stocks with no more or less than seven holes. The authors conclude that 'at some stage in Creech St Michael's history, a one-legged reprobate must have been a regular customer,'

Or perhaps they just ran out of wood. A riverside path brought me to the small village of Ham, where a suspension bridge spans the River Tone. Beyond the village, I took a road gently rising past the settlements of Knapp and Lower Knapp to reach the more sizeable village of North Curry and its magnificent church, which bears the nickname 'Cathedral of the Moors'. It's a surprising title for a church that stands just 80 feet or so above sea level, surrounded by land as flat as you can get, but it occupies the highest ground for miles. The term 'moor' here applies to the peat from which the inland levels are formed.

St Peter and St Paul's is a magnificent piece of architecture which imposes harmoniously in the landscape, and on a bright, sunny morning like this, it was showing its best. Much of the existing building is medieval and boasts an impressive octagonal tower. The north doorway is a fine example of Norman dogtooth carving, while elsewhere around the exterior can be found various examples of 'Hunky Punks', Somerset's name for the grotesque creatures, commonly found carved in the masonry of its mid to late medieval churches. Unlike gargoyles, the sculptures are purely decorative and have no function. Their origins are believed to be pagan.

Fortunately, I found that the church was open, and there was plenty to see. The fabric of the building and its bare stone walls date mainly from the 14th Century, and parts of the interior are from an even earlier time. There's an ancient parish chest of solid elm, believed to be from the Saxon period and a 14th Century tomb upon which lies the gruesome form of a cadaver carved in stone. The beautifully carved font is also 14th Century work, and a finely carved reredos is the work of Frederick Bligh Bond (see Day 21).

St Peter & St Paul's Church aligns with the Mary energy current, as does the next church along my trail at Stoke St Gregory.

Outside, I took a 15-minute rest on a bench in the spacious churchyard. The view looking north was superb despite the modest height of my vantage point. Orchards, fields and woods stretched away to the far distance in the diffused but bright light of the morning sun. I was now overlooking the Somerset Levels.

The Somerset Levels were once a vast inlet of the sea stretching between the Mendips and the Blackdown Hills. Over millennia, they gradually became inland wetlands and have been drained for over a thousand years. Hills and raised land areas were once islands in a coastal marsh, of which 160,000 acres have now been reclaimed. The nearby Willows and Wetlands Visitor Centre was closed when I walked my trail, but it's a great place to learn about the area's fascinating natural and human history. This land has a unique, almost familiar quality for me, having grown up on the edge of the Cambridgeshire Fens. I well-recall the openness of the level landscape where unhindered views extend unbroken in every direction beneath a vast expanse of sky.

With a reasonably long walk ahead, I rejoined the road and diverted onto a quiet, winding lane that brought me to the village of Stoke St Gregory. Like that at North Curry, the church is similar in age and hosts an octagonal tower, but this one was heightened in the 15th Century. The building was closed to visitors (see **Appendix, Day 20***), but a quick tour of the churchyard uncovered a set of conventional 18th Century six-hole stocks. The view south of the village stretches across West Sedge Moor, land about as flat as you can get. Just beyond, the land rises again, crowned by the 140-foot Burton Pynsent monument near the village of Curry Rivel. It's also known as the Cider Monument and commemorates William Pynsent, an 18th Century cider baron who courted financial favour from William Pitt. Capability Brown designed the urn-topped edifice.

From Stoke St Gregory, I descended north to the River Tone and the linear settlement of Athelney. The River Tone flows as a drainage channel through the flat land. The river here was banked in the 13th Century and has remained so ever since. Athelney is now a scattering of roadside houses and farms below a slightly raised area known as Athelney Hill. On it stands a prominent stone monument bearing a plaque conveying its historical significance:

> KING ALFRED THE GREAT.
> IN THE YEAR OF OUR LORD 879
> HAVING BEEN DEFEATED BY
> THE DANES, FLED FOR REFUGE
> TO THE FOREST OF ATHELNEY.
> WHERE HE CONCEALED.
> FROM HIS ENEMIES FOR THE
> SPACE OF A WHOLE YEAR.
> HE SOON AFTER REGAINED
> POSSESSION OF HIS THRONE.
> IN GRATEFUL REMEMBRANCE
> OF THE PROTECTION HE HAD
> RECEIVED UNDER THE FAVOUR
> OF HEAVEN, ERECTED A
> MONASTERY ON THIS SPOT, &
> ENDOWED IT WITH ALL THE
> LANDS CONTAINED IN THE
> ISLE OF ATHELNEY. TO
> PERPETUATE THE MEMORIAL
> OF SO REMARKABLE AN
> INCIDENT IN THE LIFE OF
> THAT ILLUSTRIOUS PRINCE.

Alfred's monastery flourished throughout the medieval period but was abandoned during the Reformation. Victorian archaeological excavations successfully located the remains, and the site came to extensive public attention in 1993 when it was surveyed and dug by the 'Time Team' television programme. In addition to the monastery, they found evidence that an Iron Age fort shared the site. In Alfred's time, 'islands' like Athelney were natural defences, and the hill is known to have been used as a fort since Bronze Age times. It was certainly adequate for Alfred. After his exiled retreat, he defeated the pagan Danish King Guthrum at Edington. Guthrum was then subjected to a forced baptism, although he went on to rule East Anglia under his Christianised name of Æthelstan. Athelney is also, of course, where Alfred burned the cakes.

From Athelney, my next objective rose above the land in full view a mile ahead of me. Burrow Mump is a small but prominent hill crowned with the ruin of a church dedicated to St Michael. Within twenty minutes, I was at the foot of the hill, and five later, I stood on the summit. The Mump and the church both have great historical significance. Overlooking the confluence of the Tone and the Parret, the hill has evidence of Roman occupation and is believed to have been used by King Alfred. Once, a Norman castle stood on the summit and then a church in the later medieval period. The mound was occupied by Royalist troops in the Civil War and again by the king's army during the Monmouth Rebellion in 1685. The remains of the present building date from 1793.

I walked around (and inside) the ruin, gaining superb views in every direction. Under the mid-day sun, the air was still, with barely a breath of wind. I spent the best part of an hour for lunch and a rest in this magical, peaceful place. Affixed to one of the walls, I noticed a slate plaque:

BURROW MUMP
This hill was given to the National Trust
by Alexander Gould Barrett
THAT THE MEN AND WOMEN of SOMERSET
WHO DIED SERVING THEIR COUNTRY
IN THE SECOND WORLD WAR MAY BE
REMEMBERED HERE
1939 IN TIME TO COME 1945

Between the node points of Creech St Michael and Burrow Mump, I'd been closely following the course of the Mary energy current while Michael had been weaving his way to the north of where I walked. Now the two energy lines crossed to form the ninth node of my trail. In the Sun and the Serpent, the authors explain that the precise node point was where the altar of the church would have been, but given the fact that an earlier church oriented at a different angle, they conclude, 'It appears to be the mound itself that anchors the energy and causes it to change orientation.'

The conventional view is that the Mump is a natural feature, but some people have reason to believe differently. The Sun and the Serpent authors point out that the red soil covering the Mump is not found locally. At the same time, in his book 'New Light on the Mystery of Glastonbury', John Michell suggests that given the Mump's shape, location and composition, it may have been constructed like Silbury Hill (see Day 27). He concludes that if artificial, 'the Mump must surely be one of these unrecognised forces commanded by ancient priests.' Silbury is known to be the largest artificial hill in Europe, yet considerably smaller than Burrow Mump.

Somewhat reluctantly, I descended the hill. I knew I had a hot afternoon trudge ahead of me, and unavoidably it would be trudged along roads busier than I'd like. My next objective was the Church at Othery, which was unfortunately locked. It's an attractive building in a beautiful setting, but I read that due to the state of the tower, it's one of many hundreds of places of worship on Historic England's Heritage at Risk Register. Looking inside the porch, I noticed a magnificent sculpture above the door. It depicts the church's patron, St Michael, thrusting a lance into the mouth of a recoiling dragon. An abandoned bird's nest rested in a convenient recess on the dragon's neck, giving the sculpture an unanticipated function and, for me, some consolation for missing the treasures beyond the door. Outside, I noticed a second sculptural depiction of Michael slaying a dragon, a statue set in a decorative niche high on the tower's wall.

Othery Church aligns directly on the Michael earth energy current and is the first landmark reached as the line travels east from Burrow Mump. Mary continues to the north to meet the church at Middlezoy, barely a mile away. I decided to divert there via some footpaths to put it on my trail before submitting to the afternoon's road walk I was now purposely trying to delay.

My detour to Middlezoy was more than worth the effort to visit the magnificent Church of the Holy Cross. Firstly, it was open for visitors, and secondly, its fascinating interior was filled with information displays that could make it worthy of the status of a museum. Thirdly, Middlezoy was associated with the nearby Battle of Sedgemoor during the Monmouth Rebellion of 1685, principally as the base for a local militia force encamped in the village. 'Zoy' means island, reflecting past the nature of the settlement.

The rebellion began when James Scott, 1st Duke of Monmouth, challenged his uncle, the reigning catholic monarch James II for the British throne. Monmouth was the illegitimate son of Charles II and intended to capture the throne and revert the crown to Protestantism. Monmouth returned from exile in the Dutch Republic in June 1685 and landed at Lyme Regis, hoping to lead an army of sympathisers from the West Country, where support for him was strong. Monmouth's forces were not regular soldiers and mainly comprised local farmworkers, which gave the uprising the alternative name, the Pitchfork Rebellion. After a series of skirmishes with local militias and regular soldiers, the rebellion ended spectacularly in defeat at the Battle of Sedgemoor on 6th July.

The king's revenge was merciless. Under the infamous Judge Jeffries (see Day 19), hundreds of rebels were captured and hung. Monmouth was beheaded on 15th July, while James consolidated his power and reigned for three more years until his protestant nephew, William III of Orange, deposed him. Sedgemoor was the last battle to be fought on English soil.

The battlefield site lies another two miles northwest of Middlezoy, between the villages of Chedzoy and Westonzoyland (see **Appendix, Day 20****)

Deferring my road walk for another half-hour, I read with interest almost the entire collection of the displayed information on the history of Middlezoy and its church. Much of the building dates from the 14th and 15th Centuries, including the impressive three-stage tower. However, one particular item grabbed my attention: an intriguing memorial to a French officer killed during the battle of Sedgemoor. A brass plaque marks his burial inside the church:

> **HERE:LYES:THE:BODY OF:LOVIS:CHEVALEIR**
> **DEMISIERSA·FRENCH:GENTLEMAN:WHO**
> **BEHAVED:HIMSELF:WITH:GREAT:COVRAGE**
> **AND:GALLANTRY18YEARES:IN:THE·ENGLISH**
> **SERVICES:AND:WAS:VNFORTUNATELY:SLAINE**
> **ONYE6THOF:IVLY1685AT:THE:BATTEL:OF:WESTON**
> **WHERE·HE:BEHAVED:HIM:SELF:WITHALL:THE**
> **COVRAGE:IMAGINABLE:AGAINST:THE·KINGS**
> **ENEMIES:COMMANDED:BY:YE·REBEL:DVKE:OF:**
> **MVNMOUTH**

The bodies of officers killed in battle were usually sent home for burial, unlike the rank and file, but this wasn't possible for the Frenchman.

Miller and Broadhurst dowsed the Church of the Holy Cross to the Mary energy line. The information on display mentions that the church was dedicated to St Lawrence and St Mary in earlier times.

Unable to put it off any longer, I made my way east along more footpaths to join the road. I was committed to walking for another five miles with no points of interest to reach a campsite near Walton, a village west of the town of Street. Had I more time, I would have visited two more nearby locations, the churches at Moorlinch and Shapwick (see **Appendix, Day 20*****), but my time and energy were running low. In the heat haze of the afternoon, I had to go carefully as the roads had no pavements. The campsite was surprisingly quiet, though, compared with the busyness of Glastonbury just a few miles further to the west. I'd be getting my share of that soon enough.

Day 21

Walton to Glastonbury

6 Miles

12.08.2020

'Ye have supped from the Pools of Sorrow,
Ye shall drink from the Wells of Joy!'
From 'At the Well – the Rune of the Water-bearer', Alice Buckton

I woke up shortly after sunrise to another still, bright birdsong-filled morning. Before I could properly think, I had a strange but warm anticipatory feeling. I intuitively knew that this day would be special. A short few miles of walking would bring me to what I knew was a climactic highpoint on my pilgrimage; Glastonbury! The word was enough to send my mind racing. As I gathered my thoughts, I decided I'd need the best of two days to scratch the surface of the place, so I'd deliberately made this an early start and a short walking day to get myself there nice and early.

The word significant far underwhelms the priceless treasure that is Glastonbury. You can spend years reading about it, but nothing compares with the pedestrian's experience of being there. Less than 10,000 people live in this small Somerset town, but it's a hub for millions of visitors annually. Pilgrims, tourists, historians, artists, spiritual seekers, trail walkers and amateur travel writers, to name but a few. Then, of course, (nearly) every year, there's a gathering of some 200.000 festival-goers, accompanied by the world's best legendary and grass-roots musical talent, well, almost; it's seven miles away in the village of Pilton.

Seen from afar, Glastonbury beckons the visitor with its magnificent Tor, dominating the town and the surrounding countryside. The Tor and nearby hills were once islands, isolated neighbours in a vast watery landscape. Small settlements formed on these islands, and the Tor and its foothills became important sanctuaries and, in due course, the earliest Christian foundation in Britain. By the Norman Era, no monastic community was more prosperous or powerful. Glastonbury has long been a significant place of pilgrimage, and in the last century or so, it has become a hub for the new age of romantic and esoteric traditions.

Glastonbury Tor has long been regarded as the mystical Isle of Avalon, featured in the vast subject of Arthurian legend. According to tradition, here was where King Arthur's sword was forged, and it was here that he was taken after being gravely wounded at his final battle against the Saxon invaders. Legend also says that Arthur sleeps beneath the Tor, awaiting the nation's time to need him again. Barely a stone's throw below the Tor, Chalice Hill is said to be where the Holy Grail was secreted by Joseph of Arimathea when he visited with it in the 1st Century. Some legends also assert Jesus himself came here as a boy. Many believe that Glastonbury is William Blake's metaphorical New Jerusalem.

Then, of course, there are the earth energies that seem to concentrate on Glastonbury and dance on its Tor, the proliferation of strange lights in the sky, and the unfathomably complex crop circles that appear overnight regularly in the immediately surrounding countryside. Some people propose that the surrounding landscape also maintains the form of a zodiacal wheel, somehow complementing the stars above. There is no end to the mystery that is Glastonbury.

Concerning the course taken by the two earth energy currents, setting the scene is complicated, but here goes:

There are no fewer than three points at which the Michael and Mary energy currents meet and cross at Glastonbury; these being the Abbey, the Tor and Chalice Well; three node points, all within a few short miles of each other along the alignment. Coming in from the east, Mary runs north of Michael. The two lines converge from different directions, snaking eccentrically around each others' paths so that Michael travels east first to join Mary at the Abbey, then at the Well and finally on the Tor. Mary approaches from the north, meeting Michael in reverse order. The two lines then leave the town, heading west, with Michael now north of Mary. The resultant pattern created by the two lines looks not dissimilar to a knot of sorts.

*I decided I would visit the three sites from west to east, thereby effectively following the sequence of the Michael line. Before reaching them, my approach to Glastonbury closely followed the Michael line's course, which also aligns with Wearyall Hill, while Mary travels further north of where I walked. Later in the day, I visited **Glastonbury Abbey** and the **Chalice Well**, the 10th and 11th nodes of the Alignment. Please note that these are numbered geographically from west to east in the order reached by the Michael energy current. They are, in fact, the 11th and 12th nodes on the course of the Mary current.*

My pilgrimage for this day was just a few miles. To reach Glastonbury, I had to road-walk through its extensive and less attractive neighbouring village of Street. I then crossed the River Brue and climbed onto Wearyall Hill, which, like many other places in the locality, has its own story.

Wearyall Hill is a long, narrow ridge immediately southwest of Glastonbury and second in height to the Tor, which stands directly east of the town. According to legend, it was here that Joseph of Arimathea thrust his walking pole into the ground, and from it sprang the Glastonbury Thorn Tree (the Holy Thorn). This somewhat controversial legend asserts that Joseph was an itinerant tin merchant. He travelled from the Middle East to Glastonbury via St Michael's Mount to trade with Cornish tin miners, sometimes accompanied by his boy nephew, Jesus. The legend suggests that Christianity first came to Glastonbury during Christ's lifetime or immediately after the crucifixion.

The Glastonbury Thorn is a unique variety of Hawthorn found in the locality. Unlike other types, it cannot be grown from seed or cuttings; it has to be grafted. Also, it uniquely flowers twice a year, in winter and spring. The British monarch is given a sprig of the flowering thorn every Christmas. There are two famous examples in the town; one on the grounds of the Abbey ruins and another in the churchyard of St John's Church. In honour of the Joseph legend, a third renowned example was planted on Wearyall Hill in 1951, but this was severely vandalised in 2010. Sadly, the landowner removed it in 2019, a year before my visit. The 'original' tree was cut down and burned in an act of superstition during the English Civil War.

On reaching the top of the hill, I gained an excellent view of the town and the Tor, bathed in the light of the (still early) morning sun. A slight haze gave the horizon a diffused, almost watery look, and I imagined what the scene would have looked like in centuries past when the hills rose as islands above the vast liquid landscape. Just east of the summit, I located the tree's dead stump, hacked and chopped at for relics by modern-day visitors.

The Authors of the Sun and the Serpent describe their experience of dowsing the Michael energy current at the Thorn:

"The flow of the current did not just pass through the Holy Thorn, but changed its direction, as if this was indeed some sort of crucial point which affected the energies'. They had discovered what they described as 'a blind spring or powerful energy spiral which is invariably present at ancient sites.'

The Michael current heads directly into Glastonbury from the hill, reaching the Parish Church of St John before turning obliquely towards the Abbey.

I descended the hill and walked into the town, taken aback by the din of the traffic and the pavements crammed with people. I decided to keep walking to get to a campsite on the edge of the town, where I could book in, ditch my gear and pitch my tent. I could then explore Glastonbury unburdened and at leisure.

Leaving the campsite, I walked back into the town. Once again, I was overwhelmed by the sounds and proximity of tourists. I tend to separate myself far from the crowd when I can (even though I'm probably just as madding), but I had no choice here, so I decided to make like the tourist I was. I immersed my mind, body and spirit in the bookshops and the health emporiums, enjoying the décor, the displays and the heady scents of herbal essences while cannily keeping my wallet closed but for the purchase of one book. I had my lunch on a bench in the warm afternoon sunshine and talked to a friendly couple who were touring the entire southwest. We shared weather talk and some amusing tales about our recent travels.

My remaining objectives for the day were a visit to the Abbey and another to the Chalice Well. These were both outdoor venues and, luckily, open to the public without pre-booking. I decided to visit the Abbey first and then walk on to the Well, saving the Tor for the first part of my walk the following day. Before entering the Abbey, I passed the Church of St John. Although closed to visitors, I noticed the long-established Glastonbury Thorn growing in the churchyard.

At the Abbey, I took my time to enjoy the comparative quiet from the bustle of the town, the spacious grassy grounds, and the magnificent stone ruins that remain of what was once the most powerful ecclesiastic location in Britain. Although Glastonbury Abbey was founded in the 8th Century, it's widely believed that the site had religious importance for many centuries going back to pre-Christian times. The Abbey's status as an important pilgrimage site was further enhanced with the claim in 1191 that the tomb of King Arthur and Queen Guinevere was discovered in its cemetery.

A fire destroyed the Abbey in 1184, and the surviving fabric dates mainly from the 14th Century in the form of two tall sections that once supported the central tower and parts of the west front, the nave and the chancel walls. All the monastic buildings have gone, but the remarkable

Abbot's Kitchen remains intact. Perhaps finest of all are the remains of the late 12th Century Lady Chapel, built under the patronage of Henry II immediately after the fire that claimed the earlier building. It stands directly on the site of the earlier church and retains a magnificently carved doorway. The chapel formed the westernmost end of the rebuilt Abbey.

In the early 20th Century, much of the architectural history of Glastonbury Abbey was researched and documented by the architect Frederick Bligh Bond (1864-1945). He believed that the dimensions of the buildings were based on gematria, a form of numeric code that originated in ancient times. In 1908, The Church of England appointed Bligh Bond as Director of Excavations at the Abbey. In his research, he somewhat controversially used the help of a medium, using automatic writing to rediscover the locations and dimensions of some of the lost architecture. He also claimed that the spirits of dead monks (and one of the Abbey's builders) had provided the information. This work was one of the first documented examples of 'psychic archaeology'. Bligh Bond also unearthed bones from a gravesite, claiming they were those of Richard Whiting, the last Abbot of Glastonbury (see Day 22). Bligh Bond revealed his paranormal sources in a published work entitled 'The Gates of Remembrance', but his employers, who strongly disapproved of his spiritualist methods, subsequently sacked him.

Inside the grounds, I quickly located what remains of the Abbey's Holy Thorn Tree, pronounced dead in 1991. the dead trunk remains in situ, with its branches cut short but supported by three props. I also found the original site of the High Altar, now open to the elements and marked by a low rectangular kerb on the ground, enclosed by a low rail. I then walked over to the reputed grave site of King Arthur and Guinevere, similarly marked and bearing a notice:

SITE OF KING ARTHUR'S TOMB
IN THE YEAR 1191 THE BODIES OF
KING ARTHUR AND HIS QUEEN WERE

SAID TO HAVE BEEN FOUND ON THE SOUTH SIDE OF THE LADY CHAPEL. ON 19TH APRIL 1278 THEIR REMAINS WERE REMOVED IN THE PRESENCE OF KING EDWARD I AND QUEEN ELEANOR TO A BLACK MARBLE TOMB ON THIS SITE. THIS TOMB SURVIVED UNTIL THE DISSOLUTION OF THE ABBEY IN 1539

Whether or not the tomb is that of Arthur and his queen is indeterminate. However, established traditions have elaborate, often multiple stories, and this one involves a 'giant'. According to legend, two skeletons were unearthed from deep beneath the ground in the Abbey cemetery in 1190 on the orders of King Henry II. One was that of a nine-foot-long man, accompanied by an average-sized female. They lay in a coffin formed from a hollowed-out tree trunk. A tradition appears to have developed with the assertion that the said remains were those of Arthur and Guinevere, later to be re-interred at the present grave site. At the time of its discovery, a lead cross was found in the tomb. The cross bore an inscription:

HIC IACET SEPULTUS INCLITUS REX ARTHURIUS IN INSULA AVALONIA

HERE LIES BURIED THE RENOWNED KING ARTHUR IN THE ISLE OF AVALON

The last documented record of the cross was in 1607.

What is not in doubt is that the tomb's existence has drawn pilgrims (and, latterly, tourists) to Glastonbury in great numbers and promoted the Arthurian legend for over 800 years. The general view of modern historians is that the 'discovery' of the tomb was a publicity stunt created to raise funds for the Abbey's rebuild following the fire. As for the cross, it's generally believed it was also part of the hoax to promote the pilgrimage gravy train, and it now also appears that the hoaxing continues. In 1981 a man claimed to have found the cross and presented it to the British Museum. Yes, after over 800 years, we're still at it!

The site of the High Altar proved to be the precise location where Miller and Broadhurst found the Michael and Mary earth energy currents crossed paths to form the node in the Abbey.

I would have liked more time to enjoy the abbey grounds, but the afternoon was passing, and I still had the Chalice Well to visit, so I made the mile's walk south and east to reach the entrance of what I knew would be a remarkable place.

The Chalice Well is a natural spring located below an elevated area of land known as Chalice Hill near the foot of Glastonbury Tor. A most attractive formal garden has been landscaped with enclosed walls, ascending walkways and terraces through which the waters of the spring channel to form a series of small cascades and pools. It's described as 'a garden of many rooms'. One of the 'rooms' is known as King Arthur's Court, which hosts a Healing Pool. Renowned for their healing properties, the iron-rich waters of the ancient spring run continuously and copiously from their source, rust-colouring the stones over which they flow. In mythology, the Well is associated with the Goddess of the Earth, symbolised by the interlinked circles of the Celtic 'Vesica Pisces'. The symbol features throughout the garden in decorative arrangements, some incorporating the addition of a sword that can equally be associated with St Michael and King Arthur's Excalibur. Traditionally, Joseph of Arimathea was said to have placed the chalice that caught the drops of Christ's blood into the Well. Twelve huts are believed to have once stood on the site, occupied by Joseph's twelve anchorite disciples.

King Arthur's Court and the Healing Pool mark the node point where Broadhurst and Miller dowsed the Michael and Mary energy currents at the Well. They describe it eloquently:

'Everybody who enters this walled enclosure becomes aware of its soothing and therapeutic effect on mind and spirit. It is as if the energies we are tracking somehow combine with those of the healing waters, and, trapped and amplified by the reservoir created by its walls, have an effect that is mentally and physically invigorating.'

The Chalice Well was initially purchased in the early 20th Century by the poet Alice Buckton (1867-1944) and is now owned and run by the Chalice Well Trust. The trust was founded in 1959 by Major Wellesley Tudor Pole (1884-1968). Both Buckton and Tudor Pole are strongly associated with Glastonbury's Celtic revival, and both were Bahá'ists. Tudor Pole is widely recognised for his writings on and explorations into religious mysticism. He is perhaps most famous for conceiving the 'Silent Minute' now conducted worldwide in honour of the fallen from both World Wars.

Less than fifty yards from the Chalice Well is another perennial spring known as The White Spring, which can also be visited as an attraction. Unlike the iron-rich content that gives the Chalice Well's water its reddish hue (and the alternative name of the 'Blood Spring'), the waters of this Well run through calcite rock. Unfortunately closed at my visit, the White Spring flows through a Victorian-built well house, forming three domed vaults describing a temple or sacred space. It now accommodates visitors, private baptisms and ceremonial bathing.

My time at the Chalice Well was too short but well worth spending. It's a magical place, and it was refreshing to pause in such peaceful and beautiful surroundings, like the drink I took from its cool, fresh water in the afternoon's heat. I reluctantly tore myself away and walked back through the town, diverting to locate one more place I had read about with interest.

I walked west of the town and onto the level countryside along a dead-straight road to the River Brue. From the riverbank, I pinpointed the raised area of land that forms Bride's Mound, on which once stood Beckery Chapel, considered the first monastic site in Britain, possibly pre-dating the Abbey site by several centuries. Bride was the Triple Goddess of the Celts, one of the most widely worshipped deities in Celtic Britain, appropriately known as the guardian of wells and streams. Christianity readopted her as St Brigid.

The chapel's remains were abandoned following Viking raids in the 9th Century, and archaeological excavations have found that the site dates back to Romano-British times. When first dug in the 1960s, some fifty skeletons were discovered, scientifically dated to the 5[t]h Century. Early Medieval scribes mention that St Brigid of Kildare visited the chapel in 488. An ancient trackway heading west from nearby Sharpham once served as a route for Pilgrims walking to Glastonbury. On the way, they would stop or pause for prayer at Bride's Mound, the western gateway to the Isle of Avalon. Near the mound, A spring known as St Bride's Well once flowed nearby, but it no longer exists. Before its demise, it had a place in events over a century ago.

At the turn of the 20th Century, a collection of people became associated with Glastonbury's Celtic revival. The Avalonians were an eclectic group of individuals who can equally be described as eccentric. They were artists, writers, poets, historians, philosophers, and esotericists. Among them were the previously mentioned Frederick Bligh Bond, Alice Buckton and Wellesley Tudor Pole, the writer Dion Fortune and a certain Dr John Goodchild. The works associated with these individuals are extensively summarised in a book by Patrick Benham, full of significance to the Glastonbury legends and legacy.

One of the early accounts concerns a Victorian travelling doctor named Goodchild, who acquired a glass vessel of great age in Italy. This vessel, or 'The Cup' as it became known, was subsequently found to have a deep and powerful significance for him and his associates. Goodchild secreted The Cup in St Bride's Well in 1889 under guidance he received during psychic communications. There it remained for ten years until its successful retrieval by two women appointed to do so following further psychic advice. The Cup was later found to have transformative and healing powers and began to attract attention in controversial press reports that connected the Cup with the Holy Grail. Later scientific examination proved that The Cup wasn't ancient. Still, for some, it continued to carry a powerful allegorical status.

Although the Well has now gone (and the decorated thorn tree that once adorned it), I had hoped to find the engraved stone that marks its location, but I failed to do so. The mound is a very different place from what it once was, now built on by industrial developments and extensive sewage works.

It was getting late by the time I returned to camp, but still quite warm. A severe thunderstorm weather warning was in place across southern England, so I was a little worried about how my night's camp would go; worried to the extent of repositioning my tent away from the power line pole I'd pitched it next to. I was anxious and slow to settle.

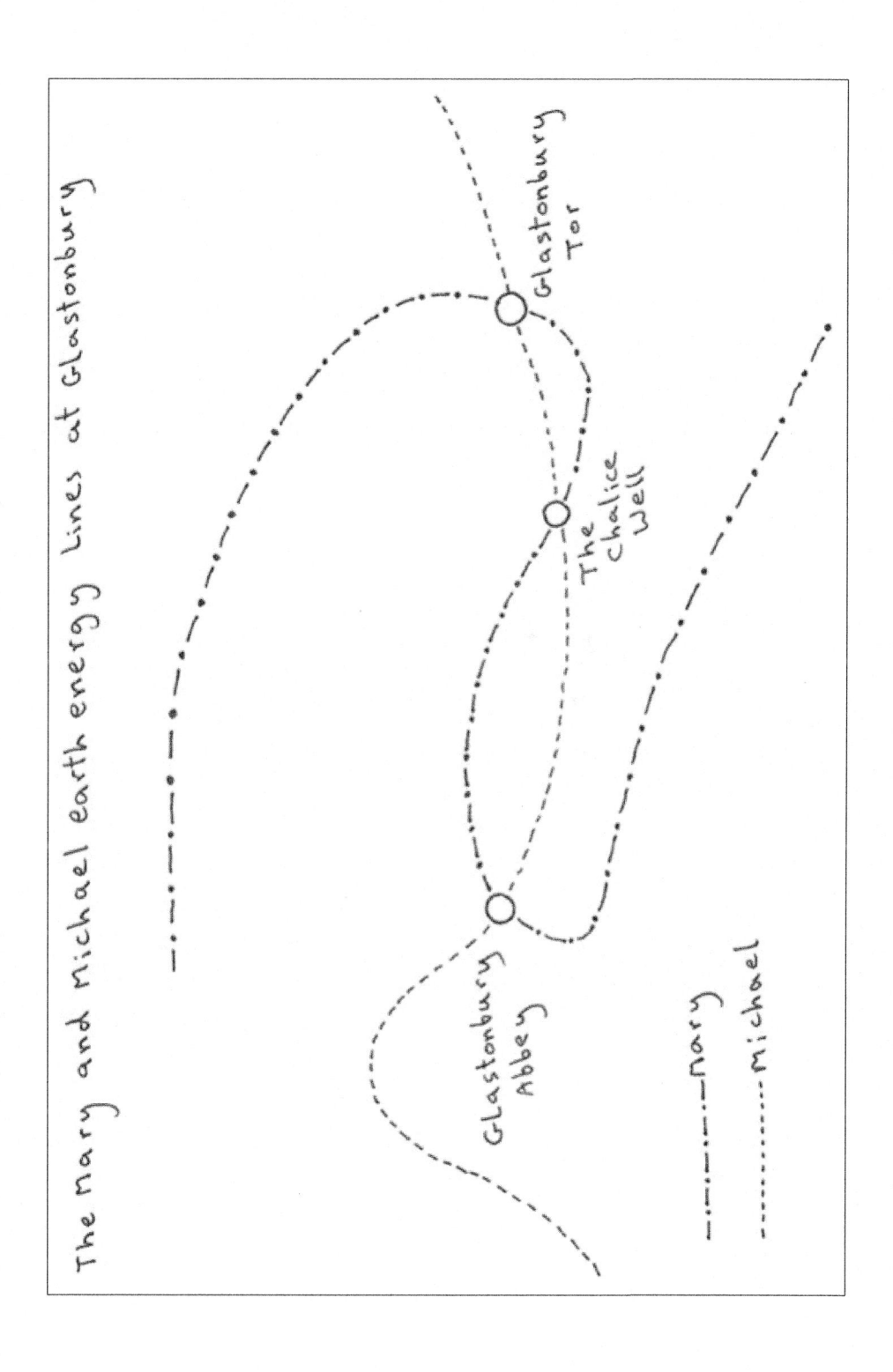

The Mary and Michael earth energy lines at Glastonbury

- Glastonbury Tor
- The Chalice Well
- Glastonbury Abbey

—··—·· Mary
············ Michael

Day 22

Glastonbury to Stoke St Michael

16 Miles

13.08.2020

'The Tower on the Tor seems to be watching our every move now as we encircle it. It's creeping closer and getting bigger.'
From 'The Long Walk to Glastonbury', Stewart Harding

I reserved my last few hours in Glastonbury for its most visible feature and one of the most famous hills in England. Rising above the Summerland Meadows, the Tor's modest height belies its commanding presence in the landscape. On its summit, St Michael's Tower is an unmistakable sight and an unmissable destination for tourists and pilgrims.

I planned my day's walk with the Tor as my primary objective, allowing myself plenty of time to immerse in its beauty and mystery. I then descended east to visit Gog and Magog, two ancient oak trees that stand below the hill to the east. From there, I headed to the villages of North Wootton and Pilton and then the historic town of Shepton Mallet. For my last few miles, I walked north along a section of the Roman Fosse Way before heading east to my final destination, a pub that allows camping in its garden.

Glastonbury Tor is the 13th node point along the St Michael Alignment, running from west to east, but due to the eccentric course of the two energy currents, it's the 11th node on the Mary line. East of the Tor, Mary continues in an easterly direction below Michael, but I mainly followed the Michael current for the rest of my day's walk. The churches at North

Wooton, Pilton and Shepton Mallet align with Michael.

I was up early for this, the 21st walking day on my trail. I felt a bit bleary, having been on anxious standby for half the night in the expectation of a thunderstorm that never transpired. A thin mist hung in the air as I left my camp, fully laden for my walk ahead. In the town, the shops and businesses were opening up for the day as I walked along my now-familiar route towards the well-trodden footpath that ascends the Tor. I passed a row of seven Tibetan prayer wheels at the foot of the hill, so I stopped (only briefly) to turn them in participation. By the time I ascended the hill, the mist had cleared.

From the path, I could see the strong form of the roofless tower above and the clearly defined terraces of the hill on which it stood. Seven distinct terraces encircle the Tor, and their origins are unknown. It's unclear whether they're natural or man-made and for what purpose, be they agricultural, defensive or ceremonial. I ascended the steep, well-maintained path to the top of the Tor, and my view from the summit was spectacular.

The most prominent feature on the summit is the tall tower; all that remains of the 14th Century church dedicated to St Michael. Earlier churches stood on the site, and there's evidence to show that the Tor was occupied from Neolithic times. St Michael's was a daughter house of Glastonbury Abbey until the rest of the church was demolished during the Dissolution of the Monasteries in 1539. The tower retains a damaged figure of St Michael on its west wall and a carving of St Bridget milking a cow above one of the two arched doorways. A notice on the wall gives a wealth of information:

GLASTONBURY TOR

GLASTONBURY RISES FROM THE LOWER LIAS CLAYS AND LIMESTONES THROUGH THE MIDDLE AND UPPER LIAS TO A DEPOSIT OF HARD MIDFORD SAND

ON THE CAP, 521 FT. HIGH, KNOWN LOCALLY AS TOR BURR. THIS IS MORE RESISTANT TO EROSION THAN THE LOWER LEVELS, MAKING THE SLOPES STEEP AND UNSTABLE.

THESE STEEP SCULPTED SLOPES, RISING DRAMATICALLY FROM THE ISLE OF AVALON IN THE FLAT SOMERSET LEVELS, HAVE ENCOURAGED MUCH SPECULATION ABOUT THE ORIGIN OF THE TOR IN LEGEND. THE EARLIEST REFERENCE IS A MID-THIRTEENTH CENTURY STORY OF ST. PATRICK'S RETURN FROM IRELAND IN WHICH HE BECAME LEADER OF A GROUP OF HERMITS AT GLASTONBURY AND DISCOVERED AN ANCIENT RUINED ORATORY ON THE SUMMIT AFTER CLIMBING THROUGH A DENSE WOOD. SCATTERED FINDS OF PREHISTORIC, ROMAN AND LATER OBJECTS SUGGEST THE TOR WAS ALWAYS USED BY MAN, BUT EVIDENCE OF ACTUAL OCCUPATION FROM THE SIXTH CENTURY AD WAS UNCOVERED IN THE EXCAVATIONS OF 1964-6. A SECOND PHASE OF OCCUPATION BETWEEN 900-1100 WAS DISTINGUISHED BY THE HEAD OF A CROSS AND WHAT WERE PROBABLY CHRISTIAN MONK'S CELLS CUT INTO THE ROCK ON THE SUMMIT.

THE TRADITION OF A MONASTIC SITE ON THE TOR IS CONFIRMED BY A CHARTER OF 1243 GRANTING PERMISSION FOR A FAIR AT THE MONASTERY OF ST. MICHAEL THERE.

THE PRESENT TOWER, THOUGH LATER MODIFIED, IS ESSENTIALLY FIFTEENTH CENTURY AND IS ASSOCIATED WITH THE SECOND OF TWO MAJOR CHURCHES WHICH STOOD ON THE SUMMIT. THE SECOND ONE WAS PROBABLY BUILT AFTER THE DESTRUCTIVE EARTHQUAKE OF 1275. THE MONASTIC CHURCH OF ST. MICHAEL, CLOSELY ASSOCIATED WITH THE GREAT ABBEY IN THE TOWN BELOW, FELL INTO RUIN AFTER THE DISSOLUTION OF THE MONASTERIES IN 1539, WHEN RICHARD WHITING, THE LAST ABBOT OF GLASTONBURY, WAS HANGED ON THE TOR

Whiting was hung, drawn and quartered in what's now regarded as a judicial murder orchestrated by the ambitions of King Henry VIII. By January 1539, the dissolution of the Monasteries was well underway. Glastonbury (which fell outside the 'Act for the Suppression of the Lesser Houses') was the only monastery left in Somerset, and Whiting refused to surrender it. An inquisition was undertaken to find the necessary 'proof' of corruption and wrongdoing, and in September, Whiting was arrested and taken to the Tower of London. Under the judgement of Thomas Cromwell, Whiting was convicted of treason. On November 15th 1539, the frail 80-year-old was dragged onto the Tor and barbarously executed, along with two other monks from the abbey. The Catholic Church (for his martyrdom) eventually beatified Whiting. Recently, members of the local community at Glastonbury campaigned for Richard Whiting to receive a posthumous Royal Pardon at the Queen's Platinum Jubilee.

Glastonbury Tor is shrouded in mystery and steeped in legend, the main one being that it's the Isle of Avalon, where King Arthur was taken, gravely wounded after his last battle, and from where he will rise to save the nation in its future time of need. Another legend claims that the Tor is magically hollow, containing the underworld kingdom of Annwyn, inhabited by fairies and led by King Gwyn ap Nudd. The entrance to this underworld is along a spiral labyrinth.

When Miller and Broadhurst first dowsed the Tor, they followed the course of the Michael energy current before discovering the existence of its feminine counterpart. Over several hours, the dowsers pursued the Michael energy current on the Tor. Arriving from the south, the current travelled up the hill in an elaborate trail along its slopes and terraces, making a snaking route towards the tower. There, the current appeared to enclose the building in a loop. It then continued back down the Tor in a similar but separate circuitous route to leave the base of the hill and continue north. In the Sun and the Serpent, the authors describe their discovery:

'The current had assumed the shape of a series of regular, rhythmical loops. Sitting down to make a sketch of what had been found so far, we plotted the sinuous path. We had stopped trying to rationalize it, but what was apparent was that it had suddenly become quite astonishingly serpentine.'

Astounded by the mysteriousness of their discovery, the authors saw parallels between the energy current and the Tor's history and traditions. Perhaps the terraces on the Tor were related to the Earth's energies and the legends concerning a labyrinth. Processional rituals would have taken place throughout its long and sacred past.

More was revealed when the authors returned to the Tor to dowse the Mary energy current. In the Sun and the Serpent, they describe their subsequent profound discovery:

The current of energy had wound around the north-eastern section of the Tor in the most exquisite manner...The Mary energy formed a container which encompassed the Michael current and its bulbous projection around the tower. The symbolism was graphic. The female force enclosed the male energy in a double-lipped cup. It was a chalice or Grail...It was a place where the male and female energies of the St Michael Line were ritually mating, the actual point of fusion apparently located at the site of the altar of the old church...We were confronted with the inescapable conclusion that what we were really dealing with was nothing less than the sexual energies of the Earth.'

The authors were aware that their profound discovery would seem outlandish, but they felt it was important to share it nonetheless:

'We knew that to reveal our findings would be to invite scorn and derision from some quarters...It was not for us to judge the significance of such a revelatory concept, or to censor it from those who may find inspiration from the discovery.'

When I stood on the Tor, I certainly felt inspired. I appreciate far more than I can understand, and I was in no hurry to let this appreciation go. This beautiful place was busy with other visitors enjoying their time at the summit. I assumed that some of them would have a good knowledge of its history, and maybe some were there for pilgrimage in whatever form it meant to them. I'm sure many were just there for a fun day out or to enjoy the view, but it was overwhelmingly apparent to me that Glastonbury Tor is a joy to experience.

From the Tor, I descended the path that follows its northeast ridge to reach a lane that led me to the famous Oaks of Avalon. These are two ancient trees known as Gog and Magog, named from the Hebrew Bible and other ancient texts, and in this case, a legend of two giants. One (Gog) is now a dead grey carcass, but Magog still grows, its large branches splaying out from its wizened trunk, hollowed out over the centuries. The trees mark what was once the traditional point of entry onto the island. A ceremonial avenue of other ancient oaks once led up to the Tor from here. Local farmers cut down the other trees over a hundred years ago, but a new avenue has recently been replanted.

Gog and Magog align with the Michael energy current, which continues north and east to reach the next significant site, the church at North

Wooton.

It took a rather tortuous route of paths and roads to get across the drained levels between Glastonbury and Wooton. Unfortunately, the church was closed to visitors. My next destination was Pilton, whose medieval church (much altered in Victorian times) was similarly closed. A lot of history is attached to the village. Before the draining of the Somerset Levels, Pilton was once a busy port. In legend, Pilton is where Joseph of Arimathea landed in Britain with Jesus (see Day 20). It was once a powerful ecclesiastical site associated with the abbey at Glastonbury. Before leaving the village, I walked down the lane to Worthy Farm.

In the last fifty years, Pilton has become famous (infamously so) for being the site of the Glastonbury Festival, which attracts upwards of 200,000 people over five days. It's run by Michael Eavis, a Pilton farmer (and his daughter, Emily), and is held nearly every year in the fields of his large farm immediately south of the village. There are occasional 'fallow' years when the festival doesn't take place, allowing a break for the land, the organisers and the local population. All of Pilton's inhabitants receive free tickets to the event. When I visited, the 50th-anniversary festival was, of course, cancelled due to the coronavirus pandemic.

By the lane in the village stands a magnificent 14th Century tithe barn owned by Michael Eavis. It was formerly used to store produce for Glastonbury Abbey and is one of four surviving barns that once served it. The building was used to train the Women's Land Army during the Second World War, but it was severely damaged by fire in 1963. In 1995 Eavis bought the ruin and presented it to the Pilton Barn Trust. A major restoration took place (costing £500,000), which saw the barn restored to its former glory.

I entered the courtyard, where I noticed a stone bench built to commemorate the Women's Land Army from the two World Wars. I then walked to the barn to find its huge wooden door unlocked. Inside the building, I was treated to a pleasant surprise. The award-winning craftsmanship and the beauty of the interior were breathtaking. I stared up and along the massive oak roof, supporting 30,000 handmade tiles. The ancient stone walls admit the daylight through deeply set openings throughout, and the floor of lime concrete is said to be the largest expanse of its kind in Europe. The barn now caters for a variety of events and functions. As I looked around, I saw examples of photographs and posters from displays that documented some of the early festivals stretching back to the first one, held in 1970.

Leaving Pilton, I made my way through the countryside, now beyond the Somerset Levels. My time at Glastonbury and walking this unique and beautiful landscape was over, and it already felt as if I'd somehow dreamt the entirety of the last two days.

By mid-afternoon, I reached the busy town of Shepton Mallet, but I didn't spend much time there. I felt tired, so I bought some provisions and continued. I halted to look at the parish church *(aligned with the Michael current)*, but it was closed. I also noticed the elaborate market cross where twelve followers of the Duke of Monmouth were hung, drawn and quartered after the ill-fated rebellion of 1685 (see Day 20).

Making my way east out of the town, I connected with a dead-straight sunken path that follows a section of the Roman Fosse Way. This 230-mile-long highway ran north from Exeter (Isca Dumnoniorum) to Lincoln (Lindum Colonia) via Ilchester (Lindinis), Bath (Aquae Sulis), Cirencester (Corinium) and Leicester (Corieltauvorum). It was constructed during the 1st and the 2nd Centuries. Just south of where I joined the path, archaeological investigations have uncovered some early burials and many finds from the Roman period.

After a mile, I left the Way and headed east to my final destination for the day, a remote country pub near the village of Stoke St Michael, where I was allowed to camp for two nights. For the next few days, I would once again be reliant on public transport to get to and from my walking objectives, so my plans were as follows:

Day 23: **Walk from Stoke St Michael to Buckland Dinham.** Bus from Buckland Dinham to Frome, bus from Frome to Stoke St Michael.

Day 24: Bus from Stoke St Michael to Frome, bus from Frome to Buckland Dinham. **Walk from Buckland Dinham to Trowbridge.** Bus from Trowbridge to Frome, bus from Frome to Stoke St Michael.

Day 26: Bus from Stoke St Michael to Frome, train from Frome to Trowbridge. **Walk from Trowbridge to Devizes.**

I checked all the times and saw it was all doable (or so I thought – see Day 24). I was beginning to feel confident about reaching Avebury on Day 28, and the first half of my trail across the most expansive land of England would be in my bag. I decided to treat myself to a shower and meal in the pub facilities before settling in for another night of blissful sleep.

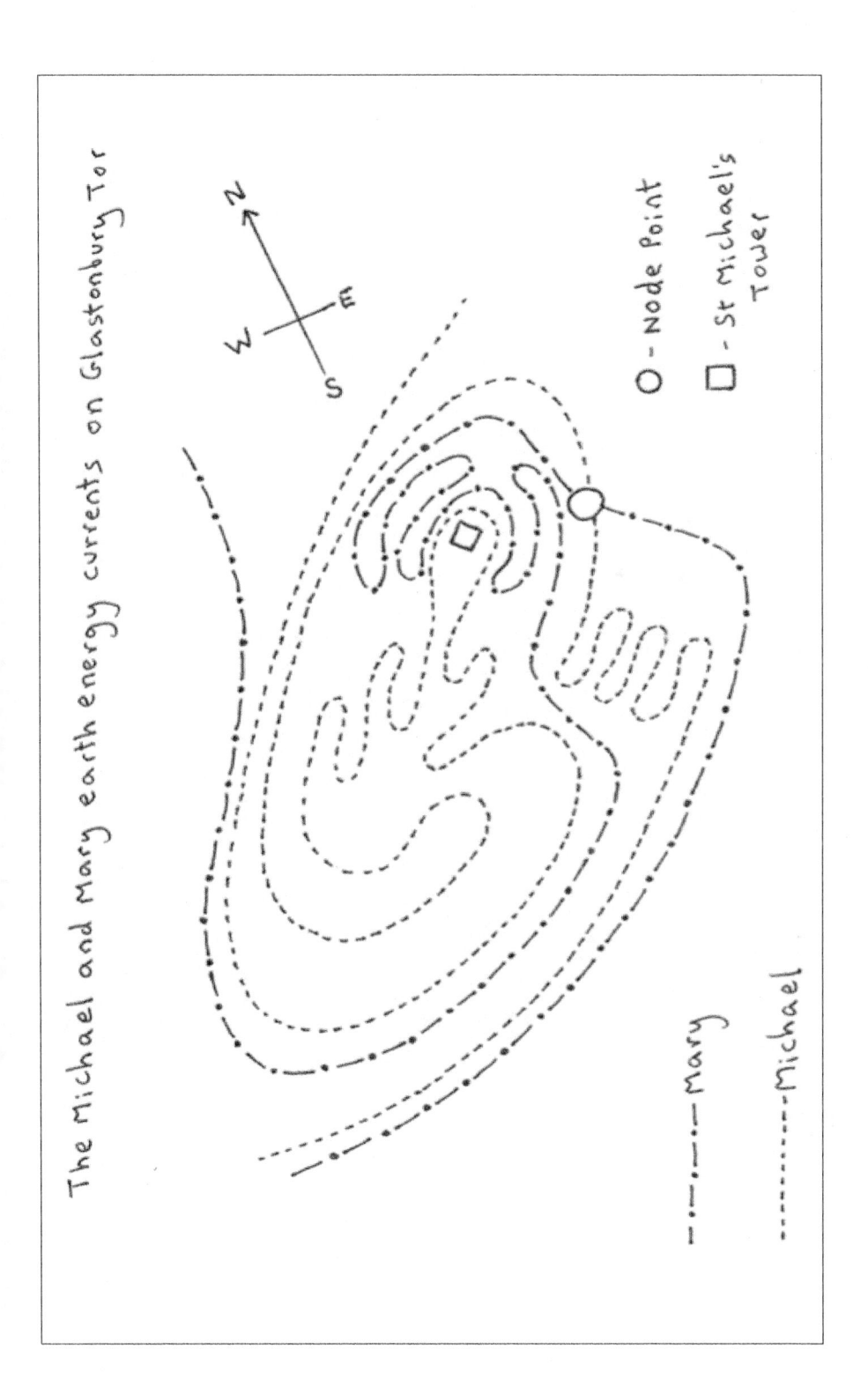

The Michael and Mary earth energy currents on Glastonbury Tor

N / E / W / S

O – Node Point
☐ – St Michael's Tower

—·—·— Mary
--------- Michael

Day 23

Stoke St Michael to Buckland Dinham

10 Miles

14.08.2020

This day was very much a road-bound walking one, taking in a series of Somerset villages from west to east; Stoke St Michael, Coleford, Mells, Great Elm and Buckland Dinham. At the end of the walk, I paid a visit to the Orchardleigh Stones, the remains of a neolithic burial chamber.

The churches of each village (except for Buckland Dinham) align with the Michael energy current, as do the Orchardleigh Stones. I followed it closely throughout my walk while Mary remained several miles further south.

My walk began early to allow for the necessary bus travel at its end. I was now in the Mendip Hills, but I could have been anywhere with the misty drizzle obscuring my views. The highest of them remained a long way to the north and east of where I walked, but at least I was in the countryside, and the roads were quiet.

Stoke St Michael was a good country mile from where I camped, and my route to the village followed a woodland footpath channelled into the ground forming a trench in places deeper than my height. It's hard to grasp the great age of ancient trackways such as these or how many hooves and feet they have served. In the centre of the village, I found the Millennium Garden, where an attractive footbridge spans a stream beyond a lych gate. The nearby St Michael's church was surprisingly open as I passed at 8.45, so I quickly looked inside. The most striking feature was a modern stained glass window depicting the winged Archangel thrusting his lance through the neck of a fire-breathing dragon. The building dates from the early 15th Century, but only the tower is original.

Limestone has been quarried extensively in the surrounding landscape. Many are long-abandoned but significant subterranean caves near the village host colonies of rare bat species, including the greater horseshoe, lesser horseshoe, and natterer's bat. The Fairy Cave Quarry is a disused limestone quarry now popular with climbers.

Coleford was the next village, and the (Victorian) Church of the Holy Trinity was closed, so I kept Walking. I now carefully followed the directions in my MMPW guidebook to the hamlet of Vobster and the next village of Mells. Like Pilton (Day 21), Mells has a 14th Century tithe barn that formerly served Glastonbury Abbey. The village was part of the abbey's estate, and many historic buildings remain. The village pub dates from the 15th Century and the imposing church dedicated to St Andrew is also medieval. It hosts a tall tower and some interesting interior features (See **Appendix, Day 23***). The church was sadly closed to visitors, but in the spacious churchyard, I located the grave of the Great War poet Siegfried Sassoon, marked by a plain white headstone bearing the simple inscription:

SIEGFRIED

LORAINE

SASSOON

1886-1967

R.I.P.

I continued walking east, following a path by the north side of the Mells River. Beyond the far bank is Tedbury Camp, a large Iron Age promontory fort naturally defended by a loop in the river. The Romans later occupied it, and in 1961 a large hoard of Roman coins was found on the site.

Soon I reached the next small village of Great Elm and its 12th Century

Church. Far smaller than its neighbour at Mells, St Andrews is substantially Norman. It, too, was closed, so I sat on a bench in the churchyard and ate some lunch. A light shower began to fall, so I retreated to the porch, where I noticed the engraved marks of a scratch dial on the church wall. The wall of the gable-roofed tower bares a more recent sundial, but the building has a wonderfully unspoilt look (see **Appendix, Day 23****).

From Great Elm, the Michael energy current continues east to the Orchardleigh Stones, the final objective of my day's walk.

Walking north from Great Elm, I arrived in the village of Buckland Dinham, where I planned to catch buses back to my campsite via Frome. I checked the time and saw that I still had over an hour to visit the nearby Orchardleigh Stones before catching my bus to Frome. I'd have to be quick, so I marched out of the village along the busy main road and then up a steep lane leading to the site on farmland at the top of Murty Hill. My objective was on private land, but an excellent and reliable website for all things megalithic advised that the landowner tolerates visitors to the monument.

Anyway, I reached the Orchardleigh Stones unchallenged. Standing in a small walled enclosure, they comprise a massive, 12-foot high standing stone and a smaller one which leans against it. More are half-submerged to ground level. Little is known about the assembly, but it's believed to have been a Neolithic burial chamber. A tale describes how a man dug ten feet into the ground to find the bottom of the stone, but it fell and crushed him before re-erecting itself.

Miller and Broadhurst observed that the site was 'immensely powerful' when they dowsed the stones on the Michael line.

With my day's walk completed, I returned to Buckland Dinham for my uneventful bus rides to Stoke St Michael and my campsite nearby.

Day 24

Buckland Dinham to Trowbridge

(First Attempt)

0 Miles

15.08.2020

'Know what day it is and learn how to read a bus timetable.'
Frank Roberts, 08.50, 15.08.2020

My first attempt at Day 24 came after Day 23, but on my second attempt, it became Day 29 (see **Day 29**).

I planned to break camp and walk to Stoke St Michael, where I would catch buses to Frome and Buckland Dinham. I'd then walk to Trowbridge, catching another bus to my next campsite just west of the Wiltshire town of Devizes...

If on a Saturday evening, you type in 'Bus from Stoke St Michael to Devizes' on your phone, the services displayed represent the NEXT buses that serve the locations without pointing out that these are, in fact, Monday services. At 08.36 the following day, I was blissfully unaware of this fact, but by 08.50, I became painfully aware of it, along with two others:

Today was a Sunday

No buses serve Stoke St Michael on a Sunday.

Realising my error with annoyance and stupidity in equal measure, I hastily amended my plans. I would now walk north to Radstock and catch a bus to Bath, then another to Devizes. My walk between Buckland Dinham and Trowbridge would have to be postponed.

My bus rides were long, and my time in Bath was short, unplanned, and, as with High Wycombe (see Day 34), jarring on my senses after all my relaxed country days and long country miles. Although my sightseeing was minimal, it was enough to appreciate the potential the city could offer had I arrived here with much more time on my hands, money in my pocket, and a lot less weight on my back. Perhaps Bath will feature on one of my future trails.

Day 25

Trowbridge to Devizes

12 Miles

16.08.20

With my trail now broken by a missing link, I had to press on, leaving eleven un-walked miles between Buckland Dinham (Somerset) and Trowbridge (Wiltshire). I knew I'd have to revisit the area to fill the gap, but I didn't know when this could happen (see Days 24 & 29).

This day's walk started at Trowbridge and finished at Devizes. The Kennet and Avon Canal links the two towns, and I spent nearly the entire day walking its towpath.

Halfway along my walk, I included a short diversion to **Bowerhill**, *where the Mary and Michael energy currents meet to form the 13th node on the St Michael Alignment.*

From my final night of camping in Somerset, I walked back into Stoke St Michael and caught the necessary buses to get me to the starting point of my day's walk at 11.00 am.

Trowbridge is a big and busy town built on the banks of the River Biss. Historically, it was a major centre for the woollen trade, and several significant buildings remain from its industrial past. One of these is the Handle House, purpose-built for drying vast quantities of teazles from the river, used in the cloth manufacturing process. The building is characterised by its perforated brickwork. Another building I noticed in the town was a small stone building known as the Blind House. This curious windowless building was a lock-up in the 18th Century before the town acquired its first police station in 1854. During a riot in 1824, the roof of the building was ripped off, and its inhabitants were 'rescued'. The roof was again torn off by German bombing in 1942.

At least 14 similar 'blind houses' survive across Wiltshire, primarily built in the 18th Century for discerning patrons of the criminal or drunk variety. They served as secure holding pens for miscreants between arrest and prosecution, presumably at weekends before the courts opened to deal with their temporary inhabitants. They could have been worse, though; the Trowbridge example had openings in the wall where friends of those incarcerated could pour 'refreshments' into the cell.

Also, in the centre of the town, I visited the parish church of St James, built in the 15th Century Gothic Perpendicular style. The building was closed, but from the outside, I noticed its tall spire rising above the pinnacles, battlements and gargoyles that feature across its length.

The Michael energy current aligns with the church before continuing north-east.

My time in the town was short, so I pressed on with my walk to Devizes. I headed north to join the towpath of the Kennet & Avon Canal, which became my walking route for the rest of the day. It was a pleasant walk, but when you use 40-year-old maps for navigation, there are inevitably a few surprises along the way. As I reached the village of Semington, I was surprised to notice the significant developments that have taken place since the printing of my map in 1981. The A 350 road has since been completely rebuilt, and now the canal crosses over it as an impressive aqueduct built in 2004.

Beyond Semington, my canal-side path ran south of the village of Bowerhill. A rather unremarkable modern development of houses now stretches to within half a mile of the canal. Still, the local community have taken steps to conserve what remains of the rural landscape. A sizeable wood now grows from 5,000 trees planted in 1993, and a large wildlife haven and picnic area have been created. An information notice lists the many animal and plant species that now thrive from this wonderful work.

I diverted north for about a mile to see the 13th of the 23 node points of the St Michael Alignment, using the directions in my MMPW guide. I located it to the corner of a field on farmland at the very edge of a new housing development. Unlike all the other node points I'd passed along the trail, this one had no historic building or geographic landmark of any description to mark it.

Miller and Broadhurst first dowsed the two currents to this location, which appears to have no documented historical significance:

'The two currents crossed at a small spring overshadowed by trees. It was half-filled with bits of old timber, utterly neglected. Yet it was unique, the only spring that marked a node in the entire quest. It must have been a particularly holy place in the past'.

Returning south to rejoin the canal, I continued east along the towpath through the village of Sells Green, passing several locks and bridges en route. The Kennet & Avon follows the natural course of its two named rivers, linking them with a constructed channel to form an 87-mile waterway between Bristol and Reading. It thus formed a continuous waterway between the Bristol Channel and the River Thames. The canal was completed in 1810, but like the Grand Western Canal (see Day 18), it was eclipsed by the development of the railways and fell into disuse during the 19th Century. It was fully re-opened in 1990 after extensive restoration.

Late in the afternoon, I reached a canal-side campsite west of Devizes. It was a convenient location to visit and explore the town, so I booked myself in for the night, pitched my tent and continued west along the canal towpath. Here my path rose alongside a sequence of 16 locks at Caen Hill. Altogether, no less than 29 locks ascend a total of 237 feet along a two-mile section of the canal. It's the longest continual flight of locks in the country after that at Tardebigge on the Worcester & Birmingham Canal. The construction of the locks was served by a tramway that ran parallel to the canal. This has long since vanished, but its tunnels remain in the four bridges that span this section of the waterway. I walked to the top of the hill. Here the channel widened into a basin filled with brightly painted and decorated barges reflecting their colours in the still water. They abundantly reflect the changing role of the canal in a new century of leisure.

A final mile of locks and bridges brought me into the town of Devizes. After Glastonbury, it has to be my favourite town on the entire trail. Modest in size, the centre is very traditional and unspoiled and has a wealth of historical architecture dating back to the Medieval Era. A Victorian castle now occupies the site of a Norman fortress that was besieged in the 12th Century and again in the Civil War. From the 16th Century, Devizes grew as an important centre for the wool trade and later in the brewing and tobacco manufacturing industries. There are two medieval churches, and scores of listed buildings line the streets. A beautifully conceived Town Trail with information leaflets and site plaques allow the visitor to walk around the town and gain an informed experience of the place. At the same time, the Wiltshire Museum on Long Street provides some fascinating displays and a wealth of knowledge on the area's history (see **Appendix Day 25***).

As I explored the town, I discovered that the large central Market Place was once within the castle's outer bailey. The imposing Market Cross was built in 1814 as a repositioned replacement of the original. On its wall hangs an intriguing, if somewhat wordy, plaque:

THE MAYOR AND CORPORATION OF DEVIZES AVAIL THEMSELVES OF THE STABILITY OF THIS BUILDING TO TRANSMIT TO FUTURE TIMES THE RECORD OF AN AWFUL EVENT WHICH OCCURRED IN THIS MARKET PLACE, IN THE YEAR 1753.

HOPING THAT SUCH RECORD MAY SERVE AS
A SALUTORY WARNING AGAINST THE DANGER
OF IMPIOUSLY INVOKING DIVINE VENGEANCE
OR OF CALLING ON THE HOLY NAME OF GOD
TO CONCEAL THE DEVICES OF FALSEHOOD
AND FRAUD.
ON THURSDAY THE 25TH OF JANUARY 1753
RUTH PIERCE OF POTTERNE IN THIS COUNTY,
AGREED WITH THREE OTHER WOMEN TO BUY
A SACK OF WHEAT IN THE MARKET EACH PAYING
HER DUE PROPORTION TOWARDS THE SAME;
ONE OF THESE WOMEN IN COLLECTING THE
SEVERAL QUOTAS OF MONEY, DISCOVERED A
DEFICIENCY AND DEMANDED OF RUTH PIERCE
THE SUM WHICH WAS WANTING TO MAKE GOOD
THE AMOUNT RUTH PIERCE PROTESTED THAT
SHE HAD PAID HER SHARE AND SAID SHE WISHED
SHE MIGHT DROP DOWN DEAD IF SHE HAD NOT.
SHE RASHLY REPORTED THIS AWFUL WISH; WHEN
TO THE CONSTERNATION AND TERROR OF THE
SURROUNDING MULTITUDE, SHE INSTANTLY
FELL DOWN AND EXPIRED, HAVING THE MONEY
CONCEALED IN HER HAND.

Feeling relieved that I wasn't the only person who writes in wordy sentences, I returned to the campsite, retracing my earlier footsteps.

Day 26

Devizes to All Cannings

9 Miles

17.08.2020

The distance between my start and finish points between these two locations is barely five miles, but my walking route for this day was further, taking in the hilltop site of Oliver's Castle and the village of Bishops Cannings. Here was the first venture of my trail onto the Wiltshire Downs and the closest thing to the wild grandeur of Dartmoor walked two weeks earlier. My final few miles were along another section of the Kennet and Avon Canal as it flows through the Vale of Pewsey, finishing at a campsite south of the village of All Cannings.

Oliver's Castle is the hilltop site of an Iron Age fort and the location of the 14th node point where the Mary and Michael energy lines meet on the St Michael Alignment. Both currents then continue north-easterly to the subsequent three nodes further east at Avebury (see Day 27). Bishops Cannings aligns with the Mary current two miles east of Oliver's Castle.

My walk began with a re-walk into Devizes once again along the canal path beside the wonderful Caen Hill Locks. The morning was wind-free, warm and sunny. On the north side of the town, I took a mile-long, tree-lined bridleway known as the Quakers' Walk, believed to date from the time of King Edward I. It traverses what was once part of a vast deer park and later the estate of Lord Roundway. A mansion stood on the site, but this was demolished in the 1950s.

Beyond the bridleway, I reached the village of Roundway and ascended north onto Roundway Down. Here, the stunning white image of the Roundway White Horse came into view, boldly carved into the side of Roundway Hill. I was now on the southern edge of the vast chalk grasslands of the Marlborough Downs. This unique landscape is being conserved largely through a rare initiative led by local landowners for the benefit of wildlife as well as humans.

Something is pleasing about the lightness of the chalky soil that forms these smooth rounded hills. People have been carving figures into the hillsides of the Downs for millennia, and in recent centuries horses have become the standard subject. In addition to the Roundway Horse, there are currently another seven white horses cut into the hillsides of Wiltshire.

As I climbed onto the Down, glorious views began to open up, and I sensed the immense. Although I only had two more days of trail walking left for this year, I knew that east of where I now stood, a whole week's worth of downland walking was waiting for me. It was a shame I couldn't carry on in one go, but the hills would still be there next year. They weren't going anywhere.

Soon the land plateaued, and I continued north with a spring in my step. I joined a short section of the Wessex Ridgeway, an extension of the National Ridgeway Trail (see Days 30-36). I continued over the Down to reach the level, grassy hilltop enclosure of Oliver's Castle. I gained some spectacular views to my west, where steep gullies fell away below me, forming a formidable, natural escarpment. Here the earthworks of an early four-acre settlement have been located along with finds from the Bronze and Iron Ages. Many similar sites have been identified all over the Marlborough Downs.

Miller and Broadhurst recount their experience of dowsing the node to Oliver's Castle, describing it as 'an exhilarating place':
'One looks down on the world like the Gods of Olympus, amused at the triviality of human lives. The entire hill is sculpted. Inside the enclosure, a rare prehistoric dewpond has survived the times when the place was

used as a fortification, and the discovery that the current crossed the centre of the platform and ran into the enclosure to a node point approximately at its centre was enough to make us realize that it is a site of considerable significance. The effect of the place even today, with its sanctity overshadowed by memories of ancient wars, is inspiring.'

Roundway Down was the scene of a battle during the English Civil War, fought on July 13th, 1643. It was the most decisive victory for the Royalists, enabling them to secure and control all of South West England until late 1645. Many of the Parliamentary cavalry plunged down these steep gullies to their deaths while being pursued by the Royalist forces during the battle. Consequently, the area immediately below Oliver's Castle is known as Bloody Ditch. Also below the 'Castle' can be found a cluster of natural springs known as Mother Anthony's Well, thought to have been the site of a Romano-British shrine.

With plenty of time on my hands, I sat beneath one of the slender trees that grew on the hill and had lunch on the dry springy turf. I stayed for nearly an hour, transfixed by the beauty of my views and the peace of the place. Yet again, I had a grandstand view of a quintessentially English summer scene unfolding before me in real time.

I was now within just seven miles of Avebury, where I planned to finish thus far my trail walk for 2020. No campsites were open in the Avebury area, however. I could have camped wild for a night or two on the Downs, but comfort and convenience brought me south to an available site near the village of All Cannings. I decided to stay for two nights to allow plenty of time to finish the walk and then spend an entire day exploring the wealth of sites in and around Avebury.

Leaving Oliver's Castle, I joined a lane leading east to meet a road that took me south off the Down and into the village of Bishops Cannings. Unfortunately, the Church of St Mary (described as one of the finest in Wiltshire) was closed, but a tour of the exterior was worth my time. The substantially Medieval building was restored sympathetically in the Victorian Era and retains a lot of stonework from the 14th and 15th Centuries.

Appropriately, Miller and Broadhurst found that the Church of St Mary the Virgin aligns directly with the Mary earth energy current as it travels west from Avebury, as does St Mary's Church at Winterbourne Monkton, six miles away. There are dozens of churches dedicated to the saint that lie either directly on the energy current or very close to the St Michael Alignment.

From Bishops Cannings, I made my way through some fields to reconnect with the Kennet & Avon Canal. I followed the towpath on its southern bank for a few miles to reach the linear village of All Cannings. I stopped at the shop for provisions and noticed its community-run, not-for-profit status. All sorts of excellent, home made food items were on sale (including a soup menu), and a machine dispensing locally produced milk. I also passed the local country pub, and seeing it was a popular dining venue; I booked myself a table for the following night. In pandemics, you have to plan!

Another mile brought me to a quiet campsite where I booked myself a two-night pitch. I was now in the Vale of Pewsey, but I would be back on the Downs for my walk the following day. Avebury was calling me, and I was excited for more highlights on my pilgrimage.

Day 27

All Cannings to Avebury

7 Miles

18.08.2020

'The whole temple of Abury may be considered as a picture, and it really is so. Therefore the founders wisely contriv'd, that a spectator should have an advantageous prospect of it, as he approach'd within view.'

William Stukeley, 'Abury, a Temple of the British Druids', 1743

Like Day 21, I woke up with a tremendous feeling of anticipation. Without a doubt, Glastonbury and Avebury were overall my two favourite places on my pilgrimage. As with Glastonbury, there's too much to see to give Avebury the attention it deserves in just one day, so my time there was planned for two days; one to walk there and complete a partial tour on foot, then a 'rest day', during which I would return by bus to visit all the remaining sites.

This final walk was short, but it included a whole bunch of ancient, sacred and historic sites. I walked north back onto the Marlborough Downs, crossing the Wansdyke and visiting the West Kennet Long Barrow. I then descended off the Down to see the Swallowhead Springs, Silbury Hill and the Sanctuary. Finally, I walked along the West Kennet Stone Avenue into Avebury village and the henge complex. Here was the termination point of my trail for the year and the precise halfway point on my entire coast-to-coast pilgrimage.

Like at Glastonbury, the alignment has three node points at Avebury. These are at **Windmill Hill** (see Day 28), **Avebury Henge** (also Day 28) and **The Sanctuary** on Overton Hill. These are the **15th, 16th and 17th Nodes**, respectively. The energy currents intertwine somewhat differently than at Glastonbury, but they are just as unique as they venture through several additional sites between each node. These other sites are all significant to the Avebury complex:

The West Kennet Stone Avenue (Michael)
Silbury Hill (Mary)
Swallowhead Spring (Mary)
West Kennet Long Barrow (Mary)
The Long Stones (Mary, see Day 28)
St Mary's Church, Winterbourne Monkton (Mary, see Day 28)

It's probably also helpful to remember that on their first visit to Avebury, Broadhurst and Miller were dowsing what they had so far believed to be the only earth energy current on the St Michael Alignment (the Michael energy current). They made their first discovery of the Mary current at Avebury Henge.

Leaving my campsite, I was travelling light, without needing all my kit, which I could safely leave behind with my tent. I walked north and crossed the Kennet & Avon Canal, but before anything else, I made a half-mile detour to visit the All Cannings Long Barrow. It sounds prehistoric, but this one is uniquely different, having been conceived and created within this very century. All Cannings Long Barrow is the first one in the country to be constructed in five and a half millennia. In 2014, a farmer with strong connections to the locality (and its distant past) decided to create a new one. It might sound like a great folly, but it was built to serve a living function for the placement of cremation urns. It's approved as a place of worship. The interior is open to the public on the winter and summer solstices and the spring and autumn equinoxes, but visitors are welcome to view the exterior anytime. I could walk around the site and see the beautifully constructed stone entrance, allowing my imagination to appreciate the passages and chambers within.

I retraced my steps to pick up a footpath taking me up onto All Cannings Down. The weather was just as perfect as the previous day, and soon my views were as magnificent. Nicely broken clouds cast their shadows over the chalk landscape, and apart from an irritating wasp sting, the natural world was in harmony with me. Ascending further, I reached the Wansdyke, a massive earthwork that channels across the downs as a ditch and bank from west to east in two sections for over 20 miles. It was built as a defensive structure in the early Medieval period, and although it's not as famous as Hadrian's Wall or Offa's Dyke it's worthy of comparison. Little is known about the who's and the whys of it, but its monumental significance is undeniable. As with many other mysteries, the Wansdyke has been linked with the Legends of King Arthur.

The Wansdyke sliced through the landscape in both directions as far as I could see, and walking just a short section of the bank gave me a taste of just how monumental these earthworks are. The work of ancient hands is visible across these uplands in the remains of barrows, tumuli and various earthworks. There are hundreds of these in the landscape on a map, and many can be easily picked out visually as raised mounds, often covered by clumps of trees (usually Beech), where the plough has naturally avoided them. Looking North from my vantage point, I could make out the hill of East Kennet Long Barrow, topped with a similar copse of trees, and nestling unmistakably in the valley of the Kennet, the neat, flat-topped cone of the incredible man-made Silbury Hill. So too, the hilltop stones of West Kennet Long barrow and a fair number of people walking around them. Avebury was calling me loudly.

Avebury is part of the UNESCO World Heritage Site known as 'Stonehenge, Avebury and Associated Sites'. Stonehenge is quite rightly the most famous of these sights, thanks to its infamous and unique assembly of sarsen stones. An important point, however, is that, unlike Stonehenge, all the Avebury sites are free to visit, and for no money, they offer a better visitor experience. Avebury is jointly owned and managed by the National Trust and English Heritage. It may not be as famous as Stonehenge, but there's much more to see. The Avebury Monument is the world's largest complex of neolithic stone circles, forming part of an extraordinary collection of Neolithic and Bronze Age ceremonial sites. Perhaps it can best be described as a ritual landscape, although there are many interpretations as to the purpose and nature of such ritual and ceremony. After all, some of the sites are over 5,000 years old, but more about all this later.

I marched as directly as possible towards the West Kennet Barrow and soon reached it along the edge of a newly harvested cornfield. This monument is one of Britain's largest Neolithic chambered tombs, but what makes it so remarkable is its extraordinary state of preservation and accessibility. A linear mound of earth over a hundred yards long contains a roofed passageway with a series of side chambers. Several enormous sarsen boulders form around an entrance forecourt. The monument dates to around 3650 BC and was used for a thousand years. When excavated in 1859, the partial remains of 46 people were found in the chambers along with cremations, pottery and various other grave goods, implements and artefacts. Following further excavations in the 1950s, the barrow was conserved and reconstructed to allow visitor access.

Observing social distancing conduct, I patiently waited for my opportunity to enter the corridor and chambers. Inside, small windows in the roof above illuminated the small, neat side chambers. I stooped into each one, pausing briefly to listen to the peaceful silence of the stones enclosing me. As with my moment under the capstone inside Trethevy Quoit on Day 9, I had a charged feeling that I was standing in precisely the same footsteps as my ancient ancestors. It's hard to put such a feeling into words.

In the Sun and the Serpent, the authors describe 'an eerie but moving atmosphere' inside the chambers and that an edifice of such magnitude and location conveyed for them a purpose far more significant than simple burial. After dowsing the Mary energy current to the site, they reported:

'Spectacularly positioned on a hill crest looking across to Silbury, it seemed that the choice of its situation could not be accidental. This was confirmed when the new serpent was found to pass right through the monumental megaliths of its facade at a diagonal angle, leaving to run down the valley. There appeared little doubt that the 'long barrow' was much more than that, and may at one time have been an important ceremonial centre and a crucial component of the Avebury complex.'

Outside, I sat down on the slope of the long barrow and looked north to Silbury Hill. Beyond the mound, I could make out the top of Windmill Hill, although the henge complex and Stone Avenue were obscured by woodland. I could see that otherwise; it too would be in full view; such was my vantage point. Of all the sites, it seemed evident that Silbury Hill would provide the best.

I now determined I'd descend towards Silbury Hill to get a closer look at this great mound, but on the way, I diverted a short distance along the River Kennet to visit another sanctuary aligned with the Mary earth energy current; the ancient Swallowhead Springs.

The Swallowhead Springs are a now much-neglected water source that feeds into the young River Kennet at a meander tucked quietly upstream away from the hoards of visitors making their way up the hill to the West Kennet Barrow. Its unique geography means it flows from spring into summer but remains dormant and dry through the autumn and winter months. This is because the spring flows from a natural reservoir within the chalk bedrock that gradually evaporates during the summer. By the autumn, the spring runs dry until sufficiently full to flow again in late February.

There is no evidence that the spring was ever Christianised as a holy well, but it has attracted much folklore through the ages, and there's a lot to a name. The upper reach of the River Kennet is called the Winterbourne, and the spring certainly 'swallows' its head with seasonal regularity. It's easy to imagine that this mysterious annual cycle would attract a potent significance to the area's early inhabitants. In his book 'Abury: A Temple of the British Druids', William Stukeley, the great antiquarian of the 18th Century, writes:

'The country people have an anniversary meeting on the top of *Silbury-hill* on every *palm-Sunday*, when they make merry with cakes, figs, sugar, and water fetch'd from the Swallow-head, or spring of the *Kennet*. This spring was much more remarkable than at present, gushing out of the earth, in a continued stream. They say it was spoil'd by digging for a fox who earth'd above, in some cranny thereabouts; this disturb'd the sacred nymphs, in a special way of speaking.'

Arriving at the spring was a pleasant surprise. Someone has constructed an archway of willow on the slope leading down from the riverbank, and an abundance of ribbons hang from the twisting branches of an old willow tree, along with various other offerings. The spring was in flow, and an attractive flight of stepping stones crossed the water that pooled from it. Standing over the trickling stream in the cool midday shade, I was reminded of my peaceful time at Alsia Well on Day 1. It was another magical pause and a welcome opportunity to refresh my senses.

Miller and Broadhurst dowsed the Mary current to the spring, noting the significance of the feminine quality of its energy:
'The horseshoe shaped head which fills with water on the return of the Goddess can have been nothing other than a sacred pool whose waters appeared miraculously to give birth to the dry bed, joining it to the stream which runs close to the Henge and around the base of Overton Hill. The fact that the distinctly feminine energies of the terrestrial current we were

tracking pass through it is even more indication of its ancient sanctity.'

After fifteen minutes of joyful relaxation, I aimed my boots for yet another ancient sanctuary, the grand mound of Silbury Hill. In less than fifteen minutes, I stood at its base. The hill stands alongside the busy A4, which inevitably spoils the setting, but nothing can be taken away from what this truly colossal monument represents. Silbury Hill is the tallest prehistoric artificial mound in Europe. It was completed around 2400 BC, and archaeology has failed to identify the true nature of its purpose. Despite centuries of excavations, no burials have been found, although William Stukeley records finding the skeletal remains of a man and Bridle in 1723. Later excavations served little more purpose than to damage the monument. In recent years, extensive work has been undertaken to stabilise the hill by filling in all the tunnels and shafts left by previous investigations.

Miller and Broadhurst summarise the fact that no studies or investigations have been able to explain the original purpose of the hill:
'So far, no-one has put forward a plausible explanation for the vast conical mound, or why the people who constructed the Henge, West Kennet Long Barrow and Silbury, all at about the same time, should have expended such enormous effort.'
The authors go on to account their experience of dowsing the Mary energy current to the hill:
'It was now heading for the massive artificial mound of Silbury. Running across the Bath/Marlborough road, it swung round to pass through the western side. Silbury, of course, is a goddess image without comparison, its enormous rounded form projecting the gentle curves of an otherwise rolling landscape.'

More is known about the how than the why, and how the early builders constructed such a massive and permanent landmark demonstrates tremendous skill. The 131-foot-tall mound covers an area of 5½ Acres and was built in stages, forming a stepped circular pyramid composed of carefully structured layers and walls of various materials, depending on the stages of the process. Some of the material was dug from ditches at the site, which were backfilled as the mound grew. Other material was imported. Astounding statistics include 35 million basket loads of chalk and 18 million man and/or woman hours. People are now discouraged from climbing the hill, and quite rightly so, as erosion from generations of youthful clambering now scars the slopes. I recall being one such youthful clamberer many years ago when I first visited Avebury. Other youthful clamberers have included Madhead, Roger and Squash in 1973:

'Then we went to and scrambled up to the top of Silbury Hill, great views from up there. Trying to imagine it shining across the landscape, all gleaming white chalk, with its deep deep ditch around it. Whatever drove the Old Ones to all this effort was a powerful force indeed, informed by a knowledge, or a belief system, that we can only puzzle over. Just imagine it struck by moonbeams in the dark silent land thousands of years ago. You'd gasp and gape for sure.'

From 'The Long Walk to Glastonbury', Stewart Harding

Today I was happy just to look up at it in wonder.

Silbury has a sister-mound five miles east along the Kennet Valley. Marlborough Mound, or 'Merlin's Mound', is a smaller structure built around the same time as its neighbour (see **Appendix, Day 30***).

My next objective was Overton Hill and the Sanctuary, which involved a short walk back towards the Long Barrow before heading east along another path, all necessary to avoid the treacherous A4. On the way, I passed by where two enormous palisaded enclosures once stood, contemporary with the other Avebury sites, but nothing remains of them above the ground. I could see the East Kennet Long Barrow hilltop mound a mile to my south. Like its western counterpart, it forms a vast mound, but it's on private land and has never been excavated. Approaching the Sanctuary, I noticed some smaller burial mounds (tumuli). The Sanctuary is now little more than a field by the busy road in which a collection of low-level concrete marker posts are positioned across the ground. Of all the ancient monuments, this wouldn't be the best introduction for a casual visitor in the 21st Century. You probably need to be a bit of a megalithomaniac to appreciate this one because the megaliths have all gone, ploughed away in the 17th Century but for a single sarsen stone.

That said, the concrete posts are colour-coded, red for timber and blue for stone. The Sanctuary was built over 4½ thousand years ago as a complex circular henge made from timber posts. Erected on the vantage point of Overton Hill, the monument overlooks all the significant sites already in existence or contemporary with its time, including the nearby West and East Kennet Long Barrows, Silbury Hill and Windmill Hill (see Day 28). The Sanctuary underwent significant changes during the many centuries of its functioning existence, expanding in size and later becoming built entirely in stone. At some point, it became linked to the main Avebury henge complex by the famous West Kennet Stone Avenue. John Aubrey first recorded the existence of The Sanctuary in 1648, and William Stukeley surveyed the site in the early 18th Century, but the stones were destroyed shortly afterwards by local farmers. Stukeley's recordings were used during the first excavations of the site in the 1930s, the finds from which included a significant amount of human remains to suggest the Sanctuary was a ceremonial site used for burial rituals.

William Stukeley boldly described the Sanctuary as a temple of pre-Roman Druidic worship, a theme he associated with the many ancient sites of this nature. He developed a theory that including the Sanctuary, the entire complex of sites around Avebury (which he surveyed in meticulous detail), was a vast ceremonial site. Stukeley saw the representation of a serpent in the stones, with its head at the Sanctuary and the Kennet Avenue representing its long neck. The central body of the beast was formed by the main Henge complex and a second avenue (now no longer in existence), its long tail trailing away to the west. Fanciful, perhaps, but as good a theory as any other from his day. William Stukeley was a remarkable man, and his detailed and illustrated publication 'Abury, A Temple of the British Druids' (downloadable for free) makes for fascinating reading. He was the archaeological pioneer of his time to whom we can be immensely grateful. The mystery prevails.

The idea of the serpent is far from fanciful concerning the characteristics of the earth energy lines the dowsers follow. Michael and Mary are identified as twin serpents, snaking and intertwining with each other across the land, and the Sanctuary is the 17th node on the St Michael Alignment. It's also where Miller and Broadhurst first discovered the Mary current while dowsing the course of Michael. In the Sun and the Serpent, the authors' experiences are testified, perhaps with a nod to Stukeley:

'The serpent ran right through the circle. There was some confusion. Another current joined it, crossing in the centre. The reactions were checked. There was no doubt. There was another serpent. One that appeared to be a different frequency but just as powerful. It entered through a group of prominent tumuli over the road, ran through the gate and the only remaining original stone, and followed the path to the centre, heading off to the south-west. The St Michael serpent entered at the neck of the stone avenue and ran towards the south-east.'

Initially, the authors had dowsed the Michael current from the tip of Cornwall to the Sanctuary, but now they had discovered Michael's female parallel. Their trail would now require pursuing both energy lines to the east coast and chasing the newly-discovered course of energy back to the beginning at Carn Lês Boel. The authors go on explain something about how and why they had only recognised Michael's energy up until this point:

'There was no mistaking that there was a different 'feel' to the quality of *the second serpent, which crossed virtually at right angles, forming a 'Celtic Cross' shape. It was just as potent, yet seemed gentler, smoother and altogether more feminine than its counterpart. In fact it was necessary to 'de-tune' from dowsing the St Michael energy to pick it up effectively, as if it were a different rate of vibration. It appeared we had only noticed it in the first place because of the especially sensitive frame of mind that existed after dawn at the Henge.'*

By the time I reached The Sanctuary, I think I was beginning to flag under the weight of my backpack and all this ancient history. I knew I stood on a sacred site of remarkable antiquity, but somehow I'd reached my saturation point. As I stood among the concrete blocks, I sensed that I didn't share the same enthusiasm as those in my midst in real-time. Besides, the day wasn't over yet. I still had the West Kennet Avenue and the most excellent highlight of the lot ahead of me; Avebury and its superlative henge complex. I already knew I'd have to come back the following day to appreciate it properly, so my write-up for the henge will be in my report for Day 28 (see Day 28!).

Flagging or not, it didn't take me long to find my second wind once I joined the avenue of stones. Here it must be remembered that although the two rows of ancient sarsen stones that still form the Avenue stand as they did nearly 5,000 years ago. People have been busy on the same land ever since. Most of the surviving stones of the Avenue are its northern section, a delightful passage across a large, attractive meadow. The southern section is now largely replaced by a road, and busy junctions interrupt the avenue's course at both ends. Nevertheless, walking the half-mile length of undisturbed stones towards the Henge was a magical experience. There's a photograph that beautifully captures the original members of the Rolling Stones walking this same avenue. This surely is conclusive proof of its great age.

My anticipation was revived. Perhaps it was the realisation that I was once again walking in the sacred footsteps of countless generations of people who processed before me along the serpent's neck. Maybe it was the realisation that the Henge would mark the physical halfway point on my full coast-to-coast trail of England's widest land, or maybe it was the recollection of what I had read of the experience of others who had walked this magical half-mile. Whatever it was, this walk between the gently curving lines of grotesquely beautiful upright boulders brought me excitedly back into the moment. This ancient promenade was too powerful for any distracting self-concern. As the tree-lined earthworks of the Henge's southern perimeter came into view, it was as if I was being guided towards the two monstrous portal stones that beckoned my entrance to this, the grandest of all the Avebury sites.

I entered the outer circle, feeling as ceremonial as I did when I paddled my boots in the Atlantic Ocean 27 days earlier. Conveniently forgetting about Buckland Dinham to Trowbridge, I sat down on the grass beneath one of the towering monoliths and took off my boots. I had arrived!

The Michael and Mary earth energy currents at Avebury

- Winterbourne Monkton
- Avebury
- The Sanctuary
- West Kennet Avenue
- Silbury Hill
- West Kennet Long Barrow
- Windmill Hill
- The Longstones
- Swallowhead Springs

—·—·— Mary
-------- Michael

Day 28

Rest Day Avebury

19.08.2020

> 'Huge druid stones surround the spot,
> Which else had almost been forgot
> By the great world without.'
>
> *Mary S Cope*

Although my walking was over, there was still plenty to see in Avebury, so I used this remaining day to uncover more of its fascinating history. The Henge complex alone was worth more time than I could muster, not to mention the rest of the other essential sites on my day's itinerary. Fortunately, there was a bus service running from All Cannings to Devizes and another from there to Avebury, so I caught the earliest running combination. I arrived in the village a little after 9.30 am and got off at the only known bus stop in the world located inside a stone circle. There are plenty of ancient stone circles in Britain, of course. Most are out in the rural landscape, and a few survive inside towns and villages, but for the centre of a village to exist inside a stone circle boggles the mind and gives a clear indication of just how massive the monument is. Sure; It's not as famous as Stonehenge, and I'm occasionally glued to the telly whenever the place turns up on my screen. There's now archaeological evidence of a 'super henge' of which Stonehenge was but a small part. The mystery continues.

What remains of the Avebury Henge is a vast circular enclosure surrounded by an enormous bank and ditch. An outer circle of large sarsen stones lines the perimeter of the enclosure, within which are two smaller (but still sizeable) stone circles. Many of the stones are missing, and many of the remaining ones have had to be relocated to their original positions following centuries of wanton abandonment and recycling. The parish church and many of the village's older buildings were constructed using stone from the Henge. The earthworks of the Henge date from around 3400 BC, and like the Sanctuary, later construction was done in phases. Most of the existing stones were completed by the middle of the third millennium BC.

Being in the village and the henge simultaneously, I decided to look around the village first. There's a handful of shops and cottages, a pub and the church dedicated to St James. One of the shops is called the Henge Shop. It's well-stocked with books on everything 'from the archaeological to the arcane' (including, of course, the Sun and the Serpent) and all sorts of associated merchandise. There's also the magnificent Alexander Keiller Museum, named after the great Scottish philanthropist and archaeologist responsible for preserving the Henge during the 20th Century. Sadly, the museum was closed (see Day 29). Keiller (1889-1959) lived at Avebury Manor, formerly a property belonging to the Abbey that once stood in the village. He was responsible for removing several of the buildings that directly occupied some of the space within the henge, and his vision was to remove all of them. With the outbreak of the War, Keiller's plans were thwarted, and the buildings and roads were retained inside the monument.

Like the museum, the church was closed. A notice explained that window repairs were underway, so I made do with a look around the exterior. St James' Church sits in beautiful surroundings. The building dates back to Saxon times, and the south door has a finely decorated Norman archway. Interestingly (perhaps not surprisingly), the church was built just outside the perimeter of the Henge, although a later 17th Century chapel exists within the circle. Until the relatively recent Age of 'Enlightenment', these ancient stones must have been viewed with fearful discomfort by the established Christian community. Perhaps it was only the enormous scale of the complex that prevented its complete destruction. When Aubrey, Stukeley and their ilk began investigating the monument, many of the stones had been removed, and most were toppled over. Under the approval of the Church authorities, local farmers systematically attacked the stones by burning them in fire pits and breaking them up; or burying them in the ground.

The destruction continued, and it wasn't until the 1930s that the lost stones were unearthed and repositioned under the patronage of Alexander Keiller. In 1938, one particular stone was excavated, and the skeleton of a man was found beneath it. The story goes that the skeleton belonged to a medieval barber-surgeon, corroborated by the fact that a pair of scissors was found beside him. Several coins dating to the 14th Century were also found, and various traditions evolved about how he came to be buried beneath the stone. Some say he was a godless villain, perhaps a murderer, thus buried on the unconsecrated, decidedly pagan ground; others that he was a medieval stone-wrecker, crushed by the stone falling on top of him, perhaps as punishment by the Devil for desecrating the stones. Whatever the truth, the stone is now known as the Barber Stone.

The Barber Stone is one of the 98 sarsen stones that formed the outer circle of the henge, although only 27 survive in place. Several are over 12 feet tall, and some weigh over 40 tons. The largest of these are the two Portal Stones flanking the southern entrance at the end of the West Kennet Avenue of stones. One is the Devil's Chair, as its shape can accommodate the visitor (if somewhat uncomfortably) in a seated position. With a diameter of 1,088 feet, the outer circle is the largest stone circle in Britain. Two inner circles of stones stand inside the outer ring. The northern circle is 322 feet in diameter, and its southern counterpart is slightly larger. Twenty-seven stones formed the north circle, of which only four remain, while only five of the original 29 now comprise the southern circle. At its centre was the largest of all the stones; a gigantic 18-foot monolith known as The Obelisk, now gone but marked by a concrete post. The massive earthen henge surrounding the complex had a depth of 29 feet.

Other stones stand as proud survivors. Some have been attacked over the centuries and impoverished, beautiful and grotesque in equal measure. But somehow, what remains of those is as worthy as the rest. All of them are well-documented, named and very well-photographed. I surmise that what remains above the ground will continue to remain, guarded and protected for as long as ever.

The individual stones appear to have two distinct shapes or forms. One is tall and phallic, and the other is wider and roughly diamond in shape. These are usually placed alternately and would seem to represent the male and the female. As to the orientation and positions of the individual stones, well, that's way out of my league. For that, you'd probably need to read up on things like sacred geometry and archaeoastrology. However, the stones appear to be positioned with their flatter sides facing into the circle's centre. If you were to hit two sticks together in the middle of the circle, you'd probably be motivated to start researching archaeoacoustics.

As with all Neolithic sites, the precise purpose of Avebury Henge will likely never be known, but its importance as a ritual site is overwhelmingly evident, as is the fact that it interrelates with the other notable sites that surround the area. The West Kennet Avenue links the henge with the Sanctuary, and although no longer in existence, a second avenue to the west connected the Henge to the Long Stones at Beckhampton. Silbury Hill and the two long barrows overlook Avebury from the south and Windmill Hill from the north. Their purposes were undoubtedly related, and we'll never precisely know what those purposes were, but they would certainly be connected with astronomy and the seasons. Every Year, upwards of 300,000 people visit Avebury and not only as tourists, pilgrims and modern antiquarians. Its popularity as a site for contemporary Druidic ceremonies and celebrations requires a rota to accommodate the various groups. It's also attracted people's attention in every field of what can collectively be described as the spiritual sciences and practitioners in the (this) field of earth energies. There's plenty of room for everyone at Avebury.

The Authors of the Sun and the Serpent describe their experience of dowsing the two energy currents to two node points within the henge, one at the Obelisk and the other between the two massive portal stones of the southern entrance to the outer circle:

'The line just missed, by a few feet, the Avebury United Reformed Church, built from smashed megaliths in 1670, and led to the concrete marker that stands at the spot where the tallest pillar of all, The Obelisk, once stood. This exact point marked a node, with the usual pentagram shape, and also changed the direction of the flow, which now made for the most gigantic of the remaining stones, set at the southern entrance.'

They continue:

'These stones also mark the spot where the exact countrywide alignment of the St Michael Line crosses the circle, as well as the point at which the West Kennet Avenue joins the Henge. It is a most significant place. In between the two towering stones is yet another node'.

No wonder I felt ceremonial at this very spot the previous day! Although I'd planned to walk my entire trail in two halves, it was only a practical solution to decide to finish the first half at Avebury, and purely accidental that I finished it at this precise spot.

With plenty of time to explore, I must have spent well over two hours wandering and wondering among these ancient stones. I was one of at least a hundred other visitors, but it didn't feel crowded here. There are no barriers or tickets, and it's all free. Quite a contrast from Stonehenge!

My time at the Henge was a joyful and powerful experience of the kind that you're never in a hurry to leave, but my explorations for the day were far from over. I now made my way west through the village and across a footbridge over the Kennet. I then walked through some fields towards two large stones visible from afar. The Long Stones are the only stones remaining of the Beckhampton Avenue. This ancient avenue of stones once ran west from the henge for half a mile, terminating at another ceremonial site called Beckhampton Cove. They stand silently in a field of grass and wildflowers, several yards away from each other. This pair of beautifully ugly, gnarled grey sarsens are the last remnants of Stukeley's serpent's tail (see Day 27). The pair are locally known as Adam and Eve, or The Devil's Quoits. An information board at the edge of the field explained that five other pairs of the avenue's stones were discovered below the ground at the turn of this century, with evidence of their burning, destruction and removal. 'Adam' is the only remaining stone from the Cove, and 'Eve' is the sole survivor of the Beckhampton Avenue.

From the Long Stones, I walked back to Avebury and continued along footpaths north of the village for a mile or two to reach the grassy top of Windmill Hill. Here I was alone at last. A warm and refreshing summer wind now whistled in my ears and shimmered the grass. Apart from a charred square foot of ground where some numpty had a barbecue, nothing indicated that anyone had ever built anything on this peaceful dome. But Windmill Hill was once the site of the largest stone age camp in the world, pre-dating Silbury Hill by a thousand years. What was once here was a Neolithic causewayed enclosure surrounded by three massive ditches with a total area of 21 acres. Most of the earthworks have been ploughed into invisibility at ground level, but much can still be made out from the air. The earthworks date from 3675 BC and are estimated to have taken at least 62,000 hours to construct.

Archaeology at Windmill Hill has uncovered a lot of animal bones, suggesting that the site was used for ceremonial feasting or possibly animal slaughter and trading. Additionally, an enclosure on the east side has evidence of being a mortuary enclosure, believed to be where human corpses were left exposed for scavenging animals before the burial of the skull and principal bones in chambered tombs. One grave was that of a three-year-old child known as Charlie, whose skeleton was unearthed in 1929. Charlie's remains are now displayed in the Alexander Keiller Museum. Charlie hit the headlines in 2010 when the Council of British Druid

Orders demanded her/his reburial at the place where s/he was found, but a public consultation determined that Charlie would remain in the museum (see Day 30).

During their visits to Avebury, Miller and Broadhurst concluded that the node points they had previously dowsed on the St Michael earth energy current were nodes where both the Michael and the Mary currents crossed. In the Sun and the Serpent, they describe their discovery on the hill after approaching it from Winterbourne Monkton:

'From the church, the current ran up to the summit of Windmill Hill, where we found ourselves standing in the exact the same spot we had been led to on our arrival in the Avebury area. The node point at the enormous tumulus pinpointed the place where the St Mary and St Michael currents crossed. The two serpents were fusing at crucial spots, always where nodes had been found: The Sanctuary, the Henge, now Windmill Hill. It was beginning to look as if the phenomena we were referring to as node points were in fact produced by this crossing of currents. Both types of energy appeared to concentrate to a fine point, enter deep into the ground and re-emerge. Something very intriguing indeed was going on.'

My quiet and peaceful time on Windmill Hill was enhanced by a magnificent vista that took in the tops of Silbury Hill, the Sanctuary and the Kennet Long Barrows, with Avebury itself nestling in the valley below. This vantage point would clearly have held a deep significance for whoever was there, and whatever was going on in those ancient days. A shiver of fascination ran up and down my spine.

The afternoon was wearing on, so I descended east to the village of Winterbourne Monkton and its church, dedicated to St Mary Magdalene. If unsurprised, I was a little disappointed to find that, like St James' in Avebury, this too was closed. It's a beautiful building with a pyramid-topped tower, set sufficiently away from the main road to afford a nice ten-minute rest in the churchyard. Intriguingly, the church's tower is supported by tree trunks visible from the interior. St Mary's was once a 'slipper shrine', where pilgrims would take off their shoes for their last barefoot mile to Avebury. Outside the church, I noticed a sizeable recumbent sarsen stone marking the grave of Rev John Brinsden, who died in 1710. The stone is believed to be from the nearby Millbarrow, a neolithic Long Barrow once sketched by William Stukeley but no longer in existence.

St Mary's Church aligns with the Mary current as it travels north of Michael between the two nodes at the Henge and Windmill Hill.

From the church, I headed south along a footpath that rejoined the route I'd taken to Windmill Hill and within half an hour, I was back in Avebury. With 30 minutes left before my return buses back to All Cannings, I bought a drink and sat outside the only known pub in the world that can be found inside a stone circle. It was the perfect end to a perfect day. I pondered on what I'd experienced with a strange sense of fulfilment.

The Stones of Avebury have had a powerful attraction ever since William Stukeley sketched his vision of a serpentine temple in his field notes and probably long before. People continue to seek the purpose of the stones, and some use them to find purpose in themselves. Perhaps this new age of mysticism and alternative lifestyles is a re-emergence of the same hopes and dreams of our ancient ancestors. After all, the stones remain the same.

Day 29

Buckland Dinham to Trowbridge

11 Miles

01.06.2021

Having got as far as Avebury the previous year, I was now ready to commence the second part of my pilgrimage. However, I still had to complete a day's walk between Buckland Dinham and Trowbridge due to a 'logistical oversight' the previous year (see Day 24). Until I finally finished this still un-walked stage, it didn't feel right to continue, so I made the time to do it here. The plan was a straightforward one; to return to Buckland Dinham, where I could camp, complete the walk and then get a bus from Trowbridge back to my starting point. Besides, this time it was a more straightforward proposition. The campsite I hoped to use in Buckland Dinham had been closed the previous year, and being vehicularly mobile, getting to my starting point was equally straightforward.

I'd picked a good day this time. The weather was fine, and I walked without the weight of all my trail and camping kit. My chosen route was to follow that of the McMillan Way to Lullington, Beckington and Rode. I could make a short diversion from Rode to visit the Devil's Bed and Bolster, a prehistoric chambered tomb. My final few miles were a walk through fields before an uncomfortable walk along the busy A361 into Trowbridge.

The Michael energy current crossed my path at Lullington, Rode and the chambered tomb before it veered north and east to rejoin my route into Trowbridge. Another neolithic site, the Orchardleigh Stones (see Day 23), also aligns with Michael, a short distance from where I walked.

Meanwhile, the Mary energy line travels further south of my trail as it had been doing since Glastonbury. Here, the two currents are far enough apart that the large town of Frome lies between the two.

I began my day's walk at St Michael's Church in Buckland Dinham. It was closed when I was last here, and today it was still closed to visitors, so I promptly located the McMillan Way path. This long-distance trail is a 290-mile-long monster, running between Abbotsbury in Dorset and Boston in Lincolnshire. It was explicitly set up to encourage people to raise funds for the MacMillan Cancer Relief charity, so it can easily be considered a modern-day pilgrimage route. I imagine it would also make a tremendous coast-to-coast trail route across southern England, but for my purposes, it would accommodate my footsteps for the first five miles of this day's walk.

Leaving the village, I followed a path over farmland to reach the delightful Orchardleigh Wood. From here, a well-defined path took me through parkland on the northern edge of the Orchardleigh estate, in which stands a large Victorian country mansion. Other buildings associated with the old house remain, including a gatehouse, stables and a boathouse. A large lake runs along the length of the estate, and there is also a church dating from the 13th Century. Much of the eastern side of the estate is now occupied by a golf course.

The next settlement was the attractive village of Lullington, where I stopped to visit the church. Substantially Norman, this lovely building's magnificent north entrance didn't go unnoticed. The beautifully decorated arched doorway (complete with a Christ in Majesty above it) commanded my attention. More gems lay within. These included a Norman font ornamented with grotesque human faces, rosettes and interlaced arcading, a Norman tower arch with zigzag mouldings and capitals carved with centaurs, bulls, wyverns and a Green Man.

I sat in the churchyard to rest and soak up the strong morning sunshine, listening to the sights, sounds and smells of the early summer. Ten minutes turned to twenty, then thirty. I would have made half a day of this, but I knew I had two buses to catch to get back to Buckland Dinham from Trowbridge, so I got back onto the MacMillan Way path. As I left the churchyard, I noticed a sign saying 'Free Tap Water' and replenished my water bottles.

From the village, I followed a path over the River Frome and on towards Beckington, where I turned north and followed the MacMillan Way to the southern end of Rode. The church here is situated right by the busy A361 road and was closed to visitors. With no need to continue into the village, I located the path I needed to take to get to the Devil's Bed and Bolster. My map indicated that it lay directly on a public footpath, but my passage was not well displayed on the ground. Summer foliage obscured what signs there were, and crops filled the fields where the paths should have been.

Fortunately, even our most obscure ancient monoliths are well-documented by a certain Modern Antiquarian on the internet, and not for the first time, his excellent directions have enabled me to find what I've been looking for. I soon found the Devil's Bed and Bolster hiding in a clump of trees near the edge of a cornfield.

At first glance, this assembly of low standing stones was almost completely hidden in the undergrowth. Closer in, I found they formed a definite and deliberate structure, perhaps an entrance or a small enclosure. Whatever they were part of countless centuries ago, they were still here. I sat among the stones listening to the birds and the wind, letting my mind slow down nicely. For ten beautiful minutes, there was no need to be anywhere else.

In the Sun and the Serpent, Miller and Broadhurst write:
'Over the fields, a grassy tump sprouted trees and boulder-like stones grew out of the undergrowth. It gives the impression of being circular, with many stones concealed in foliage, and perhaps buried. Absorbing the atmosphere of what must have surely been an important ritual site,

with the Michael current running through it, we noticed a peculiar effect which often seems to occur at these places. Above the large slab that marked the centre of the flow (presumably the Devil's Bolster), energy was pouring off, exactly like heat haze on a hot summer's day.'

The rest of my walk was uneventful, with no sites of interest, pilgrimage or otherwise; just two miles of agriculture and three more of busy roadside walking. I reached Trowbridge with plenty of time to catch a bus to Frome and another to Buckland Dinham. My un-walked Day 24 had become Day 29, walked and in the bag. The continuation of my pilgrimage was now waiting for me at Avebury.

Day 30

Avebury to Liddington Castle

14 Miles

05.06.2021

Two hundred and seventy-one days had passed by when I returned to Avebury for the second part of my pilgrimage trail. Various factors of circumstance had delayed my return, including more 'lockdowns' and coronavirus restrictions. I was back with a new pair of boots and a trail route to take me across the eastern half of the St Michael Alignment to my trail's end at Hopton on Sea. I'd returned to the same campsite at All Cannings that I used at the end of my trail the previous summer, and to start this one, I caught the same bus services to get me to Avebury for the start of 'Part Two'.

As with Day 27, I arrived in the village at 09.36 am, and again, I got off at the world's only known bus stop inside a stone circle. I was fully laden with everything I needed for the next 250 miles (or so) that lay ahead. The village and the old stones hadn't gone anywhere, and they looked as beautiful as ever, dazzling in the spring morning sunshine. It was busy (Avebury nearly always is), but not a crowded busy. It's a room for everyone and more kind of busy. I recalled my visit the previous summer when the church and the museum were both closed, so I decided to check if they were now open. I'd allowed time for this, as I limited this first day of walking to single-figure miles. I was a bit fitter this time, but I still had to carry all my trail-walking and camping gear.

As on my last visit, St James' Church was again closed, but this time with a sign at the entrance screen explaining that birds were nesting in the porch. Undaunted and strongly supportive of this measure, I chalked it up as another excuse to return again at a later date. However, the Keiller museum was open, so with permission to park my rucksack, I squeezed myself inside. This small but well-stocked building was once the stable block of Avebury Manor and is crammed with exhibits and finds documenting the history and archaeology of the Avebury Complex of sites. I spent a good hour taking in all the fascinating information. Of all the exhibits, the highlight that drew my attention more than anything else was the skeleton of Charlie (see Day 28).

Charlie was found lying in a ditch during the 1929 excavations on Windmill Hill. Scientific tests determined the remains were those of a child between two and three years old, but they couldn't determine the sex that s/he was born with. Displayed in a glass-topped coffin, Charlie assumes the position in which s/he was found. In recent years, a debate has ensued over whether Charlie should be returned and reburied at Windmill Hill, but the decision was made to keep Charlie where s/he currently lies. Charlie is believed to have died around 3350 BC.

The museum added substantially to my knowledge of the various sites, their history and the discoveries made at them. It was fascinating to learn how extensive were the excavations into Silbury Hill (see Day 27). Although much is known of its remarkable construction, we can still only surmise its purpose.

Outside, the light was dazzling as I put on my sunglasses and strapped myself back into my rucksack. I walked into the Henge and stood between the two massive portal stones that marked the extent of my pilgrimage the previous year. As the start point of this year's, it was a moment of personal ceremony for me. I turned the moment into a couple of contemplative minutes, and then I was on my way.

My first mile was a reverse of my last, which I had walked nearly a year earlier. Imagining a time before the road in front of me existed, I crossed over to continue south along the West Kennet Stone Avenue, retracing my year-old steps back to The Sanctuary. Once again, it was both eerie and exhilarating to be walking in the footsteps of many people who have taken their pilgrimages and processions for centuries. I understand people attached great significance to the times and the places they walked, celebrated and worshipped, but my timings were governed by convenience, accessibility, and commitments. If I were more committed, I'd probably have conceived and planned some of my walks to coincide with important dates and times associated with some of these ancient places. Perhaps I could have started my pilgrimage on the Beltane sunrise or aligned myself inside these sacred circles on the annual solstices or equinoxes; plenty of people still do.

On reaching The Sanctuary, I stopped for a few minutes to pay my respects to the concrete marker posts and adjust the straps on my rucksack. I was now on the Ridgeway National Trail, much of which (with a few variations) I would now walk over the next six days. The Ridgeway is a nationally recognised long-distance trail running east from The Sanctuary on Overton Hill for 97 miles and finishing at Ivinghoe Beacon in the Chiltern Hills. Sticking to the high ground of the chalk downs as much as possible, much of the route is breathtakingly beautiful.

Historically, the Ridgeway isn't exclusively defined as the Ridgeway national trail. More broadly, the historical term can be interpreted as the Greater Ridgeway. This longer route forms Britain's oldest trackway and extends from the Dorset Coast at Lyme Regis, all the way to the Norfolk coast. The entire length can now be walked as a long-distance trail by way of the Wessex Ridgeway, the Ridgeway national trail, the Icknield Way and the Peddars Way. It's also important to note that the Ridgeway can be even more broadly defined to include additional ancient trackways and their branches serving the generally accepted route.

From the 17th node point at the Sanctuary, the Michael and the Mary earth energy currents continue east, but well to the south of where I walked. Mary travels north of Michael until the two merge to cross paths at a mound within the churchyard at **Ogbourne St Andrew**. *This forms the* **18th node** *on the Alignment. Mary's route is quite direct, but Michael* takes in several sites in and around the town of Marlborough, most interestingly the large monument known as Merlin's Mound, located on the grounds of Marlborough College (see **Appendix Day 30***). Ogbourne St Andrew remained two miles off my walking route for the day, but I made a point of visiting it after completing my trail (see **Appendix Day 30****). There are two Ogbournes; surprisingly, both are node points on the Alignment. **Ogbourne St George** is the location for the *19th node*, the second in quick succession, where Michael and Mary once again cross paths, this time at a place very close to the church. I was able to visit the churchyard during the walk.

From the Sanctuary, I followed the westernmost 14 miles of the Ridgeway as far as the Iron Age hilltop fort of Liddington Castle. This first stage of the Ridgeway took me north onto the high ground of Fyfield Down. This unique landscape forms part of the Avebury World Heritage Site. Seven thousand years of human activity have left not only the famous monuments but many banks, ditches, field systems and standing stones, and most visibly, the many raised mounds and tumuli that appear nearly everywhere.

The sun continued to dazzle, illuminating the new spring landscape, uncluttered and far-reaching in every direction. Chalk downs have a joyous feel to them in any weather and time of the year, but now they were showing off. The many Hawthorns were laden with brilliant white blossom, while a sea of yellow and white wildflowers clothed the grassland throughout. The bright whiteness of the chalk rock shined with an intensity exceeding the limestone of the Yorkshire Dales. Thanks to a unique natural history, these extraordinary dry valleys are filled with sarsen stones, strangers carried in on the last ice age glaciers. These have created perfect conditions for rare and unusual lichens and an exquisite range of plant life, now in complete harmony with the nature of the downs. It was an absolute treat to be given this day as my first one back on the trail.

As the afternoon progressed, my course continued north along the highest ground, gradually veering east above the steep slope of Winterbourne Down and then up to the highpoint of Barbury Castle. This immense Iron Age hill fort dominates the landscape, and the view looking north is superb. Once reinforced with sarsen stones, earthen banks surround an enclosure of 11 acres, and I could clearly make out the entrance to the fort. Looking northeast, I could see Liddington Castle, another Iron Age hilltop fort in the distance. It would be my wild camp for the night, but I didn't know it yet.

Now heading east, I continued along the high ground for several miles, taking the form of Smeathes Ridge. Beyond here, the Ridgeway descends towards the village of Ogbourne St George. In keeping with my plans, I walked down into the village and located the church, which was unfortunately closed.

As mentioned previously, Ogbourne St George is one of two Ogbournes, the other being Ogbourne St Andrew, a smaller village a couple of miles away. Both places are significant as those where the Michael and the Mary earth energy currents cross to form the 18th and 19th nodes on the St Michael Alignment. Miller and Broadhurst describe the precise point of the one at Ogbourne St George to be a manufactured earthen mound 20 feet high, which they later discovered had been built by a local man during the Second War. Whether or not he was aware of the significance remains a peculiar mystery. After fusing with Mary at the mound, Michael enters and travels through the church itself. From the village, Michael heads east while Mary continues in a northerly direction. I remained north and east of both currents for the rest of my day's walk.

I sat on a bench in the churchyard, having failed to locate the mound mentioned above. It was now late afternoon, so I asked a man if a shop or a pub might be open. Unfortunately, there weren't any, but as we talked, he invited me to fill up my water bottles at his house along the road.

Thankful for the replenishment, I continued on my way and rejoined the Ridgeway. I was now heading north and soon crossed from Wiltshire into Oxfordshire. As I walked, I began to look out for a suitable place to camp for the night. I passed a few spots with limited potential before diverting along a permissive path through a field of yellow rape leading to Liddington Castle, an Iron Age hilltop site smaller than that at Barbury Castle and thankfully less frequented. There were some suitable options for pitching my tent, so I sat by the triangulation cairn that marks the site's highest point and spent some time enjoying the evening sunshine and attractive views. Nearby, a viewing platform hosted a panoramic direction indicator erected by the Liddington Parish Council to commemorate the Millennium. I read for an hour and then pitched my tent in a sheltered spot below the grassy bank surrounding the site. I had some food and prepared for my night's sleep. Before I knew it, I was watching the walls of my tent billowing gently in the early morning wind.

Day 31

Liddington Castle to Court Hill

15 Miles

06.06.2021

I spent this glorious day's walk entirely on the Ridgeway. After a short section of road walking near the start, I had the highest of the land and its ancient trackway at my feet. The weather was rainless and comfortably warm throughout.

Liddington Hill lies a mile west of the Mary earth energy current, which I crossed early in the day. Apart from this, I made no connection with either Mary or Michael. I kept to the Ridgeway route while Mary remained north and Michael well to the south.

The weather was misty as I dismantled my tent. I walked to the viewing platform to find the view limited to just a few acres, barely more than the width of an ancient earth-banked enclosure. I carefully ensured I left no trace of my presence and rejoined the Ridgeway path. After less than a mile, my way descended east out of the mist to join a few roads empty of traffic on this early Sunday morning. A bridge took me over the (almost empty) M4 motorway, and within another mile of roadway, the Ridgeway was a path once more. It's hard to imagine this ancient trackway was a primary route long before the invention of motors.

Soon I was back on the high ground. The sky was cloudy, but the mist had thankfully cleared, and once again, I had the spring greenery of the stretching landscape in my views, along with the mounds and hills of ancient settlement. Soon the beauty of Wiltshire turned into the beauty of

Oxfordshire as I continued east along the crest of the downs. My day's much-anticipated highlight was ahead of me: the neolithic chambered long barrow of Wayland's Smithy. I found a sign welcoming me to it, and there it was, in a tree-sheltered setting a short distance from the path.

I entered the site to find the company of several other individuals and parties, all sharing the amateur antiquarian visitor experience. Having visited the West Kennet example the previous year, I instantly recognised the monument as a long barrow, a long earthen mound with sarsen stones along its base and an entrance marked by larger standing stones. While I waited to look inside the entrance, a helpful information board gave me a brief but fascinating history.

Wayland's Smithy dates back 5½ thousand years as a ceremonial burial site. It's not as old as the West Kennet long barrow and not quite as big. The results of an archaeological investigation in 1920 (and a subsequent one in 1963) determined that the site first took the form of a stone and timber 'box' chamber with a split tree trunk at either end. Within just a century, the existing structure was built over it. Although the entire site was 'ransacked' by treasure hunters over the centuries, the 20th-century investigations proved that the initial chamber was only used for about 15 years and contained the remains of 14 people. A photograph of the site taken in the 19th Century showed the large entrance stones in their original positions.

A short, neatly constructed boulder-lined walk-in trench leads to the chamber's entrance, flanked by a row of large upright sarsen stones. I waited my turn to stoop inside the soundless stone interior and take a few photos in this special place. At West Kennet, there are four small side chambers, but here there are just two.

Wayland's Smithy was known as 'Weland's Smithy' in Saxon times. One local tradition describes Wayland as an invisible elfin smith who re-shoes your horse if you leave it tethered at the long barrow together with a small coin.

Leaving the site, I walked on, and within a mile, I found myself approaching the massive hilltop earthworks of Uffington Castle, my second Iron Age hill fort of the day. It's probably not much bigger than Liddington, but the aspect, the position and the magnificent panoramic views all come together to make it a lot more popular. And with a car park and an ice cream van, somehow, I don't think I'd get away with wild camping here.

Another apparent reason for Uffington Castle's popularity has to be what's carved on its north-facing slope. The Uffington White Horse is arguably not a horse at all, but it seems to have led in recent centuries to people cutting far inferior horses into the chalk downs. The image of the Uffington White Horse is, of course, both iconic and beautiful. It's believed to date from at least the Iron Age and possibly earlier, and the authors of the Sun and the Serpent suggest the image is that of a dragon.

Immediately north and below the White Horse is the aptly named Dragon Hill, a naturally formed mound whose artificially flattened summit exposes the bare chalk on its surface. Here, according to legend, is where St George slew the dragon. The dragon's blood spilt on the summit, and no grass has since grown there.

None of the sites I visited aligned with the Mary earth energy current. Instead, Mary travels two miles north of them through the village of Uffington and its church. However, the authors of the Sun and the Serpent mention each of them at length and clearly describe their significance. They summarise to suggest that although Mary doesn't align with the sites, she flows around them:

'The Mary current had swung right around the prehistoric centre that included the White Horse, Uffington Castle, Dragon Hill and Wayland's Smithy in the same manner that had been observed before at Avebury and other special sites, as if to enclose it.'

Not only does this collection of ancient sites have a particular and obvious significance to the St Michael alignment and its associated currents, but they also happen to be intersected by another critical alignment running the length of Great Britain along a north-south axis. The 'Belinus Line' was discovered and dowsed in recent decades by the authors Gary Biltcliffe and Caroline Hoare, who document their discoveries in their book 'The Spine of Albion'. Parallels can be drawn between the country-wide St Michael line and this country-long Belinus line. As with the former, the latter has its intertwining course of male and female earth energy currents, seeking out hundreds of sacred sites and forming its own series of node points from the Isle of Wight in the south to Balnakeil on the far northern coast of Scotland. As I stood near the triangulation cairn of Uffington Castle, I thought about it; Perhaps I might be fortunate enough to complete a longitudinal pilgrimage to complement this one? We shall see.

I sat down by the triangulation cairn that marked the highest point of the vast earthworks of Uffington Castle and the highest point of my pilgrimage since Dartmoor the previous year (see Day 12). Clouds filled the sky, adding contrast and depth to my views which were far-reaching in every direction, particularly looking north. Uffington nestled in the fields below me, and I toyed with the idea of diverting to visit the church (see **Appendix, Day 31***), but in the interests of comfort and convenience, I decided to stay on the Ridgeway path. However, I did make a quick detour to stand by the chalk carving of the White 'Horse'. Up close, it was hard to fully appreciate the aesthetic beauty of the beast, but the chalk-cut form was unmistakable. I was standing on sacred ground, ancient and beautiful.

Continuing east, the broad track of the Ridgeway path carved its course boldly across the land, flanked by hawthorns in full white blossom as far as my eyes could see. I carried on along the highest ground for mile after mile, with continually magnificent views. I passed above the Devil's Punchbowl, a sweeping cleft of land falling away to my north.

My next camp was an activity centre located directly on the path south of Wantage, and as I peeled off the afternoon's miles, I came upon a much-needed water tap and trough by a bench with a notice alongside:

DRINKING WATER
TROUGH WATER
FOR ANIMALS
NO WASHING

There are only a handful of these vital water stations on the Ridgeway; without them, there are no other publicly accessible water sources. I filled up my bottles and continued, reaching the activity centre later in the afternoon.

On arrival, I was fortunate to find I was the only person using the centre. After paying for my pitch and stocking up with supplies, the staff locked the premises, leaving details of a takeaway food delivery service. The shower and toilet facilities were left open for my use with a request that I ensure the resident cat didn't get shut inside. I pitched my tent on a grassy terrace with magnificent views and enjoyed another peacefully quiet night on the Ridgeway.

Day 32

Court Hill to North Moreton

12 Miles

07.06.2021

A morning of more downland magnificence followed by a walk further into Oxfordshire and the upper Thames valley.

In relation to the pilgrimage, I temporarily parted from the official Ridgeway route to stay more faithful to the St Michael Alignment as it heads towards the Sinodun Hills. With the Mary current to my north, I continued east to join the Michael current, roughly following its course south and east of Didcot. I then visited several sites aligned with Michael, finishing at the village of North Moreton.

    The first six miles of my day's walk were a glorious continuation of the high-level Ridgeway path above the Vale of the White Horse. Here it keeps to the high ground, north of which runs a series of ancient linear earthworks known as Grim's Ditch. This name is used for several such earthworks across southern England, and unlike the Wansdyke, they're not necessarily parts of one continuous feature. Some are of Iron Age construction, but others may be Roman. The one here is probably an Iron Age boundary rather than a defensive ditch.

    At Betterton Down, I reached the monument to Baron Wantage, built on a Bronze Age barrow. It takes the form of a cross mounted on a marble column with a stepped base. The plinth bears inscriptions commemorating the British soldier and philanthropist Robert Loyd-Lindsay, 1st Baron Wantage, who died in 1901. From here, my views north were extensive.

    Further along the ridge, I passed the tree-covered mound of Scutchamer

Knob, a round barrow where according to legend, Edwin of Northumberland killed the Saxon king Cwicchelm of Wessex in 636. The broad track of the Ridgeway continued to take me east along Bury Down, through a tunnel under the A34 trunk road and then alongside the vast expanse of horse gallops. Nearby, I passed a stone memorial:

NEAR THIS SPOT
HUGH FREDERICK
GROSVENOR
2nd LIEUTENANT
THE LIFEGUARDS
LOST HIS LIFE IN AN
ARMOURED CAR
ACCIDENT
WHILE ON
MILITARY DUTY
9th APRIL 1947
AGED 19 YEARS

I took a track heading north towards the large village of Blewbury. Despite the Didcot power station, the views north remained impressive. On the way, I managed to locate another ancient barrow, a scrub-covered mound called Churn Knob, curiously marked by a post bearing a six-pointed metal star. To reach it, I had to drag myself through a bramble-filled copse of trees. Like Scutchamer Knob, this ancient bell barrow has its share of legend. Traditionally, it's believed to be where St Birinus, the first Bishop of Dorchester, preached a sermon in the 7th Century. This tradition appears to have some stamina, for Churn Knob is still a focus for an annual pilgrimage and service. I hope the pilgrims know an easier way of getting there than I did.

Churn Knob aligns with the Michael earth energy current, the course of which I followed closely for the rest of my day's walk.

I continued north into Blewbury before following a track east onto the site of an Iron age fort on Blewburton Hill. Smaller than the hill fort sites on the Ridgeway, its level top is still sizeable, and although a modest height, the views were still appreciable.

Blewburton Hill aligns with the Michael earth energy current.

From here, I continued along a series of footpaths that followed a direct course north through the villages of South Moreton and its neighbour, North Moreton, where I could camp at a site just outside the village. This had been a relatively short walking day, so I decided to walk back into South Moreton and treat myself to a pub meal.

The churches of South Moreton and North Moreton align with the Michael earth energy current, but both were closed when I visited them on this walk.

Day 33

North Moreton to Watlington

13 Miles

08.06.2021

A steep entrenchment Castle Hill surrounds,
Once thrown up as a barrier to the foe;
Fine beech trees crown the summit's grassy mounds,
Upon its slopes the pleasant cornfields glow.

'Wittenham Hills', Emily Cozens, 1875

This day was a hot one walked through rural Oxfordshire and the Thames Valley. I visited the magnificent Sinodun Hills and the historic village of Dorchester before continuing east to reach the small market town of Watlington and a campsite where I would base myself for two nights and a day's rest.

Strictly speaking, the route I walked for this day was now north of the Ridgeway and closer to that of the Lower Icknield Way. These two ancient trackways overlap, with the Lower Icknield Way forming a lowland route north of the Ridgeway, which continues to follow the north-facing escarpment of the Chiltern Hills.

*I began the day following the Michael current north out of North Moreton before reaching the **Sinodun Hills** and the 20th node on the St Michael Alignment. I continued north and east from here, following the female current as it weaves through Berrick Salome, Brightwell Baldwin and Cuxham. Meanwhile, Michael extends further north and east through a collection of interesting sites, including the churches at Clifton Hampden* (see **Appendix, Day 33***) *and Long Wittenham* (see **Appendix, Day 33****), *which I visited at a later date after completing my trail.*

The 33rd day of my pilgrimage began sunny and still. The cloudless sky was bright, blue and full of birdsong. A short road walk soon took me alongside the 13th Century church at North Moreton, and I was pleasantly surprised to find it open shortly after 8 am. Inside I noticed the Chantry Chapel built inside the church during the 14th Century, also the east window filled with original stained glass images from the medieval period. The church also retains its original Norman font.

I continued walking north with the bold outlines of the Sinodun Hills forming the horizon, their tops crowned with woodland. Three distinct tops form this unique chalk landmass; Brightwell Barrow and two hills of a similar height called the Wittenham Clumps. A series of footpaths brought me through the village of Brightwell-cum-Sotwell and then a lane leading to the car park below the hills.

The 'Wittenham Clumps' are named after the dense-growing clumps of beech trees that clothe their summits, believed to be the oldest of such plantations in England. The southernmost is called Castle Hill, on which are the remaining earthworks of a fort that dates back to the Bronze Age. The northernmost hill is called Round Hill, and its excavation in 2004 was conducted and televised by the famous 'Time Team', during which they discovered the remains of a Romano-British house, along with the extensive remains of several Iron Age buildings and enclosures.

I reached the car park at the foot of the hill, where several nature trails and walks can be taken. An information board introduced the nearby visitor and education centre and conservation project known as the Earth Trust Centre, although it was closed during my visit.

Feeling a sense of anticipation, I made my way up to the top of Castle Hill, enjoying the widening views. Soon I was walking over the grassy ridges of the ancient earthworks to find that the wooded summit was fenced-off in the interests of public safety. I walked the wood perimeter in a full circle to enjoy more views. Nearby I noticed a stone monument on which was a bronze plaque bearing an inscription in uniquely-styled lettering. The lines reproduce a tracing made in 1965 taken from the bark of a nearby beech tree on which a poem was written in 1844 by one Joseph Tubb of Worborough Green. The poem is aptly entitled 'Poem Tree', and the words are legibly reproduced beneath the artwork:

> **As up the hill with labr'ing steps we tread**
> **Where the twin Clumps their sheltering branches spread**
> **The summit gained at ease reclining lay**
> **And all around the widespread scene survey**
> **Point out each object and obstructive tell**
> **The various changes that the land befel.**
> **Where the low bank the country wide surrounds**
> **That ancient earthwork form'd old Murcias bounds.**
> **In misty distance see the barrow heave**
> **There lies forgotten lonely Culchelm's grave.**
> **Around this hill the ruthless Danes intrenched**
> **And these fair plains with gory slaughter drench'd**
> **While at our feet where stands that stately tower**
> **In days gone by uprose the Roman power**
> **And yonder, there where Thames smooth waters glide**
> **In later days appeared monastic pride.**
> **Within that field where lies the grazing herd**
> **Huge walls were found, some coffins disinter'd**
> **Such is the course of time, the wreck which fate**
> **And awful doom award the earthly great.**

The poem encapsulates the place and its history. It nicely reflected my experience, having gained the summit at ease, adopted a reclining position and surveyed the widespread scene. The beech tree on which the original poem was carved was pronounced 'dead' in the 1990s and subsequently removed, but the stone commemorates the work.

Miller and Broadhurst dowsed the two energy currents and discovered the point at which they crossed to form the node on the hill's summit. They write of the location:
'Today it has the atmosphere of a hilltop Sacred Grove, with a ring of great trees growing within the earthen bank and ditch. It is another of those special, magical places that seem to preserve a rare glimpse of how the countryside once was, a sanctuary of ancient intimacy with nature.'

A short walk to Round Hill took only minutes, and from this second summit, the view north across the Thames valley was breathtaking. Below me, Little Wittenham looked inviting, bathed in the brightness of the summer sunshine. I descended the hill and found the church in barely ten minutes. I wandered around the leafy graveyard; the building was closed to visitors. Beyond the church, I crossed a bridge and joined the Thames Path. Half a mile away, the historic village of Dorchester-on-Thames rises from the edge of the flood plain. In less than twenty minutes, I was standing in the centre of the village, surveying its magnificent abbey.

For the unfamiliar, Dorchester on Thames is not to be confused with the larger county town of Dorset that bears its name without the 'on Thames'. Geographical clarification may also be needed to explain that the village stands on the River Thame, whose confluence with the Thames is a few hundred yards south of the village. In a further twist, the river upstream is called the River Isis, not the Thames, but this distinction is rarely made outside Oxford.

Disregarding its small size and a population of barely a thousand souls, the history of Dorchester is so significant that it could easily have become the capital of England. In the 7th Century, the kingdoms of Mercia and

Wessex largely came under the Bishopric of Dorchester at the time of their conversion to post-Celtic Christianity. However, the Bishopric was subsequently transferred to Winchester, but Dorchester remained an important ecclesiastical centre.

The present-day Abbey dates to the 11th Century, built to serve a community of Augustinian Canons until its dissolution by Henry VIII in 1536. Thankfully, the building was saved from its otherwise terminal fate when it was bought for £140 by a local benefactor. It's a large church for such a small village and makes a very welcome place to unburden one's self of a heavy rucksack on a hot day. Inside, the cool, spacious interior is substantially Norman and Gothic. Some sections of medieval wall paintings remain within the otherwise clean white plaster walls, along with pieces of sculptural stonework and a magnificent lead font.

From Dorchester, the rest of my walking day was uncomfortably warm. Avoiding all roads, I managed to link several miles of footpaths through deepest agricultural Oxfordshire, briefly taking in the villages of Warborough and Berrick Salome before becoming road-bound for my final two miles beyond Brightwell Baldwin.

Each of these villages had its church aligned directly on the Mary energy current, but all were firmly closed, with or without coronavirus restrictions notices.

My final two miles were a road walk through Cuxham (church closed) and then to Watlington, where I located a pleasant campsite on the edge of the town. The heat of the afternoon's walk had tired me, and I was glad to be taking the next day as a break from the trail.

Day 34

Rest Day

Watlington

09.06.2021

Every so often, I spend a day doing very little for no other purpose than I can. Having booked two nights at the campsite without intention, I figured I might take a bus into the Chiltern Hills or explore the delights of Oxford, but as it turned out, I was happy to walk into Watlington for some lunch, read my book and sunbathe outside my tent. I must have spent at least two hours lying on the grass under the warmth of the day, staring up at cloud formations, occasionally distracted by the beautiful sight of red kites gliding across the sky.

Sometimes kite-seeing is just as good as sight-seeing.

Day 35

Watlington to Princes Risborough

12 Miles

10.06.2021

For this walk, I joined the Ridgeway path and headed northeast on a relatively short day of walking to finish at the town of Princes Risborough.

I chose not to keep to the Ridgeway but to divert north to stay true to the Mary current as she travels in alignment with the churches at Lewknor, Aston Rowant and Chinnor. In so doing, I could walk along the course of the ancient Lower Icknield Way.

Beyond Chinnor, I took the route of the Upper Icknield Way, ending my walk by reconnecting with the Ridgeway path in the town centre of Princes Risborough. It's interesting to note that whilst not exactly parallel, the Ridgeway and the Icknield Way feature separate routes within the same landscape. While the Ridgeway keeps to the high ground, the Lower Icknield Way runs below the escarpment of the Chiltern hills. The Upper Icknield way is an ancient but relatively short branch between the two. At Princes Risborough, I finished my day's walk. However, a bus journey of 10 miles to High Wycombe was necessary to gain accommodation in a hotel, as there were no camping facilities in the area.

The sun was up and beating its heat into my tent when I woke up for this day's walk. Two red kites were soaring above the campsite as they had regularly been doing since I arrived. Having sorted out my breakfast and packed away my tent, I took my rubbish to the bins and paid my last visit to the campsite facilities. As I recall, I'd left an apple turnover pastry on the ground next to my gear, but when I returned, the pie had gone, its wrappings strewn across the grass. Instinctively I knew what had happened, and with sympathetic amusement, my campervanning neighbours gave me a verbal report of the crime. Yes, I'd been robbed, and the suspect(s) still flew brazenly above me.

From the campsite, I quickly picked up the Ridgeway path and made my way along the wide, raised track that follows the northern escarpment of the Chiltern Hills. The walking was noticeably cooler than in recent days and far more comfortable. After two delightful miles, I veered off to the north along a footpath, gradually descending to the village of Lewknor. Here I rejoined the line of the Mary current at the village church dedicated to St Margaret. The building was open, and inside I noticed several monuments, particularly the Jodrell family chapel containing a marble sarcophagus – lavishly sculpted and decorated with angels bearing wreaths. I also noticed a small wall-mounted memorial to Sir Paul Getty (1932-2003), a member of the famous American family of petroleum tycoons. Outside I rested briefly on a new-looking bench which bore an engraved dedication:

TONY SMITH–CHURCH CLOCK WINDER–DIED 2019

Time waits for no man

I sat on Tony's bench for a while and began to wonder; surely, time waits for no man EXCEPT the clock winder?

Continuing west, I soon reached Aston Rowant, and with its church firmly closed, I continued walking and arrived at a junction of paths with an information board welcoming me to 'Fiveways'.

After reading and surveying my surroundings, I soon realised I was at a significant junction of ancient trackways. I was presently standing at the crossroads of the medieval north-south Oxford to London Road (the 'London Weye') and the 3,000-year-old Lower Icknield Way. The sign also mentioned that Princess Elizabeth passed along the London Weye when under house arrest en route to Woodstock in 1553, being welcomed by the villagers of Aston Rowant as she passed. The tracks are now quiet bridleways, but the information board interestingly displays a map from

1835 alongside an aerial photo of the same area to show how things have remained or changed over the last two centuries.

From the Fiveways crossroads, I continued west along the Lower Icknield Way. This section is easy to walk and easy to locate on a map. It forms an easily recognisable dead-straight line for well over ten miles, its form altering between roads, footpaths and tracks of one type or another. It's hard to grasp that these rights of way have been precisely that for 3,000 years, but there's also something reassuring about it. Nearby, the Chinnor and Princes Risborough Heritage Railway operate steam trains along the Icknield Line, a four-mile-long standard gauge track that now shares its course with the ancient highway.

As I approached the village of Chinnor, the Icknield Way track continued as a road, and I noticed a magnificent post mill coming into view ahead of me. I was surprised to find it, as it wasn't marked on my map. Next to the mill, an information board explained that it was built in 1789 but demolished in 1967 to make way for a housing development. In 1980 a project began to restore the mill based on the salvaged material and old photographs. The mill is now completely rebuilt and soon to be fully functioning.

On reaching the village centre, I bought some provisions and stopped for some lunch in the grounds of St Andrew's Church (see **Appendix, Day 35***). Sitting on a bench amid the gravestones, I rested, watching yet another pair of red kites fly in and out of view. Under the supposition that the church would be locked, I decided to walk over to try the door. With my hypothesis confirmed, I returned to the bench, and picking up my rucksack, I noticed a brass dedication:

FEBRUARY 14TH 1964

ROBIN SEYMOUR. AGED 17 YEARS

I BURNED MY CANDLE AT BOTH ENDS.

IT WOULD NOT LAST THE NIGHT:

BUT OH MY FRIENDS AND AH MY FOES.

IT GAVE A GOODLY LIGHT.

Well, the church was closed, but it was worth the rest.

For the rest of my day's walk, I could easily have continued along the Lower Icknield Way, but the section now took the form of the rather busy B4009 road, so I picked up a footpath leading onto the higher ground of the Upper Icknield Way. An attractive woodland ascent brought me onto the Chiltern escarpment, and I crossed from Oxfordshire and into Buckinghamshire. I continued east along a quiet country lane for a couple of miles. As I passed some farm buildings, I noticed a wooden cross adorned with scores of paper tags fluttering in the breeze. Beneath it were cups containing pens and tags and a notice:

How can we pray for you?

Following the instructions, I took a tag and wrote the name of a family member before tying it to the cross.

Two more miles of road walking brought me into the prosperous market town of Princes Risborough. Unfortunately, there were no options for camping in or near the town, and the only affordable accommodation for me meant a bus ride out to High Wycombe. While waiting for the bus, I explored the town centre and sat under the shade of the Market Hall. In addition to the nearby war memorial, I noticed a collection of smaller ones to airmen who had died in various plane crashes in the town during the Second World War:

30.01.1943: RAF Anson (4 crew members killed)

13.11.1943: B-17 USAAF Flying Fortress (pilot killed, nine crew survived)

17.12.1943: RAF Spitfire (pilot killed)

21.10.1944: USAF Douglas Dakota (5 crew members killed)

In the case of the Flying Fortress and the Spitfire, both pilots managed to continue flying their stricken aircraft away from the built-up area of the town to prevent further loss of life on the ground.

After six quiet days on the trail, High Wycombe was a shock to my ambience, but the en-suite comforts of a proper bedroom (and an actual bed) were more than welcome.

Day 36

Princes Risborough to Ivinghoe

16 Miles

11.06.2021

Ivinghoe Beacon marks the end point of the Ridgeway path, and although this day's walk finished in Ivinghoe village, the route I walked was more accurately a continued walk along the ancient course of the Icknield Way. From Princes Risborough, I remained north of the Chiltern escarpment as I passed through the villages of Great Kimble, Little Kimble, Weston Turville, Aston Clinton, Buckland and Marsworth.

As with my previous walk, my footsteps mainly followed the Mary energy line for the day. All of the above villages are aligned, but the Sun and the Serpent authors make little reference to them in their writing. The Michael line continues to run in parallel, several miles further north, passing through the town of Aylesbury and a series of villages, including Hulcott, Mentmore and Slapton.

My day began with a train journey from High Wycombe to Princes Risborough, and my walk commenced where my previous one had ended, beneath the Market Hall. Like the previous one, this day's weather was cool and comfortable for walking. I was now seven days in, and as yet, no rain of any significance had fallen. There were red kites in my morning sky for the third day in a row. These birds were nearly as rare as their teeth when I was a boy, but thanks to successful reintroductions in the 1990s, they're not uncommon in parts of Wales and southern England.

My first two miles were a rather uncomfortable walk along the busy road into Great Kimble. The church, dedicated to St Nicholas, was completely restored in Victorian times. The exterior had little to attract my interest, while the interior was closed to visitors. A short walk to the neighbouring village of Little Kimble brought up what promised to be a more exciting prospect, but this church (All Saints) was also locked. A sign in the grounds indicated that within are 12th and 13th Century wall paintings and tiles (see **Appendix, Day 36***).

I continued east, following a footpath and a road to reach and pass through the tiny hamlet of Terrick, south of Stoke Mandeville. I reached a crossroads and beyond, another hamlet called World's End. Beyond World's End, the world continued in the form of Weston Turville, a historic village with a beautiful 13th Century church. The building was sadly closed, but in the churchyard, I noticed the lych gate and its intriguing 'tapsel' opening mechanism. The gate is mounted on a central pivot, operated by a pulley and counterweight. Such gates are almost uniquely found in Suffolk, but here is a scarce and attractive example in Buckinghamshire.

My next village was Aston Clinton. The late medieval church (dedicated to St Michael and All Angels) is an attractive building which was both surprisingly (and fortunately) open for visitors. I quickly looked inside and noticed a brass plaque commemorating ten American airmen killed when their B-24 Liberator crashed in the village in 1945. I also saw several carved heads and grotesque creatures on the north aisle wall.

I walked on to the neighbouring village of Buckland and was pleasantly surprised to find the 13th Century Church of All Saints also open to visitors. This is a beautiful building in an equally beautiful setting. Above the priest's door, set within the flint masonry on the south wall, there's a weathered sheela-na-gig, the pagan fertility symbol of a woman crudely exposing her genitalia. These architectural grotesques are found throughout Europe, although there are only 45 examples in mainland Britain.

I took off my rucksack and sat on the grass for twenty minutes to eat lunch. I then spent another twenty inside, enjoying the peaceful beauty of the church interior. Despite their apparent similarities, I'm always amazed at how unique I find every old English church. No two visits are the same, yet there's often a certain familiarity, often timeless and tireless. Hunting these beauties out, however, can indeed be tiresome.

Outside I had another five miles to walk to get to Ivinghoe and my next camp location. Avoiding the obvious road route, I left the church and headed north along a footpath leading to the Grand Union Canal. Here I crossed from Buckinghamshire into the county of Hertfordshire. I then followed the towpath along the south bank into the village of Marsworth (church closed). As I did so, I crossed from Hertfordshire back into Buckinghamshire, thanks to the wiggly nature of the county boundaries. The village adjoins the hamlet of Startop's End, where the Lower Icknield Way crosses the canal to take the form of the B489 for my final three miles of road walking.

The village of Ivinghoe is a historic, popular and attractive centre. It lies beneath the northernmost ridge of the Chiltern hills that terminate with Ivanhoe Beacon, Not quite the highest point of the Chilterns, but in many ways the most prominent. I intended to camp at a site a mile beyond the village and planned to do so for two nights, spending the following day as a 'rest' day, giving me ample time to explore Ivinghoe, the Beacon and the surrounding area at leisure. These days I tend to like the sound of rest days; perhaps it's an age thing?

At the campsite, I booked in. It was a Friday, so the large site was bustling, particularly with the arrival of more than one throng of Duke of Edinburgh devotees. On the plus side, my pitch featured a worthy view of Ivinghoe Beacon. It shone magnificently in the rich tones of the late evening sun. My imagination roamed back to Glastonbury Tor, Burrow Mump and Brent Tor. Surely a summit so worthy must have been crowned with a hilltop sanctuary in its distant past? It was undoubtedly an ancient signalling beacon, and there's plenty of archaeological evidence of Bronze Age activity on the hill. Ivinghoe Beacon has been featured four times in the Harry Potter films. Need I say more?

Day 37

Ivinghoe

Rest Day

12.06.2021

Northwards the vale stretches smiling and spacious,
Spurs of the Chilterns the far distance fill;
Never held dreamland a prospect more gracious:
Sunlight and shadow on Ivinghoe Hill.

From 'Ivinghoe Hill', George U. Robins

Feeling glad not to have a schedule under my feet or a pack on my back, I knew this would be a leisurely day. A steady uphill climb brought me onto the chalk uplands of the Ivinghoe Hills, and soon my views stretched away to the north. Unsurprisingly popular with visitors, the land hereabouts is owned and managed by the National Trust, and it's a haven for wildlife on the ground. Yet another pair of now-familiar red kites came into view in the air as I continued along the wide path carved into the chalk landscape.

Looking back, I had a clear aerial view of the large campsite I'd just walked up from, stretching over at least six fields. It filled a space nearly as ample as the neighbouring village of Ivinghoe immediately to the west, its church spire rising prominently in the landscape. Further west, I made out the adjoining village of Pitstone and, close by, the post and sails of the Pitstone Windmill.

I continued onto the Beacon, passing a Bronze Age burial mound cordoned off to protect it and encourage the grass to recover. It's one of several, while the Beacon's summit is the site of an Iron Age hill fort. The summit features a stone pillar and information board to mark the eastern terminus of the Ridgeway National Trail. Here the views widen further to take in those to the east and north. These include the large and unmistakable figure of a lion carved into the chalk hillside three miles away. It marks the site of Whipsnade and its famous zoo. I remember clambering over the white lion as a child during a family trip to the place.

Several groups had gathered on the beacon, and I began chatting with a family. They had come to see a flypast by the RAF's Red Arrows, scheduled to pass over or near our location within the next twenty minutes en route to wherever else. It was the Queen's official birthday, and the formation's flight was part of the celebrations. I decided to sit down and wait to witness the spectacle, but after 45 minutes, there was no sign of it. Mildly disappointed, I decided to be on my way.

I walked south, at first retracing my steps over the high ground to Moneybury Hill and the Bridgewater Monument, a 108-foot-high monumental column built in 1832 to commemorate the pioneer canal builder Francis Egerton, 3rd Duke of Bridgewater. I then walked a short section of the Ridgeway path over Pitstone Hill before taking a closer look at the post mill I viewed earlier. I then walked into Ivinghoe village, hoping to pay a visit to St Mary's Church (see **Appendix, Day 37***).

Unfortunately, the church was closed, but I noticed a trio of historical artefacts mounted on the churchyard wall: a thatch-hook well over 12 feet in length, a brass plaque commemorating the coronation of King Edward VII and a man-trap. Elsewhere in the village, I noticed the old town hall and The Meachers Brewery house, which had more recently been a youth hostel.

I spent the rest of my day back at the campsite and had an early night, knowing I had a long walk ahead of me the following day.

Ivinghoe Beacon and St Mary's Church both align with the Mary earth energy current.

Day 38

Ivinghoe to Pegsdon

16 Miles

13.06.2021

The official Icknield Way path runs from Ivinghoe Beacon in the east to Thetford in the west. However, that's just a 20th Century interpretation of the ancient original, albeit a beautifully conceived one. The miles I'd walked on days 35 and 36 followed closely a substantial part of this longer and much older route, but now I would be directly taking on a section of the waymarked version through parts of Bedfordshire and Hertfordshire. Devising a walkable trail route along a 3,000-year-old trackway is quite an achievement, but the result is by necessity very eccentric to the original, with meanderings aplenty. Nevertheless, where possible, the route keeps to the surviving traces of Britain's oldest highway. I would be directly on it for the next three days or at least never far from it.

This day's walk began with a climb back up to Beacon Hill before taking the Icknield Way path to the village of Whipsnade. I then took a magnificent walk along the crest of the Dunstable Downs before a far less glorious road walk through Dunstable and the northern suburbs of Luton. Several miles later, I reached the more conducive countryside north of the town, and a rather lovely section of the Icknield Way path brought me onto the Pegsdon Hills. I concluded my walk in the village of Pegsdon, where I had the fortunate arrangement to stay overnight with some relatives who happened to live nearby.

As on the previous day, I began this one with my now familiar walk up to Ivinghoe Beacon. The sun was shining, and without a breath of wind in the air, I suspected the day would soon be uncomfortably hot for fully-laden hillwalking. As I reached the open downland, I passed a group of three men wild camping and stopped to chat. They were on a weekend escape and asked where I'd come from. With a twinge of mild embarrassment, I pointed to the large campsite visible half a mile away. They then asked where I had really come from; it was a difficult one to answer, but I plumped for Land's End with an apostrophe. I rarely consider wild camping in central southern England as most of it's far too built-up (or agricultural) for my liking. I prefer the empty northern hills for that pastime.

My initial route was south of Ivinghoe Beacon, but now on the high ground, I spent about 20 minutes diverting onto the spur to admire the views. A slight haze in the atmosphere softened the horizon, but the panoramic vista was well worth the effort. From the summit, I headed south and east along the Icknield Way path, which led me (in a roundabout way) into the village of Dagnall. With still more indirectness (and a crossing from Buckinghamshire into Bedfordshire), I reached the village of Whipsnade, having walked alongside the perimeter fence of its famous zoo.

Whipsnade lies on the Mary earth energy line, and my walk north from here would take me onto the course of the Michael line upon reaching the town of Dunstable. From there, the Michael current and the Icknield Way are aligned.

Heading out of the village, I reached an arboretum of mature trees called the Tree Cathedral. This remarkable 9½-acre landscape was planted by just two men over nine years early in the 20th Century. Edmund Kell Blythe conceived it as a memorial to three comrades who fell in the First World War. The landscape replicates the pattern of a medieval cathedral organically. Although never consecrated, interdenominational worship and wedding blessings regularly occur within the Cathedral. Chapels, towers, transepts, nave, chancel and other features are all interpreted in the formal hedges and plantations. The result is a place of great presence and beauty.

I now headed out onto the open access land of the Dunstable Downs, and soon I was rewarded with magnificent views looking north and west from the top of the escarpment along which my path now travelled. At nearly 800 feet, this superb chalk ridge forms the highest land of Bedfordshire and is a magnet for day trippers and tourists. Because of the geography and height, the downs attract gliders, hang gliders and paragliders. Indeed, the London Gliding Club is based at the foot of the down. The cheaper option of kite flying is also popular, and the utterly free pastime of watching Red Kites also takes place, as confirmed on this, my sixth consecutive day of admiring them in the sky.

Halfway along the escarpment, I reached a large car park and visitor centre with a café, below which I noticed a large, angular metal structure composed of fin-like vents. A notice explained that this was a windcatcher operating as part of the centre's ventilation system. Air is drawn into the unit along an underground pipeline serving a fan which cools the air inside the building in summer. In winter, it assists the warm air circulation of the heating system.

At the northern end of the crest, I passed the Five Knolls, a cluster of ancient barrows first identified by William Stukeley in the 18th Century. Excavations during the 20th Century uncovered no less than 90 skeletons, with evidence of burials from neolithic times right through to the medieval period when it appears to have been used as an execution site.

My walk along the downs was too short, and on reaching Dunstable, I found myself committed to a long and uncomfortably hot walk through Dunstable and Luton's built-up areas. The only point of interest within several miles of walking was Dunstable Priory. With it being Sunday, I hoped the building would be open to visitors. Luckily, I passed by shortly after a service had just finished, and as the vicar was about to lock up the building, I interrupted her politely. She kindly allowed me a few minutes to take a look inside, and while we chatted, I explained about my pilgrimage and talked about some of the sites I'd visited.

Dunstable Priory was founded in 1132 by Henry I for the Augustinian order of canons. The priory church (dedicated to St Peter) is a magnificent example of Norman architecture inside and out. The west front is highly decorated and has a massive entrance arch; inside, the round-arched masonry is a fine example of the Early English style. Although I didn't have much time to explore the interior, I noticed the intricate 14th Century chancel screen.

Perhaps the most significant event in the Priory's long and complex history occurred within the Lady Chapel, which once formed part of the church building. Here the annulment of the marriage of King Henry VIII to Catherine of Aragon was agreed upon in 1533. Archaeologists recently discovered the chapel's original location in the Priory grounds.

Dunstable Priory aligns with the Michael earth energy current, which continues east along the course of the Icknield Way. Beyond Dunstable, it turns northward through the suburbs of Luton to the source of the River Lea, known as 'Five Springs' and the ancient site of Waulud's Bank.

After three more miles of uncomfortable road walking, I reached Waulud's Bank, a large grassy clearing in an otherwise discordant jumble of urban development. The buried earthworks are believed to be of neolithic origin, linked to the ancient Icknield Way in purpose and age.

Another two miles of noisy road walking brought me over the A6 trunk road and, at last, into some greenery at a golf course below the ridge of high ground formed by the Warden and Galley Hills. Here are the remains of Dray's Ditches, believed to have marked the boundary between two ancient tribes. Beyond the golf course, I joined the Icknield Way path, which now took me in a direct line for several miles. At my feet, I noticed the sunken path was paved with stone sets, affirming that the path I trod was very old. The tree-lined path was a joy to walk after half a day of urban chaos, and the dappled shade gave cooling respite to my tired frame of aching bones.

It was now late afternoon, and I was walking along the boundary between Bedfordshire and Hertfordshire, gently climbing onto the Pegsdon Hills, a wonderful nature reserve run by the Wildlife Trust for Bedfordshire, Cambridgeshire and Northamptonshire. I left the path to walk onto Deacon Hill, a prominent hilltop with magnificent views looking north across the Bedfordshire landscape. My original plan was to finish my day's walk hereabouts and find a secluded spot to camp for the night. However, having recently been in touch with some relatives living not far away, I took up their kind offer of a bed for the night with lifts from and to the village below the hill. All I needed to do from here was to walk down to Pegsdon and phone them for a ride to enjoy an evening of hospitality and the luxury of a proper, comfortable bed.

Day 39

Pegsdon to Radwell

12 Miles

14.06.2021

This was a shorter day's walk which involved continuing along the Icknield Way. I passed through the village of Ickleford and the Hertfordshire towns of Letchworth and Baldock, finishing at a campsite near the village of Radwell.

My route closely followed the Icknield Way and the Michael energy current. Meanwhile, Mary remained several miles to the south, linking several Hertfordshire sites as she passed between Hitchin and Stevenage.

From Pegsdon, I walked east to rejoin the Icknield Way path below Deacon Hill but still within the chalkland mass of the Pegsdon Hills. From here, I approached the Hertfordshire village of Pirton, passing an information board indicating the Knocking Hoe National Nature Reserve. This small chalk grassland site is only 7¾ hectares in area, but a reserve of nationally rare plants and a Site of Special Scientific Interest.

At Pirton, I rested briefly on a bench at the village green before continuing east along the Icknield Way path to Ickleford, situated on the northern outskirts of the town of Hitchin. The parish church (dedicated to St Katherine) is *aligned with the Michael energy current* but was closed to visitors as I passed.

Beyond the village, I continued along the Icknield Way path, crossing the River Hiz and the main LNER railway line. In so doing, I used an iron footbridge with an information notice declaring it to be a 'Reverberant

Bridge'. The accompanying piece of lengthy information gave the concept (and the bridge) considerably more kudos than it deserved. Still, I did get an echo when I followed the instructions, positioning myself and shouting as directed. Beyond the bridge, I picked up the Icknield Way path, which I followed for two miles into Letchworth.

Letchworth, or Letchworth Garden City, came into existence in 1903 as Britain's first brand-new town. This was long before the New Towns Act and the enormous subsequent building programme that revolutionised southern England's post-war landscape. Suburban to its core, this remarkably out of place place has been remarkably out of place for well over a century. Perhaps remarkably, the oldest highway in Britain (the Icknield Way) runs invisibly right through the centre of this centreless town. Walking through Letchworth is a strange experience with nothing to redeem it save for its well-keptness and Norton Common, a well-kept oasis of greenery amid its well-kept miles of brick, concrete and tarmac.

In the Sun and the Serpent, *the authors describe their experience of dowsing the Michael earth energy current through the town:*
'The sprawling housing estates of Letchworth made following the current difficult. The whole landscape had been re-styled according to the plans of modern architects. Two churches were 'dead', with no dowseable energy connections. A third, however, called the Church on the Way, was right alongside the Icknield Way, and was situated on the flow. Disguised as a series of modern roads with all the paraphernalia of the townscape, the old route carried on regardless.

Unable to identify the church mentioned, I rested for a while on Norton Common before continuing east out of the town. I crossed a footbridge over the A1M motorway, and soon I was in the centre of Baldock. This small but historic market town lies on the Icknield Way path.

Approaching from the east, Miller and Broadhurst dowsed the Michael earth energy current through the church of St Mary. In the Sun and the Serpent, they explain the significance of the place:

'The Hertfordshire town of Baldock is Templar territory. The large church of St Mary's is situated at the junction of three ancient roads, and was rebuilt and served by chaplains of the Order of the Knights Templar when they were granted lands by the Church. As guardians of the pilgrim routes and protectors of travellers on their way to the shrines of Medieval Christendom, they could hardly have chosen a better position.

We tracked the Michael current from Royston, along the Icknield Way, to the centre of town. It just scraped through a corner of the George and Dragon Pub to enter the church, where it ran diagonally through the tower and Lady Altar.'

The Knights Templar connection is an interesting feature of a number of the sites located on both the Michael and Mary lines of energy. Although not on my particular trail, the authors mention that the order is associated with a whole series of locations found directly on the course of the Mary current as it travels south of where I walked. These include the villages of Little Wymondley, Temple Disney and Preston. It's hardly surprising that the influence and representation of this powerful order of knights can also be seen elsewhere along the countrywide alignment. The most important location of all has to be Royston Cave (see Day 40).

Baldock is a town with a remarkable history. Continually occupied since the Palaeolithic era, it was the most powerful Iron Age centre in Britain and a significant settlement In Roman times, located at the junction of several of ancient Britain's most important highways. Apart from the Icknield Way, the Roman roads from Colchester (Camulodinum), St Albans (Verulamium) and Godmanchester (Durovigutum) all converged here, and in later centuries Baldock was a significant staging post on the Great North Road.

The present town was founded in the 12th Century by the Knights Templar, as was the original church, which was largely rebuilt in about 1330 by the Knights Hospitaller. On approaching the building, I was pleasantly surprised to find that it was open to visitors. Inside, my attention was drawn to the font from the original church and the medieval 'Peter's Pence' chest made from wood and iron. I noticed the finely carved 14th Century chancel screen and various tombs, clearly of great age. In no hurry to leave, I took off my backpack and sat inside the Trinity Chapel, enjoying half an hour of undisturbed peace.

Feeling calm and invigorated, I returned outside, and as I left the churchyard, I noticed an attractively inscribed wooden memorial:

IN Memory of **HENRY GEORGE** Son of **HENRY AND HARRIET BROWN**

Who Departed this LIFE **MARCH 20TH 1861** *Aged 10* YEARS *& 10* MONTHS

How soon I was cut down when innocent at play,

The wind it blew a scaffold down and took my life away.

For the remainder of my day, I shopped for food and then made my way north to the village of Radwell and a nearby campsite. I pitched up and cooked myself some food. I then took an evening walk around the village and fed the local population of ducks.

My following day would take me from Hertfordshire into Cambridgeshire. I would pass through the town of Royston and one of the most important sites in the St Michael Alignment; Royston Cave. Unfortunately, the Cave was closed due to the coronavirus pandemic, so this essential visit would have to wait until later.

Day 40

Radwell to Great Chishill

16 Miles

15.06.2021

'Where the Icknield Way crosses Ermine Street, where the ley-lines meet outside Ladbrokes, there is a grating in the pavement that kids can drop gum down and worse.'

From 'Royston Cave', John Greening

For this walk, I returned to Baldock, where I continued eastwards on a very meandering route through a series of villages to reach the town of Royston. I continued east, following the course of the Icknield Way before dropping south to finish my day at a campsite near the Cambridgeshire village of Great Chishill. The day was warm and sunny throughout.

*From St Mary's Church, the Michael energy current heads northeast out of Baldock, while Mary travels up from the south, bypassing the town. Both energy currents are heading for the same location, however. After a long crow's flight distance of nearly 60 miles and the width of two entire OS Landranger maps, the Michael and Mary energy lines finally cross to form the **21st node** on the St Michael Alignment, the first since the Sinodun Hills. The precise location is **Royston Cave**, a remarkable subterranean feature in the centre of the Hertfordshire village of Royston.*

After a brisk walk from my camp location, I arrived back in Baldock and headed out of town following the Icknield Way path. Soon I reached a footbridge over the A505 trunk road, which was a surprise, as the map

I used was printed before the road was built. Newer maps alarmingly reveal that east of here, this monstrous 21st Century highway invades the course of the ancient Icknield Way, or at least shares the same corridor along which it travelled. It's little wonder the Icknield Way trail path has to meander as much as it does to avoid such horrors.

Thankfully, beyond the bridge, I walked in the open countryside, and after two miles, I reached the isolated church of St Mary the Virgin, Clothall. The attractive and unspoilt flint-constructed church dates to the 13th Century. Inside (yes, it was open!), the clean white walls give attention to the various features within, not least the square Norman font, which stands on a central column surrounded by four stone pillars. However, the most impressive feature has to be the east window.

Best seen close-up, this exquisite piece of 15th Century work contains no fewer than seventy images of different birds, each painted within its diamond-shaped glass panel. Each has its animated pose, be it perched, walking, preening or in flight. Although many birds are represented, some are so stylised it's hard to discern the species. Some are exotic, including a parrot and an ostrich. The bird panels form around various more extensive stained glass representations of Christ, Mary and the Four Evangelists.

I retraced my steps a short distance from the church before heading northeast along a footpath that took me through some attractive countryside and farmland. After two miles, I arrived in the village of Wallington. As at Clothall, the church here is dedicated to St Mary, and as luck would have it, this too was open for visitors.

Wallington is perhaps best known for being the home of George Orwell (1903-1950, real name Eric Blair). He was married in the church and owned a cottage in the village called 'The Stores' from 1936 until after the Second World War. Inside the church, I noticed a display of text and photographs documenting Orwell's years at Wallington.

The St Mary churches at Clothall and Wallington align with the Mary earth energy current.

From Wallington, I continued to make my way east, following the rather haphazard course of the official Icknield Way path. This involved passing through the tiny hamlets of Redhill and Roe Green, then the villages of Sandon, Kelshall and Therfield. Working out my route was somewhat confusing, as there are other waymarked trails and rights of way here, including the Hertfordshire Way and the Hertfordshire Chain Walk. I certainly wasn't complaining, though. The more public footpaths, the better.

Beyond Therfield, I joined a wide lane that led me into the town of Royston and stopped for lunch. A historic crossroads marks its centre, and nearby, a famous boulder mounted on a low circular plinth bears a walk-around inscription:

THE ROYSE STONE WAS ORIGINALLY THE BASE OF LADY ROYSIA'S CROSS ERECTED IN THE XITH CENTURY AT THE CROSSING OF ERMINE STREET AND ICKNIELD WAY NOT FAR FROM THIS SPOT +

This crossroads makes Royston a significant place geographically and historically, yet an even greater significance lies directly under the tarmac and cobblestones.

In August 1742, just yards from the crossroads, workmen were digging a hole when they came upon a millstone below the ground. When they dislodged it, they found a narrow shaft with handholds descending vertically into a 30-foot-deep circular chamber that appeared to have been excavated out of the chalk bedrock. The chamber was filled with dirt and debris, which was removed over the following days to reveal deeply incised relief carvings covering the chamber's walls. These depict various Christian subjects and symbols, along with pagan elements and specific historical figures.

Since their discovery, the carvings have been extensively investigated, and much has been written about them, but their origin remains a mystery. A tunnel was later dug to allow walk-in access to the Cave, which in recent decades it has become a tourist attraction under the care of the town council. Unfortunately, due to the coronavirus pandemic, the Cave was closed throughout 2021, so I located the small grating on the pavement and peered blindly into its invisible depths from above. In due course I was able to book and attend one of the tours the following year (see **Appendix, Day 40***)

Unable to visit the Cave, I walked on to the parish church. It, too, was closed, as it was undergoing extensive restorations. However, on the road a short distance north of the crossroads, I viewed the surviving buildings of King James I's hunting lodge. The king owned an extensive collection of properties in Royston, and it was here in 1618 that he signed Sir Walter Raleigh's death warrant.

From Royston, I headed east out of the town and along a roadside path next to the busy A505. The road follows the course of the Icknield Way while also marking the county border, and so for two miles, I walked with my right foot in Hertfordshire and my left in Cambridgeshire (or so I liked to imagine). As I walked, I passed a signpost:

GREENWICH

MERIDIAN

I checked my map, and I located my longitudinal position as 0°. I soon left the roadside to continue along a wide but now thankfully vehicle-less track upon which the Icknield Way path continued. The sun continued to shine, and my afternoon was starting to feel uncomfortably hot, but I only had four miles left to walk; two more eastward ones and then a diversion south for two more to reach my destination, now firmly in Cambridgeshire, a campsite just outside the village of Great Chishill.

Day 41

Great Chishill to Brinkley

24 Miles

16.06.2021

This day's walking was as long as it was hot (24 miles, 24ºC). It was mainly of the A to B, head down/gritted teeth variety, and I took little more than a cursory interest in the places I passed. My main concern was to stay hydrated and keep moving. My route remained faithful to the Icknield Way trail throughout. My destination was the Cambridgeshire village of Brinkley, where the village pub accommodated campers.

Concerning the Alignment, the only landmark visited that actually 'aligned' was the church of St Mary in the village of Ickleton, which stands on the Michael line. This involved a two-mile detour, but to make matters worse, the building was closed to visitors. Most of my walking took place between the two energy lines separated here by a considerable distance.

My early morning walk took me east along tracks, footpaths and narrow sunlit lanes linking the small villages of Chrishall, Elmdon and Strethall. I then followed the straight course of a two-mile-long path, often obscured through fields of tall-growing crops and woodland, to reach a footbridge spanning the busy M11 motorway. Beyond the bridge, I reached the village of Great Chesterfield and diverted north for a mile to the smaller village of Ickleton and what I hoped would be the highlight of my day's walk.

The church of St Mary is famous for its medieval wall paintings, which have been restored and studied at length. Unfortunately, coronavirus precautions meant that, once again, I had to contend with a locked door and a personal promise to myself to return later (see **Appendix, Day 41***). I walked back to Great Chesterfield, adding two more miles to my already long walking day.

The Icknield Way track carves its way east for four miles between Great Chesterfield and Linton, crossing from Essex into Cambridgeshire as it does so. This stretch of walking was easy, with nice open views, although I felt the heat of the midday, mid-summer sun. As I approached Linton, I walked through the largest grain store I'd ever seen. The site is an Advanced Processing Centre (APC) serving the local farming community as a storage co-operative. Spreading across 15 acres, it has a storage capacity for over 150,000 tons of grain and an intake capacity of 10,000 tons per day.

With little time to appreciate the village, I stopped briefly to purchase my lunch in Linton. This historic place has expanded in recent decades to become a dormitory village of Cambridge, which lies only eight miles away. Continuing along the Icknield Way, I ascended Rivey Hill, the highest point of surrounding land, on which stands a large water tower.

The Rivey Tower is an impressive example of functional architecture in the Art Deco style. It was built in the 1930s and stands 98 feet high. Its dodecagonal buttressed exterior is supported by an internal framework of steel girders beneath a potable tank and topped with a slate roof. The building was extensively restored in recent years and stands out for its unusual construction in brick rather than concrete.

Beyond Rivey Hill, my Icknield Way route continued along well-established tracks through deepest rural Cambridgeshire for another six long miles as the hot afternoon progressed, now somewhat uncomfortably for my various body parts. The only other settlement on my route was the village of Balsham, above which, at a distance, I noticed a more conventional-looking concrete water tower. Here my way turned to follow a half-mile stretch of the course of a Roman road that once connected with Cambridge (Duroliponte). It now forms part of the Harcamlow Way, a 141-mile long-distance trail that takes a figure-of-eight route between Harlow and Cambridge.

By the time I reached Brinkley, I was flagging and listless. Much relieved to unburden myself of my constant shoulder-mounted fabric companion, I rehydrated myself at the pub and pitched up my tent in the beer garden, which I had all to myself. In the evening, I enjoyed the luxury of a pub meal before watching the sun set slowly over the horizon. The longest day's walk of my trail was over, and now all that remained between the North Sea and me was the entire width of East Anglia.

Day 42

Brinkley to Stonecross Green

16 Miles

17.06.2021

Thankfully, this day was cooler than the previous one and made a more comfortable walk. I made my way north from Brinkley to Woodditton and continued east for the rest of the day, crossing from Cambridgeshire into Suffolk and finishing at a quiet campsite near the tiny village of Whepstead. Most of the walking was along quiet country lanes.

I connected with the Mary energy current at the church in Woodditton and followed its course for several miles, taking in the churches at Kirtling and Ousden (also aligned). Three other historic churches also align with Mary nearby: Dullingham and Stretchworth (off-route) and Lidgate (closed on visiting). Meanwhile, Michael continues to travel south of where I walked, passing through the church sites at Withersfield and Great Thurlow.

The first hour of my morning's walk took me along a series of footpaths that form a continuation of the Icknield Way Trail while I headed north to reach the village of Stretchworth. Bearing east, I reached an isolated church which I assumed at first to be St Peter's, Stretchworth, but this turned out to be St Mary's, Woodditton. Either way, the building was closed, so I pressed on to reach the church at Kirtling, which I was pleased to find open for visitors.

The isolated Church of All Saints, Kirtling, dates from Norman times and stands close to the formal gardens that now cover the site once occupied by a 16th Century mansion. A large, moated, twin-towered gatehouse is all that remains of Kirtling Manor, built from the remains of the 13th Century Kirtling castle.

The rather austere exterior of the church gives little indication of what lies within. The porch leads to a spectacular south doorway carved ornately in the Norman style, bearing the remarkably intact sculptural form of 'Christ in Glory'. The unspoilt interior houses many interesting features, including a brick-built chapel added to the church in the 16th Century. In it stands the imposing tomb of Roger, Second Baron North. This lavish monument portrays the Baron's reclining life-sized effigy within a columned surround under a canopy rising twelve feet from the floor. Everything is highly decorated and deeply carved, depicting classical subjects and features. A remarkable sculptural representation of a dragon guards the Baron at his feet.

The Norths were a powerful family during the 16th Century. They owned Kirtling Manor, and Sir Roger was a particularly influential figure. His father had been treasurer to Henry VIII, and Roger was himself a politician at the court of Elizabeth I. He is said to have 'entertained' the Queen lavishly at Kirtling for three days in September 1578. He died in 1600, and after his funeral in Old St Paul's, he was laid to rest in his tomb at Kirtling.

The authors of the Sun and the Serpent refer to Kirtling having located this particular monument as well as sculptured images of dragons at the gatehouse guarding the entrance to Kirtling Hall:

'The tower, all that remains of the old manor house, is, along with its moat (the largest in Cambridgeshire), another indication of the one-time importance of this spot. It is difficult not to imagine some connection between the historical associations of such a place and the fact that it is built on a site through which flows the Mary energy...The fondness of the North family for dragons may well have been an allusion to this, and the

effigy of Sir Roger with his feet on a chained dragon could be symbolic of the taming of the raw Earth energy after the manner of the images of St Michael and St George.'

I now parted from the Icknield Way to connect with the Mary energy current, which veers somewhat east of it. The modern-day Icknield Way National Trail terminates at Knettishall Heath near Thetford, but this most ancient of highways has several interpretative branches, including one that (perhaps logically) extends to the equally ancient town of Bury St Edmunds. Either way, my trail was heading to Bury St Edmunds via the Michael and Mary energy currents.

It was now late in the morning, so I left Kirtling and continued east on a largely road-bound walk, crossing from Cambridgeshire into Suffolk. At midday, I reached the church of St Mary in Lidgate (closed to visitors). Another mile brought me to another church, but this time it was open.

St Peter's, Ousden, stands in pleasantly isolated surroundings with few other buildings nearby apart from an 18th Century dovecot; all that remains of Ousden Hall after its demolition in 1955. The cruciform church is characteristically Norman, with a squat tower and an unspoilt interior. On entering, I soon became aware of two pigeons repeatedly flying from one end of the building to the other, calling noisily in their trapped flight paths. Whenever I stood still or sat down, they would perch at rest on a ledge in the roof, but once I resumed my movements, they would recommence their frantic, noisy flight. I tried leaving the entrance door open for a while, but they did not attempt to reach the egress point.

Preferring the silence, I tried to minimise my movements, pitying the birds' predicament, but I did notice and approach one particular fixture that grabbed my attention. Projecting from the wall is a monument to one Leticia Moseley, who died in 1619. Within it is the striking sculpture of a skeleton in a shroud, gruesome and beautiful in equal measure, finely carved in marble.

After sitting for a while, I got up to leave while the Pigeons resumed their frantic attempts to fly to freedom. I couldn't see how they'd ever get out without some major netting operation, which I sadly deduced may not happen. It's understandable why bird screens are a common feature in church porches, along with the need to keep them closed. Prevention is the only solution.

The rest of my day's walk was a wandering eastwards along (thankfully) quiet country roads for six miles to reach a remote campsite at Stonecross Green, near the Suffolk village of Whepstead.

During these last few miles, I reached and crossed over the Michael energy current, but with no significant landmark to register it.

The weather was changing, and I felt pretty damp when I'd pitched my tent. Unbeknownst to me, some spectacularly heavy rain was waiting on its curtain call for the next day.

Day 43

Stonecross Green to Bury St Edmunds

5 Miles

18.06.2021

Unfortunately, heavy rainfall of the spectacular variety doesn't feel very spectacular when walking in it for more than an hour or so. By then, it tends to feel very wet and very miserable in equal measure. With sensible clothing, the wet isn't a significant problem, but given the right (wrong) mood and circumstances, the miserable certainly can be.

The last few miles of my previous day's walk had brought me a few miles south of Bury St Edmunds, and now I planned to approach this historic town and, on the way, travel through the Ickworth Estate. I would then spend an hour or two exploring the town before heading east, eventually arriving at a campsite near the village of Wetherden.

In pilgrimage terms, I would follow the Michael line through Ickworth and on to Bury St Edmunds, where Michael and Mary briefly merge without crossing their respective paths. My long walk east out of the town would broadly share its course with the Michael energy current.

I woke up to the sound of heavy rain on my tent and the pessimistic notion that it would be a long and uncomfortable challenge if I committed to my plans for the day. I crawled out of my sleeping bag and donned my waterproofs, and made my way to the toilet block for a quick shower. By the time I got back to the tent, I had abandoned my plans. I downgraded my 23-mile intention to a 5-mile road walk to Bury St Edmunds. I've done enough all-day walking in heavy rain to know trail walking doesn't have to be an endurance when it can be avoided. I got back in my sleeping bag, looked up a cheap hotel and booked a room using the magic of wireless technology.

On the trail, decamping in heavy rain can be tricky, but in a campsite in East Anglia in the summer, it's not life-threatening. Keeping my swearing at an inaudible level, I packed away my gear and began my soggy road march.

After nearly two hours, I reached the town and then its centre before finding my hotel. I was disappointed to be refused entry until after 2 pm and not even allowed to drop off my rucksack in advance. I had hoped to unburden my soggy body of its saturated load before exploring the town at leisure, but until 2 pm, it looked like we'd have to kill three wet hours as a soggy combination.

I decided to sightsee wherever I could indoors, so I made my way to the remains of the once-great abbey. The extensive but severely degraded ruins still retain a great Norman gatehouse and two magnificent churches. One of these is St Edmundsbury Cathedral, and not wishing to increase my sogginess, I decided to look inside.

Considering it was once a parish church, the building is enormous and looks every bit like a cathedral. It's the seat of the Bishop of St Edmundsbury and Ipswich and originated in the Norman Era, being rebuilt in late medieval times and later enlarged in the Gothic Revival style. Among the fixtures is a magnificent font designed by Sir George Gilbert Scott (1811-1878) and the equally glorious Bishop's Throne, designed by Frank Ernest Howard. I also noticed a delightfully conceived painting by Brian Whelan depicting St Edmund's Martyrdom.

St Edmund the Martyr was the king of East Anglia during the late 9th Century, but little is known of him as devastating Viking raids destroyed nearly all evidence of his reign. Tradition asserts that Edmund refused to renounce his Christian faith to his Viking enemies, so on the 20th November 869, he was tied to a tree, shot through with many arrows and beheaded. The precise location of his execution is debated but generally believed to have taken place near the Suffolk village of Hoxne (see Day 44). After his death, a popular cult grew around Edmund, and the church canonised him. Edmund, and Edward the Confessor, came to be regarded as the patron saints of medieval England until St George in the 15th Century replaced them. After his conversion to Christianity, The Danish king Canute was instrumental in founding the Abbey at Bury St Edmunds. Edmund's shrine became one of the most important pilgrimage locations in Europe. In turn, Bury St Edmunds became one of the wealthiest and most famous abbey houses.

Outside, the rain was still pouring, so I decided to visit Moyse's Hall, a remarkable 12th Century building next to the marketplace, formerly the town's gaol, workhouse and police station. Since 1899 it has served as a museum, so with permission to store my rucksack, I immersed myself in the town's past.

I enjoyed viewing a fascinating collection of artefacts and exhibits recording the history of Bury St Edmunds, including a superb collection of horology and a gallery of historical militaria from the Suffolk Regiment. My visit also included a large exhibition of artwork entitled Moments, featuring the work of (among others) Tracy Emin and Banksy. I wasn't expecting this!

By the time I'd seen everything, the rain had finally stopped, and it was after 2 o'clock. I walked back to the hotel and checked in, relieved to unpack, shower and begin drying all my wet stuff. Soon I was out again, however, as there was more to see in the town, so I made a pedestrian tour of the Abbey ruins.

The remains of the Abbey now extend over a large grassy site known as the Abbey Gardens. The very degraded and crumbling ruins leave far more to the imagination than the eyes, but concrete plaques mark some of the various locations, one of particular significance:

NEAR THIS SPOT
ON THE 20th NOVEMBER A.D. 1214.
CARDINAL LANGTON & THE BARONS

SWORE AT ST EDMUND'S ALTAR
THAT THEY WOULD OBTAIN FROM
KING JOHN
THE RATIFICATION OF
MAGNA CARTA

Further significance to near this spot is the location within the long-vanished choir of the abbey, where Broadhurst and Miller dowsed the point at which the Michael and Mary currents merge to form what I could take to be the 22nd node on the St Michael Alignment. However, in this instance, I would not be using the correct term, for they describe:

'We had half-expected to find a node in the remains of the abbey. Both the Michael and Mary currents led into the ruins, but how they performed when they met was very unusual. In the centre of the Choir, they came together, but did not cross. Rather, they 'kissed'. They joined briefly only to veer off on their respective routes. The point at which they fused was not dowseable as a node.'

The authors describe the course of the currents elsewhere in the vicinity, particularly that of Michael, which aligns directly with the great Norman tower, which curiously contains two dragon heads projecting from its wall.

While in the Abbey Gardens, I visited the Appleby Rose Garden, where I noticed a silver bench shining in the rain. It was made from the wing of a USAAF B17 Flying Fortress bomber aircraft. The garden commemorates the American service members stationed in the area during the Second World War. Nearby is the Peace Garden. It contains The Teardrop, a sculpture commemorating the murder of 57 Jews in Bury St Edmunds on Palm Sunday, 19th March 1190. The stainless steel teardrop stands on a brick base in-filled with 57 cobbles. A Holocaust Day memorial service takes place every year in the garden.

With the rain now ceased, I walked over to the Norman tower. This was the principal gateway into the Abbey and still stands impressively and unruined, one of the finest Norman structures in East Anglia. The building still functions as the bell tower for the adjacent cathedral, housing a peal of ten bells dated to 1785. A smaller, 14th Century gatehouse complete with portcullis also remains a short distance to the north.

The unexpected early finish to this day's walk had potentially set me back a day, but with time on my hands, I used the luxury of my unplanned quarters to study my maps and routes. I concluded that I could continue my trail the next day by realigning my route to omit the initially planned destination. Instead, I would continue my next day's walk to the next campsite further on. It would mean missing a few planned locations for visits, but hopefully, I'd find some attractive alternatives along the way.

Day 44

Bury St Edmunds to Thornham Magna

20 Miles

19.06.2021

Now and then, I hit a flat spot on my trail walking, and this walk seemed to fit the bill. My change of plans now meant I'd be walking further north than I originally intended. However, as ever, my progress continued inexorably east towards the North Sea coast, ever closer to my ultimate destination, now less than sixty miles away.

Looking at my camera roll for this day, I was reminded that it wasn't the most inspiring day of my trail, and although I took a route through rural Suffolk, nearly all the walking was on the tarmac. The rain came and went, but a grey overcast sky persisted, and my views were tempered by poor visibility. Still, I began my day refreshed from a long, comfortable sleep and all the en suite luxuries that come with a proper bedroom. My tent and gear were dry, well-equipped, and fully charged.

This day's route was a rather long one designed to get me from A to B and little else. Regarding the pilgrimage, no aligned sites were visited as my walking took place entirely between the two energy currents. I may have missed some interesting sites and landmarks, so after completing my trail, I later visited a few locations as a motorist. The churches at Rushbrooke (see **Appendix 44***) *and Woolpit (***Appendix 44*****) *are both aligned with Michael.*

My walk out of Bury St Edmunds allowed another walk through the Abbey Gardens and over the River Lark. I noticed the Abbots Bridge, clearly of great age, which marks the northwest corner of the abbey precincts. Soon my walk became mundane as I made my way east along the roadside, eventually bringing me to the village of Thurston. Finding little of interest, I continued east, linking up more (thankfully quiet) road routes through several similarly uninteresting villages and settlements, including Norton, Wyverstone and eventually Finningham. A final mile brought me to a campsite at Swattesfield, a short distance from the Norwich to Stowmarket railway line.

I can't imagine Gainsborough or Constable would have got much inspiration from this particular aspect of Suffolk, but I could be wrong. Not all trail days are memorable, but thankfully the vast majority are.

Day 45

Thornham Magna to Weybread

13 Miles

20.06.2021

On these final three stages of my pilgrimage, the aligned sites are predominantly churches, and there are plenty on both the Mary and the Michael energy currents. The ones I chose to visit were only a fraction of many and not necessarily the better ones. They were simply the ones I could practically see along my dedicated route. Many were closed, and at times I felt a bit 'churched-out' in two senses of the phrase.

Concerning this day, my walking route shared the course of the Michael energy current while Mary remained to the north. The aligned church sites visited were Thornham Magna, Thornham Parva, Eye, Hoxne, Syleham and Weybread. Apart from the churches, Hoxne had additional relevance and Eye, whose medieval castle also aligns with Michael.

The rain had stopped during the night, and I woke early to a bright and dry (if not sunny) morning. My nearby neighbours had enjoyed some noisy but affable fireside fun until midnight, but it didn't bother me. I could tell it was just good cheer.

I was up and dressed before the dog walkers, but I decided to hang around and cook myself a hot tent-side breakfast, probably for the first time since I was in the scouts. I didn't rank my chances of winning MasterChef, but I did have severe budgetary constraints. My motivation was to kill some time not to reach Thornham Magna too early, should the church be open for visitors. I was all done, washed up, lunch packed and on my way before my nearest neighbours had extinguished their previous night's mess and got their barbecue out.

The church at Thornham Magna nestles in the corner of Thornham Park. The estate is a popular venue for visitors who can enjoy 12 miles of way-marked countryside trails on private land (there's a parking charge). Not unexpectedly, I found the church (dedicated to St Mary Magdalene) closed on my arrival (see **Appendix, Day 45***). I continued to its neighbour, Thornham Parva. The church (St Mary's) is smaller but perhaps more charming. Its roof is thatched, as is its small tower. It was also closed (see **Appendix, Day 45****).

Not discouraged, I made my way north along a pleasant path to the next village of Yaxley and another magnificent church. Yes, you guessed. Like the Thornhams, this, too, was closed to visitors. I was disappointed but not disheartened; I could always come back again (see **Day 45*****). I Now had another mile to reach one of the highlights of my day, the historic Suffolk town of Eye.

Eye has an imposing church (St Peter and St Paul's) with a striking, tall tower, and yes, also closed. It went straight onto my revisiting list (see **appendix, Day 45******). However, the town's medieval hilltop castle remained open and approachable via a steep walk from the church below.

Little remains of Eye Castle, but the dramatic location on a small but prominent hilltop is at least enough to beckon the curious traveller. The remains of the original Norman motte and bailey are diminished beneath layers of later buildings. From its creation shortly after the Norman Conquest, the castle was subject to a series of takeovers during the civil conflicts that spanned the next two centuries. By the 14th Century, the fortification was in ruins but maintained its function as a prison. Later developments saw the motte surmounted with a windmill. During the 19th Century, the bailey became a workhouse, and a domestic house was built on the motte, known as Kerrison's Folly.

Steps lead up to the level site of the bailey, where a series of plaques set into the ground provided an illustrated history of the castle in beautifully engraved, illustrated text. A further flight of steps led to the top of the motte, where I gained fabulous views of the church and surrounding countryside.

On dowsing the Michael energy current, Miller and Broadhurst found that it ran through the castle and the church and what remains of a Benedictine priory a short distance further to the east.

The castle made a pleasant halt, after which I continued walking northeast to reach another interesting site half a mile south of the village of Hoxne (pronounced 'Hoxen').

In a field set back from the road is the St Edmund Monument, a cross surmounted on a plinth and bearing an inscription:

St Edmund

the

Martyr

AD 843

OAK TREE FELL,

AUG 1843

BY ITS OWN

WEIGHT.

The back story to this somewhat cryptic passage involves tradition, fact and a small error. The cross marks the reputed site of King Edmund's execution at the hands of Viking invaders in 843. An oak tree of great age grew here until it fell without apparent cause or warning in 1848 (not 1843). By the time it fell, the oak had a circumference of 20 feet, and later tests established it to be a thousand years old. After it fell, A metal object was found deep within the tree, taken to be an arrowhead. This served to enhance the credibility of the legend surrounding Edmund's death. Traditionally it's believed that King Edmund refused to renounce his Christian faith. He was tied to a tree by his enemies, brutally flayed and shot through with arrows before being decapitated into sainthood. The wood from the fallen tree was later used to make several items of significance to the locality, including a carved screen in Hoxne Church and furniture items for the nearby locations of Flixton Hall and Brome Hall.

At my visit, the cross was neglected behind an area cordoned off with temporary fencing. I later read that a local community group had been protesting against a proposed housing development earmarked for the site.

Leaving the cross, I made my way into Hoxne, crossing Goldbrook Bridge. Tradition states that it was under the bridge that Edmund was found and captured while hiding from his attackers. The bridge bears an inscribed stone:

KING EDMUND
TAKEN PRISONER HERE
·A·D·870·

In the village, I approached the church through its large graveyard. Dedicated to three saints, St Peter and St Paul with St Edmund's dates to the late 14th Century and was built in the perpendicular style. Its tall tower made an impressive sight, but I was even more impressed (and surprised) to find it open! Inside I noticed the ornate choir screen built from the wood of the fallen oak tree mentioned earlier. There are a series of preserved medieval wall paintings along the church walls, only parts of which remain. These include depictions of St Christopher, the Seven Deadly Sins, the Seven Acts of Mercy and the Last Judgement. I also noticed the 15th Century octagonal font sculpted with angels and other figures, their heads broken off long ago and likely during the wholesale desecrations ordered by Oliver Cromwell.

Tradition links Hoxne Church with St Edmund, as an earlier church dedicated to St Ethelbert in the 10th Century is said to have once occupied the site. Edmund's body is said to have been first interred there before its later removal to his shrine at Bury St Edmunds.

In the Sun and the Serpent, the authors write:
'At first sight, one of the most famous of English legends having a connection with Hoxne Church, through which the Michael current passes,

would appear to be nothing more than coincidence. Yet these traditions often appear to have an almost secret mythology hidden within them which is difficult to pinpoint.'

Leaving Hoxne, I made my way east along a quiet series of lanes running south of the River Waveney. Near the small settlement of Syleham, I reached a small junction marked by a wooden cross on a brick-built plinth. An information notice explained that an earlier cross once occupied this site which was once a major crossroads. The lane going north leads to Syleham Church, where it now terminates, but until the mid-17th Century, it continued over the river at a bridge that no longer exists. The cross is famously documented as marking where King Henry II received the surrender of Hugh Bigod, the rebellious 1st Duke of Norfolk, in July 1174. I took a short detour along the lane, and after a few hundred yards, I reached the church in a tranquil and picturesque setting with the River Waveney running just yards away. This was my first encounter with the river, which forms the boundary between the counties of Suffolk and Norfolk for much of its course. It would become a frequent feature on what remained of my trail.

Syleham Church is dedicated to St Margaret (of Scotland). It's mentioned in the Domesday Book, and the foundations and lower courses of the present building are over a thousand years old. Of flint construction, it has a round tower and (unusually) a chancel considerably higher than the nave. Unfortunately, the church was locked, but the churchyard was perfect for me to sit among the weathered graves and eat my sandwiches.

I retraced my steps back to the cross and continued to walk along quiet lanes and paths to Weybread, the last village on my day's route. After locating the church, I found it locked, so I continued east along a short stretch of the B1116 that shares its course with part of a ten-mile section of Roman Road. In England, you're never too far from one.

My final destination was a nearby campsite set attractively within an expanse of orchards. It surprised me that no other campers were sharing the site, but I concluded that this part of Suffolk lies outside the tourist hotspots. Also, this was a Sunday night and still three weeks ahead of the school summer holidays. I pitched my tent, and once I'd seen the self-catering options I had in my bag, I decided to walk to the nearest pub.

The next day would see me reach Norfolk and the final county border crossing on my trail.

Day 46

Weybread to Wardley Hill

14 Miles

21.06.2021

> 'Not like great rivers that hath in locks are bound,
> On whom hard man doth heavy burdens lay,
> And fret their waters into foam and spray.
> This river's life is one long holiday
> All the year round.'
>
> From 'The Waveney', Jean Ingelow

My trail continued with a day's walk heading north and east and never far from the River Waveney. I passed through Withersdale Street, Mendham, Homersfield, Denton, Bungay, Ditchingham and Broome, finishing at a campsite at Wardley Hill.

I began my walk near the Michael energy current, but for most of the day, I walked closer to that of Mary, joining her at the churches of Denton, Ditchingham and Broome. As always, many sites have to remain unvisited because there are two separate lines of energy and the practical and geographical constraints of the routes walked.

The longest day of 2021 had begun to shine its daylight well before I woke up, albeit diffused by a sky-wide covering of grey clouds. The air was still, so I surmised the sun wouldn't appear in a hurry. I attended to my morning routines using the campsite's basic facilities and prepared for my day's walk.

Following footpaths and the quietest roads I could find, I made my way east and north to reach Withersdale Street, a small village that once had its own brickworks, as did many other settlements nearby. Suffolk is famous for the history of its brick making, and genuine handmade Suffolk bricks are now a very sought-after commodity.

Continuing north, I reached the next village of Mendham, which stands on the banks of the Waveney and the Norfolk/Suffolk border. I walked along the valley to Homersfield, where I crossed the Waveney into Norfolk. I passed a tree-trunk sculpture depicting a man in a boat, his hand trailing down to touch the water below. Carved into the trunk are the words:

I DREAMED OF A BEAUTIFUL WOMAN
WHO CARRIED ME AWAY

The words refer to the river, and the work is by Mark Goldsworthy.

Now in Norfolk, I made my way towards Denton to reach the church, some distance from the village. St Mary's is another traditional East Anglian church with a round tower. However, the tower collapsed in the 1600s and, during later modifications, was rebuilt with a square extension built over what remained of the earlier one. The result is a curious combination of the two.

The church was open for visitors, and inside the spacious interior, I noticed some magnificent 15th Century roof bosses. The spectacular east window contains glass collected from different places and periods and was assembled here in the early 18th Century. The medieval font remains, but as at Hoxne, its figurative ornamentations were desecrated on the orders of Oliver Cromwell in the 17th Century.

I continued my walk along a road leading me into Bungay and promptly found myself back in Suffolk. The town rests in the neck of a loop formed by the River Waveney. As the last town on my trail, I decided to look around and get some lunch.

Naturally, the river gave Bungay a strategic defence, so the Normans built a castle here, unsurprisingly. The existing remains were rebuilt by

Roger Bigod, 5th Earl of Norfolk. Along with the curtain wall, two massive gatehouse towers survive. Elsewhere in the town are two historic churches and a ruined priory.

Re-equipped with provisions, I left Bungay and promptly found myself back in Norfolk, and without realising it, I was within the Norfolk Broads National Park for a short while. The boundaries of the Broads are informed by the network of waterways that flow through this part of East Anglia, so the maps that chart them are more relevant to the water-bound tourist than the terrestrial pilgrim. However, the Norfolk Broads are beautiful, as is this short section of the River Waveney. Here was the second and last National Park on my trail.

I followed a footpath across the floodplain to reach a picturesque footbridge over the river. Until the 19th Century, this was the site of the Ditchingham Watermill. Other mills have existed here since medieval times. George Baldry was the last occupant of the (now demolished) mill house. He built the footbridges (still in use) and hired boats and bathing huts in the 1920s and 30s, which he built himself. The writer Sir Henry Rider Haggard (1856-1925, of King Solomon's Mines fame) lived locally and frequently walked these paths.

I now continued east with just two objectives left for my walk. These were the churches at Ditchingham and Broome, although 'at' is probably the wrong word. Both stand a considerable distance from their respective villages.

I soon arrived at St Mary's, Ditchingham (see **Appendix, Day 46***), but regrettably, I found it closed. So too, the church at Broome (**Appendix, Day 46****), but my effort wasn't wasted. St Michael's stands isolated and elevated in a beautiful rural setting. I was more than happy to walk around the churchyard and rest quietly on a bench, just listening to the sounds of nature and enjoying the view.

I now had less than two miles to walk to reach my final destination, a campsite near the Norfolk village of Ellingham. After two continuous weeks of walking, I felt much fitter than I did on the Ridgeway, and I hardly noticed the weight I was carrying. I have to concede that for lack of hills, long-distance walking in the east of England is about as easy as long-distance walking can get, mainly if you keep to a sensible mile count.

The campsite was a large off-grid one, and I seemed to have it all to myself. The facilities were basic, with toilets of the unplumbed, sawdust variety. Washing machine drums were available as firepits, but when I'm on the trail, I tend to keep my tent-side antics to a minimum. My cooking (if I bother) is very elementary. If I can get a modest meal, a wash and a decent sleep in time for the next day, that's good enough for me.

My day ended much as it started. The sky was still overcast, but plenty of daylight remained by the time I fell asleep.

Day 47

Wardley Hill to Hopton on Sea

19 Miles

22.06.2021

I made an early start for this, the final day of my trail. The sky was a bit brighter than the previous two days, and breaks in the cloud cover motivated me for my last hike and my final objective; Hopton on Sea and the roofless ruin of the old St Margaret's Church.

For this final stage of my pilgrimage, I chose to follow a route mainly in line with that of the Mary energy current for most of the day, taking in the aligned church sites of Hales, Raveningham, Haddiscoe and Ashby. My ultimate destination was **Old St Margaret's Church** *which forms the* **22nd** *and* **last node** *along the St Michael Alignment. The distance separating it from the preceding one at Royston Cave (see Day 40) is approximately 100 miles, a far longer interval than any other. The Michael energy current remained south of where I walked, passing through several aligned sites, including the magnificent medieval tower at Beccles (see* **Appendix, Day 47*** *).*

In support of my plans, my chosen route was mainly along quiet roads, but with plenty of unavoidable veering both north and south to keep me on track. Yet again, I had to cross the River Waveney, whose broad flood plain now formed a formidable barrier with only one possible crossing point; a road bridge carrying the busy A 143. I also intended to make a lengthy detour near the end of my walk to reach a campsite near the Norfolk village of Blundeston. There I would jettison my gear and pitch my tent before taking an evening walk into Hopton to complete my pilgrimage.

Leaving my camp, I headed east, passing yet another round-towered church at Kirby Cane. Mature cedar trees grew around the church, enhancing the attractiveness of the scene. Although the building was closed, I noticed and admired the beautifully carved Norman doorway.

Further north along the lane, I reached the Church of St Margaret, Hales, which stands in open fields in splendid isolation from everything, including the village. Of all the churches I visited on my pilgrimage, this has to be one of the most picturesque. St Margaret's is substantially (and almost perfectly) Norman. No significant alterations have been made besides adding windows in the 13th and 14th Centuries. The church is built from flint and conglomerate stone with a round apse, a thatched roof and (yes) a round tower. Now redundant, a plaque on the wall indicated that the Redundant Churches Fund (now the Churches Conservation Trust) maintains the building.

I approached the building along an un-mowed meadow and reached the magnificent south doorway, intricately carved in the Norman style. To my delight, the door was open and inside, the simple but beautiful interior struck me. Trying not to break the silent stillness, I lowered my rucksack onto the tiled floor, sat down on one of the chairs and put my trail on hold for twenty minutes. Just for a while, I could forget about my 21st Century first-world concerns and enjoy being here and now. But for the rest of my objectives, I could have stayed there and then all day.

Looking around the sparse but beautiful interior, I noticed the simple wooden fixtures, including a gallery, the (Victorian) waggon roof, and some carefully preserved sections of medieval paintings on the plain whitewashed walls. The church information guide indicated that the two discernible figures represented St James the Great carrying a staff and St Christopher carrying the Christ child. I also noticed the octagonal 15th Century font, boldly carved with lions, angels and Tudor roses. The north doorway is also Norman and almost as ornately carved as the main entrance.

Miller and Broadhurst record that they dowsed the Mary energy current through the tower and the two Norman doors.

With some reluctance, I went on my way, knowing I still had much walking to do. The following location was Raveningham, Where the Church of St Andrew *(aligned with the Mary current)* stands within the grounds of Raveningham Hall. The park was closed, so I continued walking and passed a curious cast iron monument erected by Sir Edmund Bacon in 1831. It serves as a milestone; the distance to London 111 miles.

I now hoped to reach the village of Haddiscoe through a series of footpaths, but I found my access was overgrown and unmarked at a small settlement called Three Cocked Hat. Not wishing to waste time getting lost or cut to ribbons by midsummer foliage, I decided to bypass Haddiscoe and divert along a road route which brought me to another small settlement called Thorpe, where stands another round-towered church.

I was now on the west side of the River Waveney, separated from it by a floodplain nearly two miles wide. This former marsh is now a vast area of grassland reclaimed by a network of drainage channels. According to my map, a footpath would take me across (with footbridges over the drainage channels at two locations) and then connect me with the main bridge over the river at the village of St Olaves.

At first, my way was marked clearly, and soon I was on the open grassland. The path became indistinct, however, and try as I might, I couldn't see which of the many gates and fences served the unmarked way. Using the best of my navigation skills, I determined where my route should be, pressing on as best I thought, using my map, the landmarks I could see and, for the first time on my trail, my trusty old compass. As I scanned the land around me, I noticed a lot of wild ponies grazing and trotting in various directions nearby. I continued but realised the ponies were interested in following me. Within a minute, they were a massed herd trotting towards me with a few outliers galloping about in a very alarming manner. I was now experiencing primal fear of the fight or flight variety, but I determined to appear calm. I continued walking slowly and made my best attempt to greet the ponies with what I deemed to be my best horse-friendly tone of voice.

A few hundred yards ahead, I noticed a woman standing by a gate. She seemed to be trying to shepherd some of the ponies through the gate, so I gingerly made my way towards her. By the time I reached the gate, I was surrounded by the herd, which must have been a hundred strong. Some were nudging me with their noses, and one was biting at my rucksack, presumably to get at what remained of my lunch. I asked the woman if she was in charge(?) of the ponies, and she explained that a gate had been left open and the ponies were not where they were supposed to be. After an eternity of five minutes, they began to pass through the gate. I asked the woman if she could point out how I could get to St Olaves, but she didn't seem to know, and her manner was unhelpful. Once most of the horses were through the gate, she closed it, got into her 4x4 and drove off.

Feeling traumatised, I decided to retrace my steps back to Thorpe and down to Haddiscoe to continue my walk by the longer but comparatively safer road option.

Having returned to Thorpe, I marched down to Haddiscoe (pronounced 'Hadsker'). I had intended to visit St Mary's church on my walk (see **Appendix, Day 47****), but time was pressing on, and I wanted to consume more miles. I braved the verge of the busy A143 for another mile to reach and cross the bridge over the River Waveney at St Olaves. Two more miles of road walking brought me to an attractive two-mile section of the Angles Way. This long-distance trail route covers 77 miles from Thetford to Great Yarmouth. Many long-distance walkers use it to extend their trails to or from the Icknield Way and the Peddars Way.

After a mile, I reached yet another beautifully isolated church. St Mary's,

Ashby, is another thatched church with a round tower, but a tall octagonal one surmounts this one. The building was closed to visitors, but I was glad to sit quietly in the churchyard and lick the equine-related psychological wounds I had sustained earlier. At the end of the graveyard, I noticed a headstone-shaped monument in memory of seven American airmen killed in two separate missions nearby during World War Two.

Continuing along the Angles Way path, I reached the village of Lound and made my way south to the village of Blundeston and my campsite destination. It wasn't quite the end of my trail, but it marked the point where I joined the route of another trail I walked in 2019; Ness point, Lowestoft to Ardnamurchan Point in Scotland, the easternmost and westernmost points of land in Britain.

I now had just a couple of miles to reach Hopton, and the sun was finally shining. I made my way east, crossing the busy A12, and soon, the North Sea came into view. I passed the partially ruined Church of St Bartholemew, Corton. Its tall tower has been a roofless ruin for 300 years but remains the most prominent landmark for miles around.

On reaching Hopton, I made my way through a vast holiday park to reach the coast and the termination point of the Norfolk Coast Path. I went down and through a slipway in the sea wall to get to the shoreline. I ceremoniously paddled my boots in the North Sea as I had in the Atlantic on Day 1. I'd now walked from coast to coast across England at its widest point. Thanks to the Coronavirus Pandemic, it had taken me over a year to do this, even though it took just 42 walking days and 561 walking miles to get here.

After crossing to form the final node on the St Michael Alignment, the Mary and the Michael energy currents dip south slightly and continue east. Michael leaves the coast somewhere near here, and Mary just a few hundred yards further south. All that remained for me now was to head half a mile inland and complete my pilgrimage at the ruin of St Margaret's Church, the last of the 22 nodes of the St Michael Alignment and 'The

Last Lair Of The Dragon'.

I was hungry, so I decided to treat myself to fish and chips before visiting the church ruins.

St Margaret's Church has been a ruin since a fire destroyed it in 1865, but the Early English remains are well-preserved. They lie in grassy surrounds, the land still consecrated. The square tower survives, as does most of the shell of the building, giving the otherwise modern surroundings a feeling of great age. After the fire, a new church (also dedicated to St Margaret) was built half a mile north of the site.

Arriving at the ruin, I noticed an information board giving a documented history of the building with detailed descriptions of the architecture. An account of events surrounding the fire of 1865 explained that it started accidentally when a stove overheated, showering sparks out and into the church. A gale blowing outside soon ensured the flames roared through the church and tower and, of course, the thatch and timber roof. Extensive archaeological investigations of the site have taken place in recent years.

Having read up on the history, I located the altar site, where Miller and Broadhurst dowsed the crossing point of the two energy currents. A wooden cross marked it then, but now a slate plaque is set in the ground. It bears an inscription:

Be still, for this is sacred ground,

A place to stand and pause. Reflect

Upon the pathway here-

The lessons learned, the gifts received.

Be still, and listen to God's voice

That sings a song of unity,

Blessing the journey still to come

With love and deep humility.

I stood and paused and did what it said. My mind returned to Carn Lês Boel and my perch on the rocks above the sea the previous summer. I remembered my joy, knowing an adventure lay ahead of me. Now my pilgrimage was over, but it was time to feel that same joy and await that next journey, whatever it may be.

In a celebratory mood, I left the church and decided to spend an hour in the Turnstone, a holiday-makers' pub with a great name. I'm not a big football fan, but the Euro 2021 tournament was underway, and the match between England and the Czech Republic was being broadcast. England came away with a 1-0 win, so the cause for celebration wasn't just mine. I walked back to the campsite in the late evening twilight. The sky was clear, and the air still; Vega shined brightly above me. All was well.

Appendix

Having completed my pilgrimage in two stages over the summers of 2020 and 2021, I'd managed to walk a continuous line along the St Michael alignment from end to end, visiting many of the associated sites along the way. In planning, I endeavoured to visit significant locations aligned with the two earth energy currents, but many more needed to be included. Some essential sites were inaccessible due to the routes I committed to walking, while others were closed when visiting.

Later on, in 2021, I decided to revisit some of the places that had been inaccessible or closed when I walked my trail. Some were still closed, but I have included some brief reports of the ones I successfully visited here. These are **each referenced(*)** in the relevant day reports. These return visits continued into 2022, and all are included.

Day 3:

*Having failed to set foot on St Michael's Mount when I walked my pilgrimage, I knew I had to make a return visit to do so (29.06.2021). I bought a ticket to tour the gardens and could walk to the Mount via the causeway between the tides. The gardens were a beautifully organised riot of colour, dazzling in the late summer sunshine on the steeply terraced hillside. A network of well-laid-out steps and walkways give access, and the views were magnificent.

At the time of my visit, most of the island was strictly cordoned off, so I was, unfortunately, unable to approach and locate the rock platform on which Miller and Broadhurst discovered the precise point at which the Michael and Mary energy currents meet. This particular point of land has the added significance of being that at which the St Michael Alignment meets the Apollo/Athena Line, an intersection of great importance.

Day 4:

*After completing my pilgrimage, I got the chance to revisit Crowan (28.06.2021), and fortunately, St Crowenna's church was open to visitors. Inside, I admired its interior. Whitewashed walls with monuments concealed its greater age, but the magnificent sculpted columns and arches between the nave and the south aisle exposed it. In the north aisle is a stained glass window of St Crowenna flanked by St Michael and St George. This beautiful window is dedicated to the 23 soldiers of the parish who died in the First World War.

Elsewhere in the church, the memorials to the St Aubyn family (see Day 3) are magnificent examples of monumental sculpture, including one commemorating Sir John St Aubyn, 5th Baronet of Clowance. The work is by William Behmes, who was appointed 'Sculptor in Ordinary' to Queen Victoria in 1837. His work can be found across the country in parks and public spaces. Behmes was a very talented and successful artist and teacher, but his later life was crippled by alcoholism and gambling. He fell into bankruptcy and died in poverty.

St Crowenna's directly aligns with the Mary earth energy current. The Sun and the Serpent authors dowsed the current to and through the church and found it to exhibit an 'almost electric feeling of being beautifully balanced.'

Day 5:

*After completing my trail, I took the opportunity to visit Truro Cathedral (01.07.2021), which aligns with the Michael energy line further north of where I walked. Although it wasn't directly on my pilgrimage trail, it's far too significant not to receive a mention.

Truro Cathedral is a Gothic Revival masterpiece built in the Late Victorian Era to a design by John Loughborough Pearson. It was built on the site of an earlier church and, like its predecessor, dedicated to St Mary the Virgin. Truro is similar to Lincoln's magnificent medieval Cathedral in many ways but on a more modest scale. On my visit, I was amazed by the structure's elegance, grandeur, and harmony. Unlike Lincoln and other great medieval examples, nothing evolved, yet so much is represented in one design. Many of the magnificent monuments and works of art within are contemporary with the building, while others pre-date the building itself. The Chapel of St Mary is the only part of the Cathedral that incorporates the remains from the earlier parish church.

In the Sun and the Serpent, the authors dowsed the Mary current through the site of the original church and the Victorian chapter house.

**I'm pleased to write that I also revisited Stithians (28.06.2021) and found the granite cross mentioned by the Sun and the Serpent authors. This wayside beauty is nearly 6 feet high. It has very worn cruciform carvings on both sides. Three similar crosses are located elsewhere in the parish.

Day 6:
*My trail walk missed the church at St Michael Penkevil, but when I returned to the area after I finished the walk, I decided to visit it (01.07.2021). It's set in a beautifully remote part of Cornwall, half a mile east of the River Fal.

I was further intrigued about this remotely located church when I read of the unusual and decidedly melancholic accounts given by the authors of the Sun and the Serpent. They describe their experience of dowsing the Mary energy current at this location:
'The first thing that struck us was the depressing, burdensome atmosphere that pervades the entire place...In all our travels which had taken us to many churches and ancient sites, we had never met such a feeling of black depression...Here was a church, which should be a place of inspiration, that was so inharmonious that it dragged the spirits down into

a slough of despond. And a church where there were memorials to members of one of Cornwall's most elite families.'

The monuments are to the Boscawen family, their most notable member being Admiral Edward Boscawen (1711-1761).

Being aware of the authors' comments, I wasn't wishing or expecting to feel the 'depressing, burdensome atmosphere' they experienced. Still, I was curious to see what impressions the place would give me. I found St Michael's Church at the end of a long, narrow country lane. The large building dates back to the 13th Century but was heavily restored in the Victorian Era. Although the walls are much older, the stone was extensively re-cut and pointed, giving it an almost modern appearance. Inside, the bare, damp, unpainted plaster walls and the dim lighting give the interior a cold, austere feel, as do the many stone memorials that fill them, devoid of any colour. I didn't experience the same feelings of 'black depression' the authors write about, but I could see how here, of all places, might be where I would have done had I been attuned to the same energies.

Day 7:
*As my walk for this day followed sites along the Michael energy line, my trail route could not include sites along its Mary counterpart running further north. Among them was the St Michael sanctuary of Roche Rock (perhaps curiously) aligned with the Mary current. Given the site's powerful association with the Alignment (and its remarkable setting and location), it seemed a shame to have omitted it from my walk. After completing my pilgrimage, I returned to the area and paid a visit (28.06.2021).

Roche Rock is one of the St Michael sanctuaries of western England that take the form of a hill on which stands (or once stood) a church on its summit dedicated to the Archangel. The others are Carn Brea, Rame Head, St Michael's Mount (Day 3), Brent Tor (Day 10), Burrow Mump (Day 20) and Glastonbury Tor (Day 21). All are located on the St Michael

Alignment except Carn Brea, which lies several miles to its north and Rame Head on the southeast coast of Cornwall.

The Rock is situated in a corner of Cornwall that has seen industrial activity for centuries. A low hill rises to form a steep craggy outcrop of rocky granite, its summit topped with the ruins of a chapel/ hermitage built in the medieval period. Steep steps cut into the rock give scrambling access to the ruin, which appears to be half-hewn out of the living rock. It's an awesome-looking edifice in a perfect state of disrepair that wouldn't look out of place in a Hammer horror film.

The hermitage has many legends attached to it. The Celtic Saint Conan is believed to have taken refuge there in the 6th Century. Another 6th Century tale has Tristran, the nephew of King Mark of Cornwall, harbouring in the hermitage with the King's bride-to-be after the pair succumbed to imbibing a love potion.

I climbed up to the 66-foot summit and found myself inside the ruin. The place has a powerfully enchanting feel, and the views were better than I expected, given its modest height. The sky was overcast, and the weather was calm, but this long-abandoned rocky perch would make an ideal place to experience a wild storm.

The authors of the Sun and the Serpent describe their experience of dowsing the Rock's energy:

'To come across Roche Rock is a humbling experience. In a flat landscape, moulded into hills and valleys by heavy industry, a great crag of black rock rises over a hundred feet into the air. Its startling, stark shape makes you catch your breath. On its summit, built into the living rock, is an ancient chapel dedicated to St Michael, its eyeless vaulted window gazing out across a devastated country...The Rock itself is nature's markstone for this channel of energy, intimately connected with St Michael. Clambering up the iron ladder to the eyrie above, we found that *the current passed right through the chapel with its lower room sculpted into the rock, yet not levelled so as to disturb the natural qualities, a feature of all early rock-fast chapels.'*

Day 13:

*I decided to return to Belstone (08.07.2021) after completing my pilgrimage, and I was fortunate to find St Mary's Church open to visitors. The 14th Century building was primarily restored in Victorian times, but enough of the original granite structure survives to give it a feeling of great age. The font is the original medieval one, and in the north aisle is a large stone known as the Belstone Ring Cross, dated between the 7th and 9th Centuries. This (and similar ancient crosses found in Wales and Ireland) bears the chi-rho symbol derived from the Greek letters X (chi) and P (rho). It probably originally stood as a boundary stone or a burial marker.

Day 14:

*Although on this day I visited several sites along the course of the Mary energy current, I failed to make the detour necessary to include a remarkable Neolithic dolmen known as the Spinster's Rock. I duly returned to do so, however (28.06.2021). It stands in a field a few miles west of the Devonshire village of Drewsteignton. Three large granite boulders support a massive capstone estimated to weigh sixteen tons. It's believed to have been a burial chamber, although no significant finds have been made. In 1862 it collapsed but was restored shortly afterwards.

The word Cromlech might equally apply to this monument. Some believe it to be what remains of a larger complex of stone avenues and circles. Legend states that three sisters erected the stones one morning before breakfast.

In the Sun and the Serpent, the authors relate the legend to the monument's possible purpose as a sacred site:

'The meaning of this tradition may conceal a clue to its ancient use, for the Mary current passes right through the old stones. And in the old Celtic religion, the 'three maidens' or 'three sisters' were a symbol of the Goddess in her three distinct phases of Virgin (new moon), Mother (full moon), and Crone (waning moon).

The dolmen is hidden from the road and took some finding, but beyond a roadside gate, there it was, standing silently in the corner of a meadow, forming some shade for a cluster of sheep resting quietly in the heat of the summer sun. I walked over to the monument and could almost stand upright beneath the giant capstone. Hedges and trees largely obscured my views, but I could make out some of the heights of Dartmoor in the distance.

Day 19:

*While my entire day's walk had primarily followed the course of the Michael current, I had omitted by necessity the sites that lie along its female counterpart to the north of where I walked. These included the churches at Nynehead and Bradford-on-Tone. Later, after completing my trail (09.07.2021), I visited the church at Trull, just south of Taunton, which also aligns with the Mary current.

Now the Church of All Saints, Trull Church was formerly dedicated to St Michael. It has a magnificent, 15th Century stained glass window depicting St Margaret slaying a dragon flanked by St Michael and St George likewise in the act of killing their respective dragons. The theme is particularly pertinent to the locality, for Castleman's Hill, just two miles west of the village, is traditionally believed to be where a dragon was slain. Evidence of an Iron Age settlement has also been found on the hill. Also within the church are some magnificent carvings to the bench ends, and the pulpit is a masterly example of fine early 16th Century wood carving.

**As part of my walk on Day 19, I visited Taunton, the county town of Somerset. After completing my trail, I decided to return and give it a closer look (10.07.2021). It's too interesting a place to miss, even though The St Michael Alignment and its associated energy lines miss it by a few miles. For one thing, it has an excellent parish church (Taunton Minster) and a historic castle. Furthermore, the castle now accommodates the Museum of Somerset, one of the best provincial museums in Britain.

On reaching the town, it was easy to locate the Minster, thanks to its magnificent 160-foot tower. The present building is of the Early Tudor Perpendicular Gothic style. This can be regarded as the culmination of the development of the Medieval Gothic when English ecclesiastic architecture reached its most sophisticated. Dedicated to St Mary Magdalene, the Minster doesn't carry the same grandeur or scale of its contemporary cathedrals, and much of it was rebuilt during Victorian times. Still, the tower has to be one of the finest in England.

Taunton Castle (see Day 19) was a significant defensive and administrative centre for centuries, but now it's turned over to tourism and education in the form of the Museum of Somerset. It dates back to Saxon times. During the Norman era, it became a major defensive stronghold, owned by the Bishops of Winchester and also served as a priory. Over several centuries the castle was defended, besieged, ruined and repaired. In the 17th Century, its Great Hall became a judicial centre, and in 1685, the scene of Judge Jeffreys' Bloody Assizes following the Monmouth Rebellion (see Day 20). Over 500 supporters of the Duke of Monmouth were tried, and 144 were executed.

What remains of the castle today is the Great Hall, the inner ward and the Castle House, which now form the museum. The Great Gate also survives along with some of the outer ward buildings, now converted into castellated, ivy-clad hotels.

The museum has a remarkable collection of artefacts and exhibits, enough to keep the imprisoned visitor occupied for at least a week but certainly worth at least two hours of voluntary attention. In the Castle

House, there is a reconstructed school room from 1897 (yes, it once served as a school) and an authentic reconstruction of the interior of the nearby almshouse demolished in 1897. There's a large permanent exhibition documenting Somerset and its history with many unique items of great importance. The exhibits include a mosaic floor taken from the Low Ham Roman Villa dating from the 1st Century. It depicts Virgil's story of Aeneas and Dido and contains 120,000 tesserae, reassembled in immaculate condition. Also on display are the Frome Hoard and the Shapwick Hoard, two of the largest buried hoards of ancient coins ever unearthed. There's also a very informative exhibition on the Monmouth Rebellion. The Somerset Military Museum is located in the Great Hall, and if that's not enough, there is a gallery for contemporary art and photography exhibitions.

Finally, there is the Somerset Room. This much-altered space was originally the Bishop's Chamber, built with walls twelve feet thick over a massive barrel vault. It's the probable site where Perkin Warbeck was brought before King Henry VII after the failure of his rebellion. The room was transformed into its current plan in the 1780s. Lately, the attractive, interestingly curving white walls have been adorned with scores of quotations from people associated with Somerset and its local traditions written over recent centuries.

Admission to the Museum of Somerset is free.

Day 20:

*Deep in the Somerset Levels stands the Church of St Gregory. It was closed to visitors when I walked my trail, but as an important pilgrimage site on the Mary energy line, I paid a return visit, successfully gaining entry the following year (10.07.2021).

The cruciform building has an octagonal bell tower and dates from the early 14th Century. Inside, tall columns support the bare masonry walls with Gothic arches. Several tombs and monuments can be seen, while several recessed statues adorn the exterior, including that of St Gregory the Great.

**As the history of the Monmouth Rebellion had featured so strongly in the places I visited in Somerset, I decided to pay a visit to the Sedgemoor battle site after completing my trail (31.05.2021). It lies deep inside the Somerset Levels between the villages of Chedzoy and Westonzoyland. The latter village and its church are well-worth visiting for their historical connections with the battle. The 15th Century church (dedicated to St Mary) houses the Battle of Sedgemoor Visitor Centre, which contains information, displays and exhibits documenting the history of the Monmouth Rebellion and its final battle. The church became a prison for 500 rebel rebels captured at the battle. The prisoners were held there for several weeks in appalling conditions; some died of their injuries or treatment, and others were summarily hanged. The rest were tried at Taunton by the infamous Lord Chief Justice Jeffreys (See Day 20).

The battle site lies about a mile from the church along a signposted lane. A memorial garden is located beside a farm track amid the flat, level landscape, enclosed between two Black Poplar trees. It contains several small memorials to various wars and conflicts and a larger one with a plaque:

TO·THE·GLORY·OF·GOD
AND·IN·MEMORY·OF·ALL·THOSE·WHO
DOING·THE·RIGHT·THING·AS·THEY·GAVE·IT
FELL·IN·THE·BATTLE·OF·SEDGEMOOR
6th JULY 1685
AND·LIE·BVRIED·IN·THIS·FIELD
OR·WHO·FOR·THEIR·SHARE·IN·THE·FIGHT
SVFFERED·DEATH
PVNISHMENT·OR·TRANSPORTATION
PRO·PATRIA

***After completing my trail, I took the opportunity to explore two sites north of where I walked, the churches at Moorlinch and Shapwick. Both are dedicated to St Mary the Virgin, and both buildings date from the 14th Century, although they were previously under the authority of Glastonbury Abbey in Saxon times. Both buildings are set in attractive, quiet surroundings and on elevated land. Their towers dominate the horizon from afar. Unfortunately, the church at Moorlinch was locked, but two miles further east, St Mary's at Shapwick was open. Inside I noticed several rather austere tomb memorials.

The churches at Moorlinch and Shapwick are both dedicated to St Mary the Virgin and aligned with the Mary earth energy current.

Near Shapwick, the remains of a very ancient wooden trackway were discovered in 1970 and named after its finder, Ray Sweet. The 'Sweet Track' was constructed over 4,800 years ago. It extended to over a mile in length and would have been one of a network of Neolithic causeways that once crossed parts of the Somerset marshes long before the land was drained. The causeway was precisely dated to 3807 BC thanks to dendrochronology and is the second-oldest timber trackway discovered in the British Isles. It may only have been in use for ten years. Parts of it have been conserved both on-site and elsewhere for display purposes. Shapwick is also in second place for the largest hoard of Roman coins ever found (see also **Appendix, Day 25***). The cache contained 9,238 silver denarii discovered in the remains of a nearby villa. Like Holywell Lake further east along the trail (see Day 18), Shapwick is one of the nine 'Thankful Villages' in Somerset, where all its servicemen returned safely from the First World War.

Day 23:
*The magnificent St Andrew's Church at Mells was closed when I walked my pilgrimage, but on a later visit, I found it open to visitors (02.06.2021). I entered through the elaborate, 15th Century porch and stood within the

spacious interior, filled with monuments and memorials to fallen individuals from both World Wars. The most prominent of these is an equestrian statue of Edward Horner, who fell at the Battle of Cambrai in 1917. Several stained glass windows from the 19th Century include one by William Nicholson and a white gesso plaque by Edward Burne-Jones to Laura Lyttleton. A gilded copy of this exquisite piece can be found in the Victoria & Albert Museum.

**The interior of the small Norman church in Great Elm contrasts with that of its grand neighbour at Mells. On my return visit (02.06.2021), I was struck by its quiet simplicity. Most of the interior features and fittings are 17th Century, including a gallery for the choir, and the plaster ceiling is of a later date. The substantial structure of the building is, of course, much older.

Day 25:

*Among the many historic settlements of Wiltshire, the market town of Devizes is well worth visiting. While doing so on my trail, I noticed that it's home to the Wiltshire Museum, which contains an archive, library and gallery run by the Wiltshire Archaeological and Natural History Society. For pandemic reasons, it was closed when I walked through the town on my trail, but I made arrangements to visit it the following year (03.06.2021) before starting the second part of my pilgrimage.

A two-hour museum tour enhanced my knowledge of the sites I'd visited on my trail the previous year. It also educated me on the wealth of other ancient places within the county, not least Stonehenge and Salisbury. Furthermore, I was completely unaware of the existence of another henge which once lay between Avebury and Stonehenge. Although nothing now remains of it, Marden Henge is the largest neolithic henge enclosure so far discovered in Britain. It once contained a monumental mound approximately 15 metres high, completely levelled in the 19th Century. There is archaeological evidence of a round timber structure; bones found at the site were radiocarbon-dated to 2450 BC.

Two notable names feature in the archaeological history of Wiltshire; William Cunnington (1754-1810) and Sir Richard Colt Hoare (1758-1838). These two wealthy individuals established a very disciplined approach to the new science of archaeology in the 19th Century, based on 'facts not theories'. The Wiltshire Museum contains a fascinating record of their work, and the collection of finds from the county's Neolithic and Bronze Age sites is genuinely remarkable. The remains of several individuals were discovered at some of these sites. These people were given appropriate names, and many of the finds that accompanied them are on display in the museum:

The Roundway Archer

Buried on the crest of Roundway Down (see Day 26), this individual lived soon after Stonehenge was completed and was buried with weaponry and other prized possessions believed to have come from central Europe.

The Marlborough Lady

An elderly Bronze Age woman of high status, buried in a round barrow with her gold and amber jewellery and other valuable possessions.

The Master of Ceremonies

An individual buried near Stonehenge along with a musical instrument, a bronze ceremonial goad and a bone headdress.

The Shaman

Buried in a barrow and wearing a ceremonial cloak decorated with pierced animal bones. Beside him, an axe made from Dolerite, a toolkit for tattooing (a fine bronze point and flint cups) and stone tools for burnishing metal.

The Lady with the Amber Necklace

This burial was discovered near Upton Lovell. The woman's remarkable gold and amber necklace has been reassembled and displayed along with other items of gold.

The Bush Barrow Chieftain

A burial from 1950 BC. The chieftain is accompanied by a remarkable bronze dagger, its pommel decorated with thousands of tiny gold studs set in a zigzag pattern.

What is clear from these and many other burials is that Neolithic and Bronze Age Wiltshire people were highly skilled and well-travelled across Europe. Their leaders were of great wealth, power and authority, and much has been learned about their movements.

In addition to this remarkable collection of ancient artefacts, the Wiltshire Museum has a fascinating record of objects from the Iron Age, Romano-British, Saxon, Viking and Medieval periods of the county's history, and (of course) King Alfred the Great. Among the unique items on display are the Marlborough Bucket, a large funerary vessel constructed from staves of yew and bound by iron hoops, richly decorated with imagery embossed onto its bronze surface. It's considered one of the finest examples of Celtic art ever found in Britain.

Day 30:

*On my tour of some places I had missed on my pilgrimage, I felt obliged to visit the Marlborough Mound (17.05.2022). This extraordinary artificial hill is contemporary with its near neighbour, Silbury Hill (see Day 27). Both are situated in the valley of the River Kennet. The Marlborough Mound is considerably smaller than Silbury, but at 62 feet in height, it's still much larger than any other comparable monument of its time or type in Britain.

Like Silbury, little is known about the hill's purpose, but it was constructed around 2500 BC. It has a varied history, as has the site on which it stands. In the Norman period, it was the motte for a castle and a royal residence until the death of Henry III. It later became a landscape feature as a garden mound for a stately home. A spiral path led to a summer house on the summit, below which were a grotto and a cascade fed from a water tower above. It now stands within the grounds of Marlborough College and its famous Chapel. Structural conservation has taken place in recent years to restore the Mound and what remains of these historic features.

In legend, Marlborough Mound is said to be the burial place of the wizard Merlin; locally, it's known as 'Merlin's Mound'. The motto of the town is 'Ubi nunc sapientis ossa Merlini' ('Where now lie the bones of wise Merlin')

On their quest, Broadhurst and Miller dowsed the Michael earth energy current to and through Marlborough College Chapel, but given its significance, they were surprised to find it missed the mound by just 50 metres. In the Sun and the Serpent, they explore what may account for this:

'We wondered whether the serpent currents of the Earth could actually move. If they were organic, then there was every likelihood that they were also dynamic. Perhaps the path of the current had shifted at some point in the past, and the College Chapel had become a later replacement for the spiritual use of the energy?'

My attempt to visit the Mound and the Chapel was disappointing but not wholly surprising. They stand in a strictly private setting, and I had made no attempt to contact the college in advance to seek permission. I did manage to see them from a distance, and I could discern what remains of the terraced walkways encircling the mound, which appeared attractively landscaped with bushes and trees.

**After completing my trail, I visited the Church of St Andrew in the hamlet of Ogbourne St Andrew. Unfortunately, it was closed when I visited, but I could locate and stand on a tree-covered mound within the church grounds.

This mound forms the precise point at which the Michael and Mary energy currents meet to form the 18th node on the St Michael Alignment, as described in the Sun and the Serpent:

'There, a large prehistoric mound was, along with the church, located within a raised bank. In the middle of the mound was another node. Trees swayed and tall wildflowers whispered gently in the breeze in another of those magical places that underestimate their true significance.'

The church and the mound, a bowl-barrow dating from the Bronze Age, remarkably demonstrate how the comparatively recent era of Christianity in Britain was built upon the rites of our far more ancient human history.

Day 31:
*Just a mile or two north of the Uffington White Horse lies the Church of St Mary in Uffington village. Having bypassed it on my walk, I returned to see it the following year.

St Mary's Church stands on the course of the Mary current, complete with dragon references in the form of a magnificent sculpture of St George slaying the beast in a niche next to the entrance. Inside are more dragons decorating the font.

The church dates from the 13th Century and was built from imported sandstone. Much of the fabric suffered ruination during the English Civil War, and in 1740 the steeple was destroyed during a storm. An octagonal tower later replaced this. The church retains the workings of its clock built in 1701, but it didn't have a face. A rhyme is associated with the church:

> **Oh, Uffington – poor people,**
> **Got a Church without a steeple,**
> **But what is more, to its disgrace,**
> **Got a clock without a face**

Day 33:

*Beyond the Sinodun Hills (the 20th node on the Alignment), I followed the Mary line closely. This took me away from the course of Michael, which extends further north of where I walked. Inevitably I missed a series of sites worth visiting, but after completing my pilgrimage, I was fortunate to visit two of these in May 2022; the churches at Clifton Hampden and Long Wittenham.

St Michael & All Angels, Clifton Hampden stands on the north bank of the River Thames, or as my Ordnance Survey map indicates, the River Thames or Isis (or as those local to Oxford would say, the River Isis). Sir George Gilbert Scott extensively rebuilt this late Norman chapel in what has to be a masterpiece of Victorian church architecture.

This elegant spire-topped church stands on attractive grounds, rising above the north bank of a leafy section of the young River Thames. The architectural elements span nearly a millennium here, but the overall effect is perfectly harmonious. The medieval bays and pillars perfectly complement the rebuilt chapels and windows, and the 19th Century choir screen carved and adorned with St Michael and his angels is a magnificent work of art.

Outside, the enclosed churchyard is landscaped beautifully with exquisite views down to the river and beyond. It contains the grave of Major John Howard, who led the Pegasus Bridge glider raids on D-Day. I also located the gravestone of William Dyke, which bears the inscription:

> IN MEMORY OF
> WILLIAM DYKE
> OF THE GRENADIER GUARDS
> WITH WHICH REGIMENT HE
> SERVED AT THE BATTLE OF
> WATERLOO
> HE WAS FOR MANY YEARS
> A CONSTANT AND DEVOUT
> WORSHIPPER AT THIS CHURCHYARD
> DIED FEB 28TH 1866
> AGED 71 YEARS
> BE THOUGH FAITHFUL UNTO DEATH
> AND I WILL OWE THEE A CROWN
> OF LIFE

Parish records indicate that Dyke was a private soldier who accidentally fired the first shot at Waterloo. Consequently, he was dismissed from the army. However, continued interest and research have uncovered records from more than one source suggesting that Dyke's discharge was honourable.

**From Clifton Hampden, I took the opportunity to visit St Mary's church at Long Wittenham, also aligned with the Michael current. Here I noticed the ancient oak porch, its walls and supports gnarled and weathered with great age. Inside, the original font is made from lead, one of only a handful in England.

Day 35:

*16.05 2022: Driving across Oxfordshire a year after completing my trail, I had to visit St Andrew's church at Chinnor. It was closed to visitors when I walked my pilgrimage, but now it was open. The sun was shining, and the trees in the churchyard were laden with blossom as I approached and entered the building.

Inside, two women were busy cleaning but stopped to welcome me in. I shared about my pilgrimage and why I was revisiting the church. Much intrigued, they invited me to look around and ask any questions I might have. They pointed out the early 14th Century rood screen, one of the oldest surviving examples in the country. I looked around and noticed the prominently positioned stone font. It was made to replace an earlier, 14th Century one which still stands within the church. On mentioning this detail in conversation, one of the ladies directed my attention to yet another stone font; small, lead-lined, plain and cylindrical. It was hidden beneath some stacked chairs in the corner of one of the aisles. This font was the earliest of the three, dated to the 13th Century, and I'd never have noticed it.

Besides these and many other interesting features, the most striking has to be the beautifully decorated and illustrated stone pulpit. It has six faces, each with a scene carved in relief within an upright oval frame. One is of Jesus, and a different landscape scene in each of the others. There are palm trees, flying birds, fields of corn, rising and setting suns and roads winding into the distance. Each one is exquisitely conceived and beautifully executed. The images convey biblical imagery and represent the English landscape.

From the Sun and the Serpent:
'At St Andrews, Chinnor, a superbly carved pulpit showed the winding pilgrim route stretching over the verdant countryside. At the point where the road disappeared into the horizon, the sun rose in great splendour. It was difficult not to see in this a profound symbolic representation of the old Icknield Way and its connection with the forces of the Earth and the Sun.'

Day 36:

*Small, hidden away gems are easy to overlook, and All Saints Church, Little Kimble, has to be a fine example. When I walked my pilgrimage, it was closed to visitors, but I determined I would pay it another visit later (16.05.2022).

Tucked away along a quiet country lane, this small building is easy to miss. It dates from the 13th Century and consists of just a chancel and an aisleless nave. There is no tower, just a gable housing two bells. Inside, all is quiet, unspoiled simplicity, but the walls are adorned with the remnants of paintings from the 14th Century. Time has undoubtedly faded their colours and erased much of the work, but there's enough left to give a glimpse of the visual feast places like these must have provided for their attendant congregations.

The surviving images cover some of the chancel and much of the nave walls. Some figures, such as St George in chain mail, are easy to identify, complete with his cross and shield. Others were fortunately explained on a helpful information board that could double up as a table tennis paddle. The surviving fragments of imagery represent, among other scenes, a bearded St James, complete with knobbed staff and pilgrim's hat, St Margaret being tortured and then executed, and St Christopher carrying the Divine Child on his shoulder. Also represented are St Lawrence, St Francis and St Clare.

All Saints Church aligns with the Mary earth energy current.

Day 37:

*St Mary's church was closed when I passed through Ivinghoe on my pilgrimage, but I gained entry on a subsequent visit (16.05.2022). It stands prominently as the focal point of the village, as it has done for 800 years. Its most notable interior feature is the 15th Century tie-beam roof, adorned with carved angels. Beneath it (at a touchable level), the finials of the pews (dating from the same age) allow a close-up visual and tactile experience. If they were in a museum, they'd be behind glass, but here as functional as they were 600 years ago.

Apart from the permanent stone monuments and monumental brasses, I noticed a more vibrant display of work documenting the church's history illustrated by local children.

St Mary's church stands on the Icknield Way and directly aligns with the Mary energy current.

Day 40:

*Royston Cave has to be one of the most important of the St Michael Alignment sites, and having waited patiently for nearly a year, I finally got to stand inside this mysterious and venerable chamber (15.05.2022). Although I'd completed all my walking almost a year before, somehow, my pilgrimage remained unfinished until I could finally bear witness to the place.

Having booked my tour of the Cave, I joined my fellow tourists assembled outside the small entrance. Soon we were led along the narrow passageway (dug in 1790) that leads into the artificially lit bell-shaped chamber and its sculpted walls. Hitherto, having seen the carvings only in photographs, finally seeing them three-dimensionally in the living rock was breathtaking. The deeply carved figures and images cover every inch of space in the lower part of the chamber. The sculptural quality was unquestionably crudely executed, yet the overall effect was remarkable. As I looked up into the space above me, I could see the narrow shaft that formed the original opening, while another shaft at the top of the chamber led up to a grille in the street pavement above. Several recesses halfway up the chamber wall once accommodated a wooden platform structure. How such a large cavern could have been created with no historical reference to its existence and remain undiscovered until 1742 is a complete mystery, mainly as it lies directly beneath such an essential junction of ancient highways (Ermine Street and the Icknield Way).

The carvings on the walls represent significant religious and historical figures. Our guide helped point these out in a panoramic sequence as follows:

Two knights riding on a horse (believed to represent the Templar Seal).

St Christopher carrying the child Jesus.

Two crucifixion scenes.

St Catherine, complete with her wheel of martyrdom.
King Richard I and his wife Berengaria (a crown floats above her head, representing her uncrowned status).

A large cross or sword.

The pagan symbols of a horse and a Sheela-Na-Gig (a female fertility symbol).

Three figures believed to represent Jesus, Mary and Joseph.

St Laurence and the gridiron upon which he was martyred

A figure with upraised arms believed to be King David of the Psalms.

A figure believed to be Jacques de Molay, Master of the Knights Templar, who was burned for heresy in 1314.

A knight or military saint believed to be St George or St Michael.

Two figures believed to represent either St John the Baptist and St

Thomas of Canterbury (as seen on the Seal of Royston Priory) OR Heraclius, Patriarch of Jerusalem and Templar Grand Master Gerard de Ridefort, depicting their meeting in 1185.

A small carving of a figure holding a skull in one hand and a candle in the other, possibly representing a candidate for initiation.

This collection of imagery gives many clues to the origin and purpose of the Cave. Traditionally, the consensus suggests it was used by the Knights Templar, notably because they founded nearby Baldock (see Day 39). Beyond the carvings, there have been no significant archaeological finds to determine the Cave's origins or use. When it was discovered in 1742, the chamber was filled with debris, all subsequently removed. Only a skull, a small drinking vessel and a piece of brass were retained. Other theories have suggested the cave was an early Freemasons' Lodge, an Augustinian storehouse, a private chapel and a wayside hermitage.

Concerning the pilgrimage, Royston Cave marks the 21st and penultimate node on the St Michael Alignment. Apart from the location, the pagan and Christian symbols on the chamber walls and the representation of St Michael all point to the Cave's relevance as a St Michael sanctuary. In the Sun and the Serpent, the authors write of their own experiences here:
'Anybody standing in the uniquely magical atmosphere of the Cave cannot fail to experience its potency. Its shape, that of an inverted womb, and its images, predominantly female, mark it as a place to honour the Earth Goddess. Directly in the centre of the Cave was a node. The Michael and Mary currents crossed, for the first time, in a chamber cut into the Earth itself...There was no doubt in our minds that Royston Cave was one of those mythical entrances into the Otherworld, situated at a place where the earth currents fuse to create energies that may be used to penetrate

the veils of matter, traditionally a spot where illumination may be experienced. Now virtually forgotten, it is, in its way, a powerful place of transformation as many of the more well-known structures that mark centres of transcendent change. Such a rare example of early rites, complete with its tapestry of magical images, emphasizes once more the crucial role of the Earth's energies in the prehistoric and early Christian religions. We were again led to wondering what other secrets the Earth may conceal directly beneath similar places where nodes existed.'

Royston Cave had a powerful effect on me. To spend time in this magical place, undisturbed for centuries and steeped in so much mystery, is awe-inspiring. Surrounded by many deeply symbolic images hewn in the living rock sparked my imagination. I surmised that the Cave was a secret sanctuary for the Knights Templar when the order was being persecuted out of existence during the early 14th Century, but that's just wishful want-to-know on my part. The real beauty of this place rests in the unknowing.

Day 41:
*When walking my pilgrimage, I included St Mary's, Ickleton as a significant objective along the way. It was disappointing, therefore, (but not entirely unexpected) to find the church closed. To miss St Mary's would mean missing some magnificent medieval wall paintings, so I revisited the place after completing my trail (15.05.2022).

Dedicated to St Mary Magdalene, the church was once a Benedictine priory. The present building dates from the early Norman Era, but parts of it are built from the material used in Roman times. Hidden for over 400 years, the extensive wall paintings covering much of the nave were only discovered following an arson attack in 1979.

The paintings were created in the 12th Century. They are more extensive than those at Little Kimble (Day 36) and more complete. They're considered to be among the best examples still in existence. The artwork extends across both walls of the nave, forming a two-tier frieze above the arcades.

Scenes of Christ's Passion are depicted, as well as the martyrdoms of several saints. The once vibrant colours have faded to pale yellow, red and ochre.

St May's church directly aligns with the Michael earth energy current.

Day 44:

The final four stages of my trail were in East Anglia, and most of the pilgrimage sites were churches. Many were off-route or closed to visitors, but I took the opportunity to revisit some of them later after completing my trail. Two locations on the Michael energy current that fell within the range of where I walked on Day 44 were the churches at Rushbrooke and Woolpit. I took the opportunity to visit these on 15.05.2022.

*The medieval church at Rushbrooke is dedicated to St Nicholas and was extensively restored in the 19th Century, but the result is far from what would be expected. The doorway leads into a vestibule, and other screens and partitions carve up the space of the interior, giving the place a private and intimate feel. Dark wooden screens, pews and choir stalls are offset by whitewashed stone walls which bear the arms of Henry VIII (the only example in the country). The restoration was the work of Colonel Robert Rushbrooke (1779-1845), who lived at nearby Rushbrooke Hall, the largest moated Tudor mansion in Suffolk. The Hall was destroyed by fire in the 1960s. The church contains several monuments to the Jermyn family, who owned the Hall.

**The Church of St Mary, Woolpit *(also on the Michael line)* is a magnificent building. Crowned with an ornate and elegant spire, St Mary's has a superb hammer-beam roof adorned with beautifully carved angels. The original roof was extensively damaged in the 1640s, as were many others at the hands of the iconoclastic puritan movement, but an extensive restoration took place in the 1840s. Equally magnificent carvings of animals form the bench ends of the pews.

  Woolpit is famous for its legend of two children who lived in the village in the 12th Century. They were believed to be brother and sister, and their skin was green. They ate nothing but raw broad beans and spoke in an unknown language. The boy was sickened and died, but the girl grew to learn English. She explained that she was from a land of twilight where everything was green. Later accounts of the tale included the novel 'The Green Child' by Herbert Read.

Day 45:

*On the edge of Thornham Park is St Mary's Church, Thornham Magna. It was closed to visitors when I passed by on my trail, so I decided to return and pay it another visit (14.05.2022). Dedicated to St Mary Magdalene, the church is mainly of 14th and 15th Century work. It features a Green Man carving over the south porch, two fonts (one medieval and a later Victorian replacement), a striking stained glass window by Edward Burne-Jones and several beautifully carved monuments and memorials.

**Just down the lane from St Mary's is a church dedicated to St Mary the Virgin at Thornham Parva, which I visited on the same day. Pre-dating its neighbour, it has Saxon stonework within its walls and a thatched roof and tower. Inside the small building are some early 14th Century wall paintings, but perhaps the most striking (and unique) feature is the Thornham Parva Retable, a 14th Century painted altarpiece. Nearly all of such pieces were destroyed during the reformation on the orders of Henry VIII. However, this one survived when it was removed from Thetford Priory and secreted away by the Dukes of Norfolk. Its whereabouts were unknown until 1927, when it was found in the loft of the stables at nearby Thornham Hall. It was then given to the church at Thornham Parva and installed in its present position. Carefully restored during the 1990s, The Thornham Parva Retable is Britain's largest and most complete altarpiece.

Both of the above churches align directly with the Michael earth energy current.

***Also revisited on 14.05.2022 was St Mary's, Yaxley *(aligned with the Michael energy current)*. This beautiful medieval church dates to the 14th Century and has a substantial medieval porch to match. Inside there's a wealth of early features, including a Sexton's wheel above the south door. There are only two of these throughout East Anglia. Six threads are attached to the wheel, which was spun to determine on which of the six feast days of the Virgin Mary a penitent would fast. There's also a painted chancel screen and what remains of a medieval 'Doom' wall painting over the chancel arch. A depiction of the devil with his tongue hanging out can still be discerned. The stained glass windows are magnificent, as is the Jacobean pulpit.

****St Peter and St Paul's, Eye, was closed when I passed through the town on my trail, but I decided to include it on my return visit (14.05.2022). Barely a stone's throw from the castle, the Church of St Peter and St Paul has to be one of Suffolk's grandest. The building was developed in the 15th Century from an earlier foundation and demonstrates the late Gothic decorated and perpendicular styles. Its tall flint-faced tower rises almost as high as the adjacent castle mound.

The interior contains a magnificent 20th Century loft and rood screen, the base of which is original work from the early 1500s. Various saints are depicted, many of them female. The wooden roof is also impressive, with intricately carved bosses restored or replaced from the originals.

Day 46:

*Upon crossing the River Waveney from Suffolk into Norfolk on Day 26, I soon arrived at St Mary's Church outside the village of Ditchingham *(aligned with Mary)*. The building was unfortunately closed, but I made my return on 14.05.2022. St Mary's is a substantial, square-towered church built in the 15th Century. Inside is a magnificent painted ceiling and a tall war memorial of black marble. A life-sized soldier lies beneath a tablet bearing the names of those from the parish who fell in the First World War. Also, at the time of this visit, I was fortunate to be directed to the chancel. There, beneath a carpet runner, I found a black marble stone commemorating the family of Sir Henry Rider Haggard. It contains the ashes of the writer, along with those of his family. Part of the inscription reads:

HENRY RIDER HAGGARD
KNIGHT BACHELOR
KNIGHT OF THE BRITISH EMPIRE
WHO WITH A HUMBLE HEART STROVE TO SERVE HIS COUNTRY
BORN AT BRADENHAM, NORFOLK ON JUNE 22. 1856
DIED MAY 14. 1925

A striking coincidence (for me) was that my visit marked the 97th anniversary of the writer's death and my 63rd birthday.

A stained glass window in the north aisle commemorates the writer. It contains imagery both intriguing and perhaps relevant to the church's alignment with the Mary energy current. This was noted by the authors of the Sun and the Serpent:

'A memorial window to the author Henry Rider Haggard contained many interesting images, including St Michael holding a flaming sword, the pyramids of Egypt, sacred Druidic leaves, a chalice, serpent and a six-pointed star.'

**St Michael's, Broome *(aligned with the Mary energy current)* was a memorable enough location on Day 46 of my trail to warrant a return visit (14.05.2022). Set in a remote and beautiful setting with no other buildings in sight, I parked my car and approached the building along the same tree-lined lane I'd walked the previous year. The church is substantially medieval, dating to the 13th Century, but much of it has been altered and restored over the intervening centuries. The peaceful interior is an attractive space. There are monuments and hatchments to the De Brome family, who owned a moated manor house that stood nearby. This was demolished in the 19th Century, and only traces of the moat remain. A small war memorial stands in the churchyard.

Day 47:

Following the Mary line closely during my final two days of walking my trail, I was aware that many sites aligned with Michael had yet to be visited. One of these was the massive tower in the Suffolk market town of Beccles and having read about it, I decided it warranted a post-trail visit (12.05.2022). Miller and Broadhurst dowsed the Michael current to the tower, which stands appropriately next to St Michael's Church.

Beccles was once a prosperous town and trading port. The tower was built as the bell tower serving the adjacent church dedicated to St Michael. The tower is 97 feet tall and has 100 steps which (when open) can be taken to view the town and surrounding countryside from the top. The building was constructed in 1500 in the Perpendicular Gothic style with much attention to detail in the stonework. There are clocks on the tower's north, east and south faces but not on the west face, which overlooks the border of Suffolk towards Norfolk across the River Waveney. Tradition states that this is because the people of Norfolk would not pay for it, and the people of Beccles didn't want to give the time to the people of Norfolk for free.

**Having failed to access the Church of St Mary, Haddiscoe, on Day 47, I took the opportunity to pay another visit (14.05.2022). It stands elevated above the marshes that bear its name on the Norfolk side of the River

Waveney. This traditional, round-towered church is notable for the distinctive black and white chequered stonework on the upper courses of its 11th Century tower. The south doorway is a magnificent example of Norman work, elaborately carved with chevrons and scallop patterns, and above it, a Christ in Majesty. Inside are some 14th Century wall paintings and a magnificent font, boldly carved with angels and winged beasts. Also, an extensive display documenting those from the parish who served in the First World War.

A stone ledger on the south aisle floor is of further interest. Inscribed in Dutch, it honours one Barbele Jans, who died on the second day of December 1525. She was the wife of Pier Piers, a Dutch engineer who was instrumental in draining nearby marshes during the 16th Century. Without such expertise, much of East Anglia could still be underwater today!

Appropriately, St Mary's aligns with the Mary earth energy current.

Bibliography/References

Publications:

Benham, Patrick, *The Avalonians*, Gothic Image Publications, 2006

Biltcliffe, Gary, and Caroline Hoare, *The Spine of Albion*, Sacred Lands Publishing, 2012

Bottomley, Frank, *The Church Explorer's Guide*, Kaye & Ward Ltd, 1978

Broadhurst, Paul, and Hamish Miller, *The Sun and the Serpent*, Mythos Publishing, 1990

Burton, Anthony, *The Ridgeway*, Aurum Press Ltd, 2008

Dealler, Richard, *Carn Les Boel to Brentor A walker's guidebook*, michaelmarypilgrimsway.org, 2015

Dealler, Richard, *Brentor to Glastonbury & Glastonbury to Avebury A waker's guidebook*, michaelmarypilgrimsway.org, 2015

Dunn, John, *Walking Ancient Trackways*, David & Charles, 1986

Harding, Stewart, *The Long Walk to Glastonbury*, Amazon Publishing, 2022

Jones, Lawrence E, *The Beauty of English Churches*, Constable and Company Ltd, 1978

Michell, John, *New Light on the Ancient mystery of Glastonbury*, Gothic Image Publications, 1990

Michell, John, *The New View over Atlantis*, Harper Collins, 1983

Ordnance Survey (by licence), *Michael & Mary Maps*, Penwith Press

Stukeley, William, *Abury, a Temple of the British Druids*, 1743

White, Rupert, *The re-enchanted Landscape, Mysteries, Paganism & Art in Cornwall 1950-2000*, Antenna Publications, 2017

Also: Excellent church guides and histories available at churches from Cornwall to East Anglia

Websites:

ancient-origins.net (various articles)

britishpilgrimage.org (Useful information about the Mary Michael Pilgrims Way)

causleytrust.org (The Charles Causley Trust)

cornishbirdblog.com (various articles)

earthwisdomearthscience.com The Michael Mary Line: Part I, Dartmoor: Connecting the Mary Line (Part II), The Michael Mary Line Part 4: White Horses and Dragons

icknieldwaypath.co.uk (the oldest road in Britain with the newest updates)

idwa.org.uk (Useful information about the Mary Michael Pilgrims Way, including an extended route in Oxfordshire)

legendarydartmoor.co.uk (various articles)

marymichaelpilgrimsway.org (currently not active but deserves to be)

megalithomania.co.uk (Many relevant articles in a vast and growing archive about the condition and everything associated with it

suffolkchurches.co.uk (various articles)

themodernantiquarian.com (Information on nearly all the megalithic sites)

Documentaries/Podcasts:

wessexarch.co.uk 'Beyond the Stones'

BBC; 'In Our Time', 'Megaliths'

Index of places visited
(by counties from west to east)

Cornwall:
Alsia Well, 4, 28
Blind Fiddler, 9, 11
Bodmin Moor, 45, 64
Boscawen-un, 9-11
Carn Lês Boel, 2
Cheesewring, 49, 50
Come-to-Good, 29
Cosawes, 27
Cowlands Creek, 29, 32
Creed, 31, 34
Crowan, 23, 24, 246
Daniel Gumb's House, 50
Eden Project, 36, 38, 39
Germoe, 18, 20
Godolphin Cross, 14, 18, 20-23
Golitha Falls, 46
Goonzion Down, 40, 43
Hendra, 26
Hurlers, 48, 49
Kelly Bray, 51
Kerris, 12
Kennal Vale, 27
King Harry Ferry, 31, 32
King Doniert's Stone, 46
Kit Hill, 51, 52
Livery, 40, 41
Longstone Cross (Long Tom), 47, 48

Lostwithiel, 40-43
Luxulyan, 40, 41
Marazion, 12, 15-18
Menacuddle Holy Well, 36, 37
Minions, 48, 49
Nancegollan, 23
Nanjizal Bay, 4
Old Kea, 26, 29-31, 33
Penzance, 8, 9, 12, 13
Perran Sands, 19
Perranarworthal, 26-28
Perranuthnoe, 17, 19
Perranwell, 29
Philleigh, 33
Polcrebo Downs, 23
Ponsanooth, 29
Prussia Cove, 19
Resugga Castle, 31, 34
Roche Rock, 37, 248-250
Roundwood Fort, 31, 32
Ruan Lanihorne, 31, 33
Stithians, 25-27, 247, 248
Stowes Pound, 48, 49, 50
St Austell, 31, 36, 37
St Buryan, 1, 2, 4, 5, 8, 9
St Cleer, 46
St Michael's Mount, 12-19
St Michael, Penkevil, 33, 247, 248
St Neot, 40, 43, 44
St Neot's Well, 43, 44
St Piran's Well, 27
Teffrey Viaduct, 40

Tredavoe, 12
Tregonning Hill, 18, 20, 21
Tregony, 33, 34
Tregony Bridge, 33, 34
Trenow Cove, 18
Trenant, 40, 44
Trethevy Quoit, 46, 47
Wheal Rock, 25

Devon:
Ayshford Chapel, 92, 93
Belstone, 67-69, 250
Belstone Cleave, 69
Bickleigh, 83, 85, 86, 88, 89
Bickleigh Bridge, 86, 87
Brent Tor, 52-54, 56
Cadbury, 86
Cadbury Castle, 81, 83, 85
Chagford, 75, 76
Clifford Bridge, 77, 87, 82
Cosdon Stone Rows, 69, 70, 75
Dartmoor, 63-65, 67-70, 72, 74, 79
Devil's Cauldron, 55, 56, 57, 58
Dunsford, 78, 81-83, 87, 88
Fingle Bridge, 76, 77
Fitz Well, 66
Gidleigh, 67, 71, 72, 74
Grand Western Canal, 88, 89, 93
Halberton, 89
High Willhays, 65
Holcombe Rogus, 92, 93
Kes Tor, 75

Kitty Tor, 75
La Wallen Chapel, 72
Lowdswells Lock, 92, 93
Lydford, 55, 56, 59, 60, 64
Lydford Bridge, 55
Lydford Castle, 59
Lydford Gorge, 55, 56, 57, 58, 60, 69
Nine Stones Circle, 68, 69
Okehampton, 66, 67
Posbury Clump, 79, 80
Round Pound, 75
Scorehill Stone Circle, 72, 73
Shobrooke, 83, 84
South Zeal, 67, 69
Spinster's Rock, 74, 250, 251
Stampford Peverell, 89, 90
Sticklepath, 69
Sydenham Damerel, 53
St Boniface's Well, Crediton, 81
St Libbet's Well, Crediton, 81
St Mary's Well, Uton, 80
St Swithin's Well, Shobrooke, 83, 84
Tedburn St Mary, 79
Thorverton, 83, 84, 85
Throwleigh, 67, 70, 71
Tiverton, 88, 89
Tiverton Castle, 89
Tiverton Parkway, 88, 91, 92
Venny Tedburn, 79
White Lady Falls, 57, 58
Widgery Cross, 64, 65
Yes Tor, 65, 66

Somerset:
Ash Cross, 91, 94
Athelney, 103, 104, 105
Beckington, 167
Bride's Mound, Glastonbury, 118, 119
Buckland Dinham, 132, 134, 135, 166, 168
Burrow Mump, 100, 105, 106
Chalice Well, Glastonbury, 112, 114, 117, 118
Coleford, 132, 133
Corfe, 95, 98, 99
Creech St Michael, 100, 101
Devil's Bed and Bolster, 167, 169, 170
Glastonbury, 110, 111, 112, 122
Glastonbury Abbey, 112, 114-116
Glastonbury Tor, 112, 113, 123-127
Great Elm, 133, 134, 256
Greenham, 92
Greenham Lift, 94
Ham, 100, 102
Holywell Lake, 92, 94
Knapp, 102
Lowdswells Lock, 94
Lower Knapp, 102
Lowton, 98
Lullington, 167-169
Mells, 133, 255, 256
Middlezoy, 101, 107, 108
North Curry, 102
North Wooton, 122
Orchard Portman, 95, 99
Orchardleigh Stones, 132, 135
Othery, 101, 106, 107

Pilton, 123, 128
Pilton Tithe Barn, 128, 129
Pitminster, 98
Rode, 167, 169
Sellick's Green, 98
Shapwick, 109, 254, 255
Shepton Mallet, 123, 129
Stoke St Gregory, 102, 103
Stoke St Mary, 95, 99
Stoke St Michael, 129, 132, 133, 135
Street, 112
Taunton, 94-96, 252, 253
Thorne St Margaret, 94, 95
Thornfalcon, 100, 101
Trull, 94, 251
Vobster, 133, 134, 256
Walton, 100, 108
Wearyall Hill, Glastonbury, 112, 113
Wellington, 92, 94-96
Wellington Monument, 92, 94, 96, 97
Westonzoyland, 108, 254

Wiltshire:
Avebury, 144-149, 157, 159-164, 166, 1171, 172
All Cannings, 146, 148, 171
All Cannings Long Barrow, 147
Barbury Castle, 175
Beckhampton Avenue, 162, 163
Bishops Cannings, 142, 144, 145
Bowerhill, 137-139
Caen Hill Locks, 139, 142
Devizes, 137, 138, 140-142, 256-258

Kennet and Avon Canal, 138-140, 145, 147
Liddington Castle, 174-176, 177
Marlborough Mound, 258, 258
Ogbourne St Andrew, 173, 175, 259, 260
Ogbourne St George, 174, 175
Oliver's Castle, 142-144
Roundway, 142
Sanctuary, 146, 147, 153-156, 162, 172-174
Sells Green, 139
Semington, 138
Silbury Hill, 146, 147, 153-156, 162, 172-174
Swallowhead Spring, Avebury, 146, 147, 150, 151
Trowbridge, 137, 138, 166
Wansdyke, 146, 148, 171
West Kennet Avenue, 146, 147, 150, 154, 156, 157, 162, 172, 173
West Kennet Long Barrow, 146-150
Windmill Hill, 146, 150, 154, 164, 165
Winterbourne Monkton, 147, 165, 172

Oxfordshire:

Aston Rowant, 191, 192
Berrick Salome, 185, 189
Blewburton Hill, 184
Blewbury, 183, 184
Brightwell Baldwin, 185, 189
Brightwell-cum-Sotwell, 186
Castle Hill, Wittenham Clumps, 186, 187
Chinnor, 191, 193, 262, 263
Churn Knob, 183
Clifton Hampden, 183, 261, 262
Court Hill Activity Centre, 181, 182
Fiveways, 192

Grim's Ditch, 182
Lewknor, 192
Long Wittenham, 186, 188, 262
North Moreton, 182, 184, 186
Round Hill, Wittenham Clumps, 186, 188
Scutchamer Knob, 183
Sinudin Hills, 182, 185
South Moreton, 184
Uffington, 179, 180, 260, 261
Uffington Castle, 179, 180
Uffington White Horse, 179
Wantage Monument, 182
Warborough, 189
Watlington, 185, 189, 190
Wayland's Smithy, 178

Buckinghamshire:
Aston Clinton, 196, 197
Bridgewater Monument, 200
Buckland, 196, 197
Great Kimble, 196, 197
Ivinghoe, 198, 199, 264, 265
Ivinghoe Beacon, 196, 198-202
Little Kimble, 196, 197, 263, 264
Marsworth, 196, 198
Princes Risborough, 191, 194, 196
Pitstone Windmill, 200
Terrick, 197
Weston Turville, 196, 197
World's End, 197

Bedfordshire:
Dray's Ditches, 204, 205

Dunstable, 201, 203
Dunstable Downs, 201, 203
Dunstable Priory, 203, 204
Luton, 201, 203
Pegsdon, 201, 205, 206
Pegsdon Hills, 201, 206
Waulud's Bank, 204
Whipsnade, 202

Hertfordshire:

Baldock, 206-208, 210
Clothall, 211
Ickleford, 206
Kelshall, 212
Knocking Hoe Nature Reserve, 206
Letchworth Garden City, 206, 207
Radwell, 209
Royston, 212, 213
Royston Cave, 209, 210, 212, 213, 265-268
Sandon, 212
Wallington, 211

Cambridgeshire:

Balsham, 215
Brinkley, 214, 216
Great Chishill, 210, 213
Ickleton, 214, 268, 269
Kirtling, 217, 218
Linton, 215
Ousden, 217
Rivey Hill, 215
Stretchworth, 217
Woodditton, 217

Essex:
Crishall, 214
Elmdon, 214
Great Chesterfield, 214
Strethall, 214

Suffolk:
Beccles, 238, 273
Bungay, 234, 235, 236
Bury St Edmunds, 219, 221-227
Ditchingham, 234
Eye, 228, 229, 271
Eye Castle, 229, 230
Finningham, 227
Goldbrook Bridge, Hoxne, 231
Homersfield, 234, 235
Hoxne, 223, 228-232
Ickworth, 221
Lidgate, 217, 219
Mendham, 234, 235
Norton, 227
Ousden, 219
Rushbrooke, 226, 269
St Edmund Monument, Hoxne, 230
St Edmundsbury Cathedral, 222
Swattesfield, 227
Syleham, 228, 232
Thornham Magna, 228, 229, 270
Thornham Parva, 228, 229, 271
Wardley Hill, 234
Wetherden, 221
Weybread, 228

Whepstead, 217, 220
Withersdale Street, 234, 235
Woolpit, 226, 269, 270
Wyverstone, 227
Yaxley, 229, 271

Norfolk:
Ashby, 241
Blundeston, 238, 242
Broome, 236, 272, 273
Corton, 242
Denton, 234, 235
Ditchingham, 236, 271, 272
Haddiscoe, 240, 273, 274
Hales, 239
Hopton-on-Sea, 238, 239, 242, 243
Kirby Cane, 239
Raveningham, 240
St Olaves, 240
Three Cocked Hat, 240
Thorpe, 240, 241

Printed in Great Britain
by Amazon